Contents

Exam Overview

TEST 1

PART 1

Reading (1 hour 15 minutes)

You are going to read an article about hot air balloons. Choose the most suitable heading from the list **A–I** for each part (**1–7**) of the article. There is one extra heading which you do not need to use. There is an example at the beginning (**0**).

Mark your answers **on the separate answer sheet**.

A	Involving balloon passengers
B	Qualifying as a balloon flyer
C	The price of balloons
D	Balloons for special occasions
E	The joy of achievement
F	Restrictions on passengers
G	Flying your balloon: practical considerations
H	The superiority of balloons
I	The inventors' expectations

Tip Strip

- Read the text quickly for general understanding.
- You only need to understand the main point of each paragraph. Don't worry if you don't understand every word.
- Read each paragraph, decide what the main point is, then find the best heading. Be careful – the headings won't use the same words as the text.
- When you have read all the paragraphs, go back and check your answers.

Paragraph 3: This refers to rules and limitations. Can you find a similar phrase in the headings?
Paragraph 7: Who is this advice for?
Heading A: What does 'involving' mean? Participate?
Heading B: 'Qualifying' suggests you need to take exams. Which paragraph mentions this?
Heading H: This heading suggests comparison. In which paragraph are balloons compared to other means of transport?

It's up, up and away

Eileen Shaw on the joys of ballooning

0 | *I* |

Mostly it's about hot air – for without that, balloons are just big empty bags with baskets on the bottom. The Montgolfier brothers had great hopes when they made the first manned flight. They thought balloons would take off as a viable means of commercial flight. Instead, they have remained the province of sport, adventure and enjoyment.

1

Modern balloons are a lot more sophisticated than their ancestors, but they still retain the essential characteristics which makes them so attractive. A plane is claustrophobic and very noisy. Balloons are so gentle and majestic and silent when the burner's not working. 'It's the most marvellous form of aviation,' says Chris Boyd, managing director of *Hot Air Balloons*.

2

Hot Air Balloons offers balloon trips suited to the requirements of customers, with unlimited possibilities. Celebrations are high on the list of reasons for booking a balloon flight. 'Birthdays, anniversaries, we even had a couple who wanted to get married during the flight, but we told them that wouldn't be allowed,' says Chris.

3

He takes parties of four to twelve, the maximum number allowed, and there is no age limit at the upper end – he has had a 92-year-old customer. The only other rule is that you have to be at least one metre tall, so small children are not allowed on board. This is because the side of the baskets is adult chest height and youngsters might be tempted to climb up to look out.

4

An ordinary flight lasts about an hour and a half and can reach over 1,000 metres. The cost of a flight covers four hours and includes a certificate for first-time flyers. The important point is that you don't just turn up and climb on board. You are invited to take an active part, so before the flight you spend about 45 minutes helping to inflate the balloon and getting to know it.

5

At the end of the trip, passengers are served with champagne and nibbles. Champagne is traditional after balloon flights. 'Most people are very happy that they have done it because they might have been a bit anxious before they set out, so they are glad to celebrate the experience,' he says.

6

So, taking a trip is one pleasure, but what if you fancy owning your own balloon? First, you will need a balloon licence. To get a licence you can train with a company like *Hot Air Balloons* and do 16 hours' flying with an instructor. Then you have to take written exams in the technical aspects of the balloon and other subjects.

7

When you own a balloon, you will need a trailer to store it and tow it to the launch site and someone to follow you to pick you up when you land. You may need a landowner's permission to start your flight, but it is possible to start from a very large garden. You can read all about how to get started in a new quarterly magazine for balloon enthusiasts published by the Balloon and Airship Club.

PART 2

You are going to read a newspaper article about the sport of inline skating. For Questions **8–15**, choose the correct answer **A**, **B**, **C** or **D**.

Mark your answers **on the separate answer sheet**.

Inline Skating

Tracy Winters is on a mission to change the image of inline skating in this country

In her skates there is no stopping Tracy Winters. She spends most of her time teaching, consulting, examining or campaigning on behalf of this country's ever-growing number of inline skaters.

Busy as she is, Tracy did manage to spare an hour early one Saturday morning to give me a lesson in the local park. The slight unease I felt at never having used inline skates before was not helped, however, by her emphatic disapproval as I pulled a pair of brand-new skates from my bag.

'Oh dear,' she said with a frown. 'You've been sold what we call 'aggressive' skates, which are no good for the sort of skating that you want to do. They're too heavy for twists and turns and the wheels are too small. And you've no brake.'

'But I was told that all I need to do to stop was drag my leg behind me,' I protested.

'No, no, no,' said Tracy. She explained how she was currently helping a girl who has been off work for a year with a damaged leg after following similar advice. Tracy is drawing up a list of guidelines for selling inline skates based on ability, budget and type of use, which she wants to see all retailers use. She has seen the purchase of inappropriate skates all too often before. 'What you should have been sold is recreational skates,' she told me.

Ordinarily, those who turn up with the wrong skates suffer the added annoyance of missing out on a lesson because Tracy will not teach them. I was more fortunate and, after a small **ticking off** for not having knee pads, my lesson began.

Away from the critical eyes of more experienced skaters, she started me off gently, simple skating up and down a track on the edge of the park.

'Hands out,' Tracy told me repeatedly. **This** was not just to help break a fall, but to prevent my tumbling altogether. Ice skaters, Tracy pointed out, keep their arms in front not only to look elegant: it actually keeps them balanced.

To help get rid of my fear, Tracy insisted that a fall would be good for me, but that I would need to relax for this to reduce the chances of injury. I was not so keen, but obeyed each time she reminded me to keep my back straight and chin up. 'You don't look at the ground when you're riding a bike,' she said.

Apart from ice-skating and bicycle riding, inline skating has similarities with ballet and skiing, which makes it attractive to a wide range of people. An estimated sixty percent of inline skate owners use them every week and more than half are recreational skaters. In this country the sport is regarded as something for the young and as potentially dangerous. Tracy, together with the National Inline Skating Association, is trying to change this impression, in the first instance by emphasising the importance of insurance and the wearing of protective clothing in case of accidents. She would also like to see the sport more widely catered for in sports centres and health clubs, possibly through the building of indoor skating arenas.

Having been on wheels almost every day of her life since the age of five, Tracy is well-versed in the virtues of skating and, she claims, she never tires of the sport. 'It is the feeling of moving, of gliding, I can't quite pin it down, but it makes me feel good,' she says. Like the hundreds who start skating every week, I now know what she means.

8 How did the writer feel before her inline skating lesson?

    A a little nervous
    B quite confident
    C very frightened
    D extremely excited

9 What was wrong with the skates which the writer bought?

    A They were of poor quality.
    B They were not suitable.
    C They did not fit her well.
    D They didn't work properly.

10 Why is Tracy writing a set of guidelines?

    A to help people who have been injured
    B to advise people who are buying skates
    C to provide information to sales staff in shops
    D to tell her students what to bring to lessons

11 'ticking off' in line 32 means

    A checking something.
    B waiting for something.
    C giving someone a reward.
    D telling someone they're wrong.

12 What does 'this' in line 37 refer to?

    A simple skating
    B repeated instructions
    C use of the hands
    D avoiding falls

13 Tracy compares skating and cycling in terms of

    A the fear people feel at first.
    B the need to learn how to fall.
    C the need to relax to keep balanced.
    D the correct body position to adopt.

14 How would Tracy like to change the idea people have of inline skating?

    A by encouraging older people to do it
    B by discouraging recreational skating
    C by stressing the need for safety
    D by forming a national association

15 After the lesson, the writer agrees with Tracy that inline skating

    A is easy to learn.
    B is rather tiring.
    C is hard to teach.
    D is very satisfying.

Tip Strip

- The questions follow the order of the text.
- Read the text carefully. Don't worry if you don't understand every word.
- Try to answer the question, or complete the sentence, before you look at options A, B, C and D.
- Underline key words in the question, e.g. 'How did the writer feel before ...' then find the part of the text where the answer is and underline words there, e.g. the slight unease I felt.
- Find the option which best matches the text, e.g. in paragraph 2 'slight' means 'not much' and 'unease' is a negative emotion, so the right answer is 8A.

Question 10: Be careful! Tracy mentions 'retailers', which is another word for ... ?

Question 11: What type of person is Tracy? Does she think the writer is well-prepared for the lesson?

Question 12: Does 'this' refer to something earlier or later in the text?

Question 13: When does Tracy mention cycling? Why?

Question 14: What idea *do* people have of the sport? What does Tracy think about this?

You are going to read a magazine article about the Hebrides Islands in Scotland. Seven sentences have been removed from the article. Choose from the sentences **A–H** the one which fits each gap (**16–21**). There is one extra sentence which you do not need to use. There is an example at the beginning (**0**).

Mark your answers **on the separate answer sheet**.

BRITAIN'S WILDEST PLACE

by Jon Orchard-Smith

It was just after 5 a.m. and the summer sun was rising over the mountains as the *Marguerite Explorer* sailed out of the loch into the calm waters of the sea. I was at the wheel – under the watchful eye of the captain. A few of the other dozen passengers and crew were on deck, clutching mugs of coffee. **0** | **H** | In the morning light, a dozen dolphins, grey and graceful, were swimming straight towards us.

The Hebrides, a group of islands off the Scottish coast, offer tourists a diversity of wildlife and scenery with few equals in the UK. **16** | | In places it is possible to see such marine animals from the shore, but to have the best views, you need to be on a boat.

17 | | The *Marguerite Explorer* was the first boat to offer whale-watching holidays throughout the Hebrides. Under the command of Christopher Swann, the crew of the *Marguerite* have worked with some of the world's leading sea-life scientists. They are very knowledgeable guides to the islands.

The Hebridan archipelago stretches nearly 250 miles from top to bottom, covers over a hundred miles from side to side, and has about 2,500 miles of coastline. **18** | | This relative lack of people, together with freedom from pollution, helps to make the Hebrides a haven for rare flowers and plants.

19 | | Some of the islands are under threat from mining and throughout the islands, developments such as fish farms, which are vital to the local economy, affect the environment too.

The Hebrides have their share of problems, but they are unbelievably beautiful. Why, then, aren't they packed with tourists? While visitors are an increasingly important part of the island economy, tourism is still low key, compared with some other parts of Britain. The answer may be that the prevailing Hebridan climate is wet and windy. **20** | |

Another discouraging factor is the wildlife the tourists least want to see – the insects, especially the mosquitoes. Particularly between July and September, visitors can expect to be severely bitten. Like so many wild places, the Hebrides can be hard on visitors. **21** | | And you will feel you will want to return to them, as I felt when I approached the end of my journey in the *Marguerite Explorer*.

A There are now a number of companies offering such trips.

B However, only about 40 out of the hundreds of islands are permanently inhabited.

C This is more than enough to put off the casual guest.

D And in the waters around them you can find not only dolphins but whales and the mighty sea eagle as well.

E But once you've watched dolphins leap through the dazzling water around your boat, you'll think they are paradise.

F Moreover, the fate of the islands and their people are bound together.

G Despite being relatively unspoilt, the Hebrides are also facing many pressures.

H Suddenly someone shouted: a splash in the water, half a mile away.

Tip Strip

- Read through the base text for general understanding.
- Read the text around each gap carefully.
- Read the sentences and find one that fits in with the meaning of each part. Check for topic and language links before and after the sentence.
- Reread the paragraph again to check that it makes sense.

Question 16: It is followed by 'such marine animals'. Can you find these animals in the sentences?

Question 18: The sentence following the gap mentions 'lack of people'. There is nothing about people in the sentence before it. Is 'People' the missing link?

Question 19: Look at the paragraphs before and after. Should this sentence introduce more of the same information or new information?

Question 21: Before the gap is 'can be hard', and after the gap 'You will want to return'. Do you need a 'but' in the middle?

You are going to read an article about the artists who draw animated cartoons. For Questions **22–35**, choose from the people (**A–D**). The people may be chosen more than once. There is an example at the beginning (**0**).

Mark your answers **on the separate answer sheet**.

A	Dan Taylor
B	Colin Grey
C	David Hoxton
D	Carl Hughes

Which artist

used to consider drawing was a pastime?	**0**	*A*
went abroad to find work?	**22**	
helped an arts school financially?	**23**	
thinks the ability to tell a good story is essential?	**24**	
thinks people who are good at drawing find jobs easily?	**25**	
thinks computers will replace skilled cartoonists?	**26**	
wants to attract adult audiences?	**27**	
says some artists are afraid of losing independence?	**28**	
thinks art schools do not teach students basic skills?	**29**	
runs a course for trainees?	**30**	
says many good cartoon artists work in advertising?	**31**	
will display his work for the public to see?	**32**	
likes being part of a large team?	**33**	
used to do drawings for colleagues?	**34**	
has invested in new equipment?	**35**	

Tip Strip

- You do not need to read the whole text first.
- Read each question and underline the key words.
- Read the text quickly and find the information. Remember the text is long and contains information which you will not need.
- When you find the relevant part of the text, read it carefully.
- Questions and text will not contain the same words. You need to look for the meaning, e.g. Question 23 'helped financially' = 'has given funds'.

Question 22: 'went abroad'. Be careful! The answer is not in paragraph 4.
Question 26: Look for a similar way of saying 'will replace'.
Question 29: Look for a similar way of saying 'basic skills'.

Jobs in cartoon animation

The future seems bright for animators, the artists who can make cartoons come to life. Four cartoonists give their impressions.

Dan Taylor is delighted that TV shows are now often inhabited by 'animated' cartoon characters. 'On paper the character you create is just a drawing,' he says, 'but then you give it movement, and it becomes a real TV personality.' Dan passed his art exams when he was at secondary school, but for many years he treated his drawing as a hobby. He would create images for his work mates, to be stuck on motorbikes or leather jackets. Eventually, he signed up at the Arts Institute to start a career as an animator. 'There is plenty of work around for people who can draw because cartoon shows can win sizeable audiences around the world,' he says. Dan would like to create cartoons that cross the boundary from children's animation to animated characters for grown-ups, with issues that interest them. Many of his ideas for future series will be on show at the annual animation festival in Bradford next September.

As head of animation of Grant Studios, **Colin Grey** sees his work load grow day by day. 'There is a huge public taste for animation,' he says, 'but we still lack skilled artists because the publicity industry has employed lots of people who are now busy designing ads.' Recognising the need to encourage training, Grey has just given some funds to the university for an arts school qualification in animation. 'This is a good investment of some of our profits,' he says. Grey believes another problem is that many animators are often reluctant to go for jobs in the big organisations. 'They fear large-scale projects will take away their freedom of action,' he says. He is trying to bring a bit more of the US way of working to bear on his current projects. 'Of course production methods have changed since Walt Disney put together his first animation. Now studios can create a character and have it animated in a different country.'

Despite the recent demand for cartoon artists in Europe, **David Hoxton** found that the only way to get his ideal job was to leave England and try his luck in the USA. 'Their way of working is with large numbers of people working on each series of drawings,' he says, 'I'd always dreamt of working in such a way, producing the thousands of drawings necessary to bring characters to life.' Hoxton thinks his job requires excellent drawing techniques, something he feels is often neglected in schools. 'Colleges of art encourage independent thinking, which is good, but some of them have lost their way when it comes to teaching the essentials.' He admits that computers can now do the translating of a drawing into a moving image, but he is convinced the skilled artist will always be in demand.

Carl Hughes is the owner and chief animator of Manton Hall Films, one of the biggest animator outfits in Europe. In the last three years, he has spent £10m on new machines to compete with international rivals. The reward has been a string of contracts to animate US shows at its offices in England. 'We believe training our staff is very important,' he says, 'I offer them a series of classes within a 12-week intensive programme. After that, they join the teams on particular shows.' Hughes believes what he needs most is artists who have artistic potential, not so much the ability to draw as the ability to develop the plot of a narrative, an interesting plot that will interest the audience. He knows that many people in the industry are crying out for highly-skilled animators to get involved in the development of shows, but he thinks the future of all that area of work lies with computers. 'Eventually they will do away with the need for artists,' he says.

PAPER 2   Writing (1 hour 30 minutes)

You **must** answer this question.

1   You are organising an adventure weekend holiday for a group of friends. You have seen the advertisement below, but you need to know more. Using the notes you have made, write to Adventure Weekend, giving relevant details and asking for further information.

experience needed?

canoeing?

food?

e.g.?

Adventure Weekend

A DIFFERENT HOLIDAY...

- Mountain climbing, sailing, walking and many more options!
- Our prices include almost everything
- All you need to bring is appropriate clothes
- Send us details about your group's age, interests and level of fitness, and we can suggest the best adventure weekend for you ...

Write a **letter** of between **120** and **180** words in an appropriate style. Do not write any addresses.

Tip Strip

- You don't have to be imaginative. Read the instructions carefully and underline key words and phrases, e.g. <u>give relevant details</u> or <u>ask for further information</u>.
- Read the input material. What information does the advertisement ask for?
- Base your answer on the input material, but try to use your own words.
- Think about who you are writing to. Which style is best: more formal or less formal? Should you use *Yours sincerely*, *Yours faithfully* or *Best wishes*?
- Plan your answer. Paragraph 1: express your interest in the holiday and give information about your group; Paragraph 2: request the extra information about the holiday (based on the hand-written notes).
- When you've finished, read the input information again. Have you included everything?
- Check the word limit, but don't waste time counting every word.
- Check your grammar and spelling.

Write an answer to **one** of the Questions **2–5** in this part. Write your answer in **120–180** words in an appropriate style.

2   This is part of a letter you receive from an English friend.

> *In your last letter you said you were organising a surprise party for a friend. Was it difficult to organise? What did your friend say? I'd love to hear how it went.*

Write your **letter**, answering your friend's questions and giving relevant details. Do not write any addresses.

3   You have been asked to write a story for your school magazine. The story must **begin** like this:

Peter opened the door and saw Jack standing in the doorway. Jack had returned, and Peter was frightened.

Write your **story**.

4   A magazine for young people called *Pastimes* has asked you to write about your favourite hobby. Write an article, describing your hobby and explaining why you would recommend it to other readers.

Write your **article**.

5   Answer **one** of the following two questions based on your reading of **one** of the set books.

Either   (a) 'I don't like the way this story ends.' With reference to the book you have read, write a **composition**, saying whether you agree or disagree with this statement.

Or   (b) Which character from the book do you feel could be your friend and why? Write a **composition**, describing the character you chose and saying why he/she could be your friend.

Tip Strip

- Read the questions carefully. Choose a question you have ideas and vocabulary for.
- Underline key points in the question and include them in your answer.
- Before you start writing, think of the main point you will include in each paragraph.
- Pay attention to organisation: all options require you to write in paragraphs.
- Check for spelling and grammar mistakes.

Question 2:
- Answer **all** your friend's questions.
- Use an informal style, but start and end the letter in an appropriate letter format.

Question 3:
- Think of how your story will develop **before** you start writing.
- Check your verb sequences, e.g. simple past / past perfect.
- Remember: no greeting, no headings.

Question 4:
- Use a neutral style, you do not know the reader.
- Introduce your topic in the first paragraph and summarise what you have said in your final paragraph.
- You are asked to describe your hobby and explain why you recommend it. Use vocabulary related to hobbies and leisure, and the language of description, opinion and explanation.
- Avoid repeating the same adjectives, e.g. nice, good.

Question 5(a):
- Say why you agree or disagree using examples from the book/story.
- Make notes on what to include in each paragraph **before** you start writing.
- Use a neutral to formal style.

Question 5(b):
- Describe a character **and** say why .... You can answer both parts in different paragraphs or combine both in each paragraph. Your answer should be a balance of both elements.

Use of English (1 hour 15 minutes)

For Questions **1–15**, read the text below and decide which answer **A**, **B**, **C** or **D** best fits each space. There is an example at the beginning (**0**).

Mark your answers **on the separate answer sheet**.

Tip Strip

- Read the text for general understanding.
- A, B, C, D are all grammatically possible, but only one fits the gap.
- The word must fit in the context of the text as a whole.
- Check the words before and after the gap. Some words can only be used with certain prepositions, some words will be part of set expressions.
- Read through the text and check that your answers make sense.

Question 2: Which verbs are usually used with 'role'? Which one is best in this context?

Question 5: Which phrasal verb means 'release'?

Question 7: All these words can follow 'in', but only one makes sense in this sentence.

Question 10: Which word completes the linking expression with 'what'?

Question 13: Which of the words is often found after the preposition 'under'?

Example:

0   **A**   dating   **B**   ageing   **C**   growing   **D**   stretching

0	A	B	C	D
	▨	▢	▢	▢

TREES FOR LIFE

Trees are amongst the biggest and longest-living things on Earth, some (**0**) ..... back longer than the oldest buildings. But (**1**) ..... being nice to look at, trees also (**2**) ..... an important role in improving the quality of our lives.

On a world-wide (**3**) ....., forests help to slow down the effects of global warming by using up the gas (**4**) ..... as carbon dioxide and giving (**5**) ..... the oxygen we need to breathe. At local neighbourhood level, trees also (**6**) ..... important environmental benefits. They offer shade and shelter, which in (**7**) ..... reduces the amount of energy needed to heat and cool (**8**) ..... buildings; at the same time, they also remove other impurities from the air we breathe.

Urban trees are especially important because for many people they provide the only daily (**9**) ..... with the natural world. What's (**10**) ....., urban trees also provide a home for birds, small animals and butterflies. (**11**) ..... the trees we would lose the pleasure of seeing these creatures in our cities. Regrettably, (**12**) ....., trees in cities are now coming under (**13**) ..... There is a limit to the level of pollution they can (**14**) ..... and, down at street level, their roots are being seriously (**15**) ..... by the digging needed to make way for modern telephone, television and other cables.

1	A	as far as	B	as long as	C	as soon as	D	as well as
2	A	play	B	show	C	act	D	serve
3	A	scale	B	size	C	range	D	area
4	A	called	B	known	C	titled	D	referred
5	A	in	B	away	C	up	D	out
6	A	bring	B	make	C	take	D	find
7	A	turn	B	place	C	order	D	reach
8	A	opposite	B	close	C	next	D	nearby
9	A	junction	B	touch	C	contact	D	taste
10	A	more	B	else	C	most	D	other
11	A	Throughout	B	Beyond	C	Without	D	Outside
12	A	therefore	B	whilst	C	however	D	despite
13	A	risk	B	threat	C	danger	D	warning
14	A	stand in for	B	face up to	C	put up with	D	fall back on
15	A	concerned	B	disturbed	C	interfered	D	involved

For Questions **16–30**, read the text below and think of the word which best fits each space. Use only **one** word in each space. There is an example at the beginning (**0**).

Write your answers **on the separate answer sheet**.

Example:	**0**	*take*

FIT FOR SPORTS

It's not always easy to decide which sport to (**0**) .... up. When choosing, it is important to remember that excellence in sports results (**16**) .... a number of factors. For some sports, the body shape and structure with (**17**) .... you are born are important. Top runners are typical examples of individuals (**18**) .... have selected a sport because of their natural body type. Many other sports are more dependent (**19**) .... training and technique, and anyone following a well-structured and appropriate training programme should do well.

The aim of all sports training (**20**) .... to improve fitness and skills, and to develop training programmes that are both safe (**21**) .... effective. To do (**22**) .... properly, an understanding of (**23**) .... physical demands of sport is needed. All sports require a combination of strength, speed, endurance, agility and flexibility to varying degrees. (**24**) .... is important is how these elements are combined to build up the skills of the sport (**25**) .... question. Other factors to be (**26**) .... into account in a training programme are diet, the importance of avoiding injuries, your general state of health, and the nature and role (**27**) .... other team players.

Bearing (**28**) .... considerations in mind, anyone prepared to work (**29**) .... it can expect to progress to a very reasonable competitive level, even (**30**) .... only a few people will go on to break world records.

Tip Strip

- Read the text for general understanding.
- The word must make sense in the context of the text as a whole.
- Decide which type of word each gap needs, e.g. preposition, relative, conjunction, verb, adverb, etc.
- Look out for fixed expressions, dependent prepositions after certain verbs and linking words and phrases.
- Read through the text and check that your answers make sense.

Question 16: What type of word goes here? Which two words are possible? Which one makes most sense with what comes before and after?
Question 18: Which type of word goes here? Are 'individuals' places, people or things?
Question 20: The writer is talking about something in general. Which tense should be used?
Question 28: The word you need refers back to the last paragraph. Is it singular or plural?

For Questions **31–40**, complete the second sentence so that it has a similar meaning to the first sentence, using the word given. **Do not change the word given.** You must use between two and five words, including the word given. Here is an example (**0**).

Example: **0** You must write all you personal details on this form.

fill

You must .... with all your personal details.

The gap can be filled by the words 'fill in this form' so you write:

0	*fill in this form*

Write **only the missing words** on the separate answer sheet.

---

31 I'd love to go on holiday in March, but that's my busiest month.

wish

I .... go on holiday in March, but that's my busiest month.

32 'Harry, I think you should cancel the concert if this rain continues,' John said.

advised

John .... the concert if the rain continued.

33 Not many students attended Dr Brown's lecture on politics.

number

Only .... students attended Dr Brown's lecture on politics.

34 City residents are going to organise a campaign to reduce street noise.

be

A campaign to reduce street noise .... by city residents.

35 After the accident Brenda was confused and did not recognise her brother.

so

After the accident Brenda .... did not recognise her brother.

36 Peter hasn't seen his aunt Lucy for years.

saw

It's .... his aunt Lucy.

37 The police said John had stolen the money.

accused

The police .... the money.

38 Tania has a mobile phone because her son may need to contact her.

in case

Tania has a mobile phone .... to contact her.

39 The reason Gloria didn't tell us the truth is that she was afraid of our reaction.

if

Gloria would have told us the truth .... afraid of our reaction.

40 The students organised a show but they postponed it due to lack of funds.

put

The students organised a show but they .... of lack of funds.

For Questions **41–55**, read the text below and look carefully at each line. Some of the lines are correct, and some have a word which should not be there.

If a line is correct, put a tick (✔) by the number **on the separate answer sheet**. If a line has a word which should not be there, write the word **on the separate answer sheet**. There are examples at the beginning (**0** and **00**).

Examples:	0	*of*
	00	✔

0	....	On lovely sunny days in the summer, many of people in London
00	....	go along to one of the beautiful parks. Most of them go there
41	....	just to sit around and relax themselves with friends, but I prefer
42	....	something such more active. For me, one of the most exciting
43	....	things to do is flying a kite. It's amazing how much fun you
44	....	can have with a small and piece of material on a long piece of
45	....	cord. The best thing about kites is that, unless you will want
46	....	one that can do lots of fancy tricks to impress your friends,
47	....	they don't cost a very lot of money. You need a day when
48	....	there's a good strong breeze. To get it the kite flying, you have
49	....	to unwind a few metres of the cord and then get a friend to
50	....	hold the kite up while you to get a good grip on the handles.
51	....	Then, you start running towards the wind, that making sure your
52	....	friend lets go at the more right moment. As the wind catches
53	....	the kite, unwind the cord and watch the kite climb by higher
54	....	and higher. Keep a good hold so you don't lose it and, of
55	....	course, avoid trees, unless you're be good at climbing!

For Questions **56–65**, read the text below. Use the word given in capitals at the end of each line to form a word that fits in the space in the same line. There is an example at the beginning (**0**). Write your answers **on the separate answer sheet**.

Example: | **0** | *explorer*

FLORIDA

When the famous (**0**) ...*explorer*..., Columbus claimed Florida for Spain in   **EXPLORE**
1492, he had never (**56**) .... eyes on it. The area's most important   **LAY**
early (**57**) .... thus set a pattern that has continued for centuries.   **VISIT**
There is a general (**58**) ..).................. amongst people, apparently quite   **BELIEVE**
(**59**) .... with whether or not they've been there themselves, that   **CONNECT**
Florida is a good place to go.

In fact, it is almost (**60**) .... not to enjoy yourself in Florida today,   **POSSIBLE**
given the wonderful (**61**) .... of facilities available to tourists. Some   **SELECT**
of the world's most popular tourist (**62**) .... are located in the state   **ATTRACT**
whose (**63**) .... beaches welcome 40 million people each year.   **SAND**
These days it seems (**64**) .... to describe Florida's geography and   **POINT**
climate. After all, few people would have (**65**) .... in finding it on a   **DIFFICULT**
map and most would know what weather to expect there.

Tip Strip

- Read the text for general understanding.
- Decide what type of word you need for each gap (e.g. noun, adjective, etc.).
- Look at the whole sentence, not just at the line containing the gap.
- You should make no more than two changes to the word.
- You may need to add a prefix or suffix to some words.
- Some words may be positive or negative. Check the meaning of the passage!
- Read through the text and check that your words make sense.
- Check your spelling.

Question 56: What's the past participle of this word?
Question 58: Is a noun, verb or adjective needed here?
Question 62: Is this word going to be singular or plural?
Question 64: Read the text to the end. Is this word going to express a negative or positive idea? Will you add a prefix or a suffix?

PAPER 4   Listening (40 minutes)

You will hear people talking in eight different situations. For Questions **1–8**, choose the best answer **A**, **B** or **C**.

Tip Strip

- Read the **question** before the options and underline key words.
- Each question is based on a different listening text with a separate mark.
- Relax and concentrate on each new text, don't think of the one you have just done.
- Decide on one of the options after the first listening.
- Use the second listening to check that you are correct.
- If you are not sure, guess. You may have understood more than you think.
- Do not listen for single words, but for the general meaning.
- Don't worry about words that you don't know.

Question 3: The listening text mentions paint, photography and stone figures, but which are in the collection?

Question 4: What can be learnt as you go along?

Question 5: The customer has a guide book, but does he use it?

1 You hear part of a radio play.
Where does this scene take place?
A   in a restaurant
B   at a police station
C   in the street

| | 1 |

2 You turn on the radio and hear a man talking.
What are you listening to?
A   a competition
B   a lesson
C   an advertisement

| | 2 |

3 You hear a woman talking about an exhibition.
What can you see in the exhibition?
A   paintings
B   photographs
C   sculptures

| | 3 |

4 You hear a manager talking about the skills young employees need.
What skills are essential in his opinion?
A   problem-solving skills
B   writing skills
C   computer skills

| | 4 |

5 You hear a hotel manager talking to a customer.
Where did the customer get the information about the hotel?
A   from a guide book
B   from the Internet
C   from a friend

| | 5 |

6 You hear a young girl who spent a month in a foreign country talking about her experience.
What was good about it?
A   She became self-confident.
B   She improved her language skills.
C   She travelled to many places.

| | 6 |

7 You hear a woman talking about a book on the radio.
What is the book about?
A   healthy eating habits
B   the history of food
C   teenagers and food

| | 7 |

8 You hear a young woman giving advice on going night clubbing.
What is her advice?
A   Think about what you will wear.
B   Be prepared for extra expenses.
C   Check the music is what you like.

| | 8 |

You will hear an interview with the dancer, Darren Faiweather. For Questions **9–18**, complete the sentences.

Tip Strip

- The questions follow the order of the text.
- Before you listen, read the questions. Think about the type of information which is missing.
- The words you need to write are on the tape, but not in the same order as the question sentences. It is not a dictation.
- Write 1–3 words in each space. Don't repeat the words and ideas already used in the sentence.
- Check that your word or phrase is grammatically correct and makes sense.
- Check your spelling.

Question 9: Are you listening for a noun or a verb for this gap, or both?

Question 13: What type of places could Darren work? Listen to check your ideas.

Question 15: Listen for the word he uses to describe her. What sort of word will it be?

Question 17: What type of information are you listening for in this question?

Darren's father thought that dancing classes would enable him to

[*fut*] **9** well.

The idea of dancing classes came from a [*teacher*] **10** who lived nearby.

Darren was successful as a dancer in both local and national

[ ] **11**

In London, Darren found it difficult to [ ] **12** at the College of Dance.

Darren worked in the college [ ] **13** to pay for his classes.

As Darren lived outside London, he spent as long as

[ ] **14** each day travelling.

Darren describes Lily Partridge as a [ ] **15** teacher.

Darren thinks that Lily liked him because they often had

[ ] **16**

Darren first became famous dancing in a ballet called [ ] **17**

Darren is now well-known as a dancer who likes to perform

[ ] **18**

You will hear five different women talking on the subject of happiness. For Questions **19–23**, choose from the list **A–F** what each speaker says. Use the letters only once. There is one extra letter which you do not need to use.

A   She talks about her good news.

Speaker 1 [　] **19**

B   She starts each day with a decision.

Speaker 2 [　] **20**

C   She laughs at every opportunity.

Speaker 3 [　] **21**

D   She praises the people she likes.

Speaker 4 [　] **22**

E   She finds time for extra leisure activities.

Speaker 5 [　] **23**

F   She concentrates on a few activities.

Tip Strip

- There are five different speakers talking on a similar topic. You hear all five once, then all five repeated.
- Read the instructions carefully. What will the people be talking about?
- Before you listen, read options A to F.
- On the first listening, note down the speaker's main idea. Mark the option closest to this idea.
- On the second listening, check your answers. You may need to change some of them.

Sometimes a word in the prompt occurs in several extracts, for example:
A: 'Good news' is mentioned by speakers 1 and 4, but neither 'talk about good news'. Listen for another way of saying this.
C: Laughing is mentioned by four of the speakers. But which speaker laughs a lot?
D: Speaker 2 mentions that people 'praise' her. But which speaker praises other people?

You will hear an interview with the television actor, Simon McGregor. For each of the Questions **24–30**, choose the best answer **A**, **B** or **C**.

Tip Strip

- The questions follow the order of the text.
- Before you listen, read through the questions and underline key words.
- Listen to find the answer to the question, then choose the option (A, B or C) which is closest.
- The words in the options will be different from the words you hear.
- Most questions will be about people's ideas, opinions, feelings, etc.

Question 24: 'Reason' is the most important word here. What does Simon say he lacked?

Question 25: Listen for the adjective Simon uses to describe his first job.

Question 27: Why is 'busking' in commas? This word is probably explained on the tape.

Question 29: What does 'According to Simon' mean?

Question 30: Whose opinion are we listening for here?

24 What reason does Simon give for not going into acting straight from school?

   A He didn't want to study any more.
   B He was not brave enough.
   C He lacked the necessary qualifications.

          24

25 How does Simon feel now about the careers advice he was given?

   A He is grateful for the opportunity it gave him.
   B He regrets not mentioning his real ambitions.
   C He wishes he hadn't trained as an accountant.

          25

26 What led Simon to give up accountancy?

   A He found the work boring.
   B He had developed other interests.
   C He realised he wasn't going to qualify.

          26

27 Why did Simon take up 'busking'?

   A to earn extra pocket money
   B to pay the fees for his course of study
   C to support himself while he studied

          27

28 How did Simon's grandmother influence him?

   A She encouraged him in his ambitions.
   B She organised plays for children.
   C She had been involved in the theatre.

          28

29 According to Simon, people who are shy

   A prefer to be on their own.
   B really want to be accepted.
   C find acting comes easily to them.

          29

30 Simon thinks that it is better for actors if they

   A can identify with the characters they play.
   B have to work hard to convince audiences.
   C are not too similar to the characters they play.

          30

PAPER 5

Speaking (14 minutes)

Tip Strip

Part 1

- The examiner will ask you questions in turn. Don't try to learn a little speech about yourself. This will not answer the examiner's questions properly.

Part 2

- A minute is quite a long time to talk. Don't panic, don't go too fast.
- Don't interrupt your partner's turn. Listen so you can comment afterwards.
- Don't give separate descriptions of each picture. Compare and contrast them from the beginning.
- If you don't know a word in one of the pictures, describe what you mean using other words.

Part 3

- Ask your partner for his/her opinions, don't just say what you think.
- You have to talk for 3 minutes, so don't decide or agree too soon – talk about all the pictures first.
- You don't have to agree with your partner.

Part 4

- The examiner may ask you questions in turn, or may ask general questions for you both to answer.
- You don't have to agree with your partner, but try not to interrupt; let your partner finish, then say what you think.

PART 1 (3 minutes)

The examiner will ask you both to talk briefly about yourselves by answering questions such as:

Where are you from? Tell us something about the area where you live.
What type of work do people do in your area?
What is there for young people to do in your area?

PART 2 (3 or 4 minutes)

You will each be asked to talk for a minute without interruption. You will each have two different photographs to talk about. You will also have to answer a question after your partner has spoken.

Newspapers (compare, contrast and speculate)

Turn to pictures 1 and 2 on page 151 which show people reading newspapers.

Candidate A, compare and contrast these photographs, and say why you think the people are reading newspapers. You have a minute to do this.

Candidate B, do you often read newspapers?

Parents and children (compare, contrast and speculate)

Turn to pictures 1 and 2 on page 152 which show parents and children.

Candidate B, compare and contrast these photographs, and say how you think the people are feeling about each other. You have a minute to do this.

Candidate A, did you often get into trouble as a child?

PART 3 (3 or 4 minutes)

You will be asked to discuss something together without interruption by the examiner. You will have a page of pictures to help you.

Jobs in television (discuss and evaluate)

Turn to the pictures on page 153 which show different jobs students could do in a television company to gain work experience.

How popular do you think these jobs might be with young people? In which two jobs would they learn the most useful skills?

PART 4 (3 or 4 minutes)

The examiner encourages you to develop the discussion in Part 3 by asking questions such as:

Would you like to work for a television company? Why (not)?
Why are people worried if children watch a lot of television?
How much are we influenced by what we see on television?
What do you think of television programmes for young people in this country?

PAPER 1   Reading (1 hour 15 minutes)

You are going to read an article about a man who works as a professional shopper. Choose from the list **A–H** the sentence which best summarises each part (**1–6**) of the article. There is one extra sentence which you do not need to use. There is an example at the beginning (**0**).

Mark your answers **on the separate answer sheet**.

A	Bryan successfully avoids some of the problems that shoppers encounter.
B	Bryan's success may be related to a recognised trend.
C	Bryan's experience allows him to predict bargains.
D	Bryan makes his terms and conditions clear.
E	Bryan's initial success was not anticipated.
F	Bryan's clients are offered special treatment in shops.
G	Bryan's strategy is to provide a flexible service.
H	Bryan feels fortunate that he is able to combine work with pleasure.

Tip Strip

Another task in Part 1 asks you to match summary sentences to parts of an article.

- Read the text for general understanding.
- Read each paragraph, decide what the main point is, then find the sentence which is the best summary of it.
- The sentences won't use the same words as the text.

Sentence B talks about a 'trend'. Which paragraph talks about things which are changing?

Sentence D talks about 'terms and conditions'. Which paragraph describes what you get for your money if you use Bryan's service?

Sentence G says that Bryan's service is 'flexible'. Which paragraph tells us about different ways in which Bryan's service will help you?

THE GOOD BUY MAN

So, you don't want to get your toes crushed in the summer sales? Michele Dalton meets a man who'll do your shopping for you.

0	H

Bryan Bonaparte is that rare find – a man who loves shopping. Indeed, he loves it so much that he's set up an agency to provide a shopping service for those people who don't share his enthusiasm. 'I get a real buzz out of shopping,' admits Bryan. 'It's a challenge to track down what people want and to find new and interesting things on their behalf. People say to me, "I can't believe you enjoy doing this", but I do. And it's great to get paid for it as well.'

1	

Bryan's agency, called Ace, started in a small way one Christmas. It was meant to be just a seasonal thing, but it turned out to be so successful that he carried on throughout the year. It seems there are always gifts to buy for weddings, birthdays, anniversaries and retirements.

2	

A survey published in the *London Evening News* last year found that many people are getting increasingly depressed at the prospect of shopping, and this may go some way to explaining Bryan's success. The survey pinpointed crowds, bad weather, choosing the right present and carrying heavy bags as stress triggers.

3	

Planning a shopping trip with military precision is Bryan's solution. 'A lot of people go shopping, especially during the sales, with no idea what they are looking for,' he explains. 'It's no wonder they find wandering around the stores frustrating and exhausting.'

4	

The shopping stretch covered by Ace runs through most of London's West End shopping districts. Bryan, or another member of his team, is happy to take anyone shopping within this area or to visit stores on their behalf, delivering goods to clients' homes or offices at a convenient time, including evenings and weekends. If you don't actually know what you want, Ace will make suggestions, buy the items, then return to the shops to exchange them if you are not completely satisfied.

5	

A flat charge of £15 per hour applies to either service. Clients with a list of requests are given a quote based on the amount of time involved. The only thing Bryan won't do is buy food. For sales shopping, customers need to be specific about size, colour, style and designer labels. Details about the normal price and the discount that clients want are required, and Bryan warns that shops generally won't exchange items bought in sales.

6	

Bryan's specialist knowledge means that clients usually get a good deal. 'I've come to know how long the sales will run for, the stock that will be carried and whether old stock will be brought back in at sale time. If I know the store will reduce prices after a month, then I'll hang on before buying. Sometimes, prices can be slashed by up to 70% a few days before the sale ends. With Bryan to guide you, will shopping ever be the same again?

You are going to read a magazine article about an artist. For Questions **7–14**, choose the correct answer **A**, **B**, **C** or **D**.

Mark your answers **on the separate answer sheet**.

The Ballet Sculptor

Delicate figures ready to begin a dance or caught in mid-flight – these images dominate the work of sculptor Suzy Jordan

Young sculptor Suzy Jordan is fast developing an international reputation for her beautifully-crafted figures which are made from a mixture of clay and metal. People love dancers, particularly ballet dancers, and Suzy has a fascination for them too. 'I used to long to be a dancer when I was younger,' she says. 'There's something amazing about all those graceful movements that, unknown to the audience, can be so painful for the dancers. I'm glad I didn't go in for it, but just watching them gives me so many ideas.'

Suzy has been in touch with some leading ballet companies to see if they'll allow her to sit and draw their dancers during rehearsal time. Her dream is to join forces with them, do a series of life-size sculptures and then hold an exhibition in the foyer of the theatre where the dancers perform.

Most of her sculpture is of figures. 'If I get the chance to sculpt from life, it's really great because I can work more quickly and I'm not guessing shapes or turning to reference books,' she told us. But most of her work has to be done from drawings. After graduating from Art School, Suzy taught drawing for a number of years before setting up as a sculptor, so at least she has the necessary skills.

Most of Suzy's works are individually commissioned and one piece can take as long as four or five months to complete. All of the work is done in a small shed in the garden of her family home in the country. This tin space, about 3 square metres, contains her main **worktop**, plus all her other gear. Suzy uses terracotta clay to form her sculptures and applies a mixture of lacquer and crushed metal powder, usually bronze, on top. This makes her pieces less expensive than solid bronze figures would be. She then adds a layer of resin or wax to give her work an aged look.

One of Suzy's biggest commissions came from a school in Sweden. They wanted three specially-designed life-size figures to suspend from the ceiling in their gymnasium. Hard to imagine how she did **it**, but each one was made in her garden shed. They had to be made of plaster so that they wouldn't be too heavy to hang up. Suzy travelled to Sweden with the sculptures to help direct their installation. One of the drawbacks of working to commissions rather than on mass produced pieces is having to work out what sort of price to charge. 'I used to be such a softie,' she confides. 'If someone fell in love with something I'd made, I'd accept a lower offer or let them pay for it in instalments, just so that it went to a good home. But I've learnt not to do that anymore.'

Suzy's work starts at around £100 for the smallest figures, but large sculptures can cost as much as £3000 each. But as she doesn't make copies of her work, each person has an original, so they must be worth having as an investment. As she explains, 'All artists want some kind of recognition for their work. I don't think many of us do it for the money. I have a friend who says she can't wait to see my work in ten years and see how it's progressed. I'm very lucky to be doing the sort of work where that kind of progression shows.'

7 How does Suzy feel about dancers?

A inspired by the way they move
B upset by how much they suffer
C sad that she didn't train to be one
D impressed by how they react to audiences

8 Suzy has contacted certain ballet companies because she'd like to

A find a job in a theatre.
B sell sculptures to them.
C be invited to performances.
D co-operate in a joint project.

9 Why would Suzy prefer not to work from drawings?

A She's not good at drawing.
B Books advise against it.
C It takes a long time to do.
D She'd like to develop new skills.

10 What is a 'worktop' (line 29)?

A a type of building
B a piece of equipment
C a surface to work on
D an article of clothing

11 Why does Suzy not make her figures wholly from metal?

A They would look too new.
B They would cost too much.
C It would make them too heavy.
D It would require more space.

12 What does 'it' in line 39 refer to?

A producing the figures
B designing the figures
C delivering the figures
D hanging the figures

13 Why has Suzy's attitude towards her work changed?

A She now produces larger quantities.
B She now only works to commission.
C She no longer has problems selling it.
D She has become more businesslike.

14 What does Suzy find satisfying about her work?

A Each piece is unique.
B She makes a good living.
C Her work is rising in value.
D People appreciate what she does.

You are going to read a magazine article about a man who works as a diver. Six paragraphs have been removed from the article. Choose the most suitable paragraph from the list **A–H** for each part (**15–20**). There is one extra paragraph which you do not need to use. There is an example at the beginning (**0**).

Mark your answers **on the separate answer sheet**.

THE GOLFBALL FROGMAN

Professional diver Adam Tranter was thrilled when some friends invited him for a round of golf at an internationally famous course. If he did well, he might be allowed to join the socially-prestigious golf club.

0	H

Unwilling to give up the idea of joining the golf club altogether, Adam hit upon the idea of using his diving skills to make himself useful. He put on his wetsuit, strapped a couple of air tanks to his back, and began retrieving lost balls from the lakes on the course.

15	

And you can't really blame them because there is something a bit ridiculous about a grown man wandering around a golf course in a rubber suit and goggles, jumping into ponds. But for Adam it's a serious business and, apparently, he's also providing a valuable service to golfers.

16	

Of course, Adam does also come across less distinguished balls and plenty that look a bit knocked-about. These also have a price, however, he cleans them up and sells them at second-hand sales and to other less prestigious golf clubs.

17	

Most of the lakes are only five or six feet deep, but on the bottom it's impossible to see a thing, you just have to feel around in the mud for the balls. Adam has to be very careful too, because you get all sorts of things down there – bottles, cans, all sorts of junk. If he were to cut himself, he could be out of action for weeks.

18	

Fortunately, Adam's never been in any kind of difficulty. Nonetheless, he always has someone with him, keeping watch just in case. 'A golf course can be a fairly lonely place,' he explains. 'You can be a long way from help should you ever need it.'

19	

Despite all these hazards, Andrew insists that the job is great fun. 'I was under a lot of weed a couple of weeks ago and all you could make out from the surface was my air tank. A young guy, searching the banks of the lake for his ball, spotted me and ran to the clubhouse shouting, "There's a monster in the lake!"'

20	

Luckily, nobody at the club has complained about Adam's activities, however, and one suspects that given his notoriety in the golfing world, his membership is now secure.

Tip Strip

Another task in Part 3 asks you to insert paragraphs into an article.

- Read through the base text for general understanding.
- Read the text around each gap carefully. Look at the whole paragraph, before and after the gap.
- Read paragraphs A–H. Check for topic and language links with paragraphs in the base text.
- Reread the text and the paragraphs to check that it makes sense.

Paragraph B talks about 'another such danger'. Which paragraph in the base text talks about dangerous things?

Paragraph D begins with 'But'. It is making a contrast with something in the previous piece of text. Which paragraph in the base text tells us something about money?

Paragraph G talks about 'people' and their reaction to Adam's job. Which paragraph in the base text explains why this happens? It uses a pronoun instead of 'people'.

A   He makes a good living out of it too. Adam can collect anything from 1,000 to 2,000 balls during a day's diving. A lot of them are good quality with hardly a mark on them and can be sold to professional golfing shops, which in turn sell them back to golfers.

B   Another such danger is weed. The water in the lakes tends to be stagnant and so plant matter tends to build up very quickly. A diver can easily get tangled up, therefore. Adam is well-aware of the danger and, as a professional, knows better than to take unnecessary chances.

C   Another thing to look out for is golf balls themselves. 'I usually dive while play is going on and quite often I can be in a lake when balls are landing in it,' says Adam. 'Getting hit by one of those things would be nobody's idea of a joke.'

D   But Adam wouldn't want us to get the impression that it's easy money. 'I don't want kids thinking that they can earn extra pocket money by doing this,' he insists. 'It is dangerous, dirty, cold and smelly.'

E   Apart from that, Adam has few regrets about his decision. Indeed, he has become more involved in the world of golf than he bargained for.

F   On another occasion, when he was covered in weed, he surfaced just behind some poor unsuspecting golfer and yelled 'Boo!' The poor man apparently went very white and no one has seen him at the golf club since.

G   As a result, Adam has become something of a celebrity on the golf courses of southern England – as a frogman. 'When I tell people what I do, they just fall about laughing,' he says.

H   It didn't take him long to realise, however, that although he was a natural in the water, he was quite out of his depth on the green. He had no future as a golfer.

You are going to read some interviews with women who have unusual jobs. For Questions **21–35**, choose from the people (**A–D**). The people may be chosen more than once. There is an example at the beginning (**0**).

Mark your answers **on the separate answer sheet**.

A	Dina Dorset
B	Angela Bell
C	Claire Dorn
D	Dolly Masons

Which interview is with someone who

works part-time?	**0**	*A*
had a better salary in an earlier job?	**21**	
cannot make friends at work?	**22**	
will get a university qualification?	**23**	
has to pretend she is always happy?	**24**	
writes to her customers?	**25**	
meets her customers socially?	**26**	
organises activities for older people?	**27**	
was promoted at work?	**28**	
does not like to use her voice?	**29**	
has a job that affects her health?	**30**	
had an earlier job as a teacher?	**31**	
thinks attitudes towards her work have changed?	**32**	
has the job she had always wanted?	**33**	
considers work more important than family?	**34**	
has responsibility for quality control?	**35**	

Women in unusual jobs

Dina Dorset

is a disc jockey in a night-club in London. A few years ago she thought her future was in tennis. 'For a while I trained promising young players on a full-time basis, but one day a neighbour who was a radio producer took me down to his radio station and I became involved in the music scene,' she says. There are lots of late nights for Dina but surprisingly the job doesn't offer her much in the way of a social life. 'I don't have any real contact with the large numbers of people I meet,' she says. She particularly likes the fact that she now only works four hours a day. 'The one thing I resent is having to appear cheerful all the time even when I feel down,' she says. She hopes to be able to produce her own records one day but she has given up her ambition of going to college. 'You can't do everything in life,' she says.

Angela Bell

is a clown, she paints her face white and wears funny clothes to entertain people. She decided clowning was the job she wanted after seeing a clown show. 'I said that was it. It involved no talking, and that suited me down to the ground,' she says. She soon realised that women only introduced the act and were on stage for a few minutes because it was considered a job for men. 'That is changing now,' she says. 'But from the beginning I decided to call myself Chris on the programmes instead of Angela so that the audience don't know if I'm a man or a woman.' Angela had to choose between family and work. 'I liked my work too much to think of children,' she says, 'and I have no regrets.' She says the secret of her success is that she is a very happy person, which is what you need to be a good clown.

Claire Dorn

works on a cruise liner, a floating luxury hotel which is her home for eight months of the year. She is the ship's secretary and has responsibility for all information customers may need while on board, as well as acting as secretary to the captain. 'He is very demanding but I have no complaints from him,' she says. Losing touch with the real world for so long is no problem because the ship's officers can take advantage of the activities provided for the entertainment of passengers. 'I've made many lasting friendships here,' she says, 'we get customers of all ages and backgrounds.' Her previous work experience as a Personal Assistant to a manager prepared her for the demands of this job. It was better paid than her present job but she gave it up because she had always liked the idea of working on a ship. 'The only disadvantage is that there are constant time changes when you go round the world and it makes you feel physically unwell,' she says.

Dolly Masons

has worked in a chocolate factory for the past twenty years. 'I was nearly sixteen when I joined,' she says. 'My parents both worked here at the time, so it had become a kind of family tradition. My first job was as an assistant and I've since climbed the ladder to become customer relations manager.' Her present job involves a number of responsibilities, from performing taste tests for all chocolates to ensure their flavour is the same, to organising events for retired employees, including parties and excursions to the seaside. 'I like to have variety in my job,' she says, 'any comments from customers will be forwarded to me to deal with. Of course, I'll never meet them personally but they will all get a written response from me.' She admits that at the moment she is finding it difficult to concentrate on the degree course in marketing she started last year, but is confident she will finish it by June.

PAPER 2   Writing (1 hour 30 minutes)

PART 1   You **must** answer this question.

1   You and a friend want to find a summer job abroad. Your friend has sent you a letter with an advertisement. Read the letter and the advertisement together with the notes.

> *This sounds interesting, just what we want. I've made some notes on it but I'm too busy with exams. Can you write to them for more details? Maybe you can think of other questions, too.*
>
> *See you soon*

FCE level

waitress?

food?

SUMMER JOBS AGENCY

★ Do you speak English well?

★ We have summer jobs in hotels and restaurants in the USA and Australia.

★ Accommodation provided. ——————— where?

★ Travel expenses covered.

★ Free time allowed.

★ We arrange travel to and from your country.

Write a letter to the Summer Jobs Agency asking for the information which your friend suggests and adding any relevant questions of your own.

Write a **letter** of between **120** and **180** words in an appropriate style. Do not write any addresses.

Write an answer to one of the Questions **2–5** in this part. Write your answer in **120–180** words in an appropriate style.

2   You have received this invitation from a magazine called 'Animal Life'.

> *We have heard you know a lot about animals. Could you write an article for us explaining to our readers which animals make good pets and how to look after them?*

Write your **article**.

3   You have been doing a class project on traditional festivals in your country. Now your teacher has asked you to write a composition on the following subject:

My favourite local festival

Write your **composition**.

4   You have just come back from a visit to a local museum organised by your school. The Principal has asked you to write a report about the museum and what you saw there, saying whether it is of interest for all age groups in the school.

Write a **report** for the Principal.

5   Answer **one** of the following two questions based on your reading of **one** of the set books.

Either   (a) Write a **composition**, comparing two characters from the story you have read and saying which of the two you prefer and why.

Or   (b) 'I would have preferred to see this story on film and not to have read it.' With reference to the book you have read, write a **composition**, saying whether you agree or disagree with this statement and why.

Use of English (1 hour 15 minutes)

For Questions **1–15**, read the text below and decide which answer **A**, **B**, **C** or **D** best fits each space. There is an example at the beginning (**0**).

Mark your answers **on the separate answer sheet**.

Example:

0 **A** became **B** turned **C** appeared **D** succeeded

| 0 | A | B | C | D |

POLAR ADVENTURER

In March 1999, Amyr Klink, a Brazilian yachtsman and polar adventurer, (**0**) ..... the first man to circle Antarctica while staying south of 50 degrees latitude. He (**1**) ..... the most dangerous sea route in the world. Klink was already (**2**) ..... known because in 1984 he had rowed across the Atlantic in a small boat. The book which he wrote, based on his (**3**) ..... on that trip, had by then (**4**) ..... millions of copies.

For his polar adventure, Klink built his (**5**) ..... boat. He (**6**) ..... off in 1998 from South Georgia and he arrived back there 88 days later – although he (**7**) ..... eleven of those days on dry land in Antarctica. He did not stop there out of (**8**) ....., but because he wanted to see the Antarctic Peninsula.

Klink knew that his (**9**) ..... would be dangerous. On the way he had to be careful to (**10**) ..... huge floating blocks of ice. These icebergs, as they are called, were everywhere and (**11**) ..... one of them would have been a disaster. As Klink knew that any rescue mission would have been impossible in the rough seas, he did not (**12**) ..... to take a life-boat.

When he sailed into (**13**) ..... winds 750 miles south of Tasmania, he met waves that were twenty-five metres high. This meant staying awake most of the time. He only managed to sleep for twenty-minute (**14**) ..... at a stretch. But he succeeded in the end, (**15**) ..... all the difficulties that he had to face.

1	**A**	went	**B**	took	**C**	had	**D**	made
2	**A**	really	**B**	widely	**C**	broadly	**D**	thoroughly
3	**A**	events	**B**	incidents	**C**	happenings	**D**	experiences
4	**A**	sold	**B**	printed	**C**	bought	**D**	produced
5	**A**	proper	**B**	individual	**C**	own	**D**	single
6	**A**	set	**B**	put	**C**	left	**D**	got
7	**A**	passed	**B**	lived	**C**	spent	**D**	remained
8	**A**	necessity	**B**	demand	**C**	urgency	**D**	requirement
9	**A**	excursion	**B**	tour	**C**	voyage	**D**	cruise
10	**A**	expect	**B**	avoid	**C**	escape	**D**	refuse
11	**A**	crashing	**B**	breaking	**C**	knocking	**D**	hitting
12	**A**	consider	**B**	mind	**C**	bother	**D**	accept
13	**A**	fast	**B**	strong	**C**	heavy	**D**	hard
14	**A**	periods	**B**	times	**C**	occasions	**D**	lengths
15	**A**	as far as	**B**	apart from	**C**	according to	**D**	in spite of

For Questions **16–30**, read the text below and think of the word which best fits each space. Use only **one** word in each space. There is an example at the beginning (**0**).

Write your answers **on the separate answer sheet**.

Example:

0	*at*

GOOD AT LANGUAGES

At school, Sarah Biggs says she was very bad (**0**) .... languages. Now she speaks English, Spanish and Italian and works (**16**) .... a bilingual secretary in a travel company in England. (**17**) .... several foreign languages at work is not easy, but for Sarah, and other multi-lingual secretaries (**18**) .... her, it is all standard practice.

Sarah comes from Spain, (**19**) .... she attended school and college. But it was time spent abroad after college (**20**) .... encouraged her interest in languages.

In her job, Sarah has (**21**) .... great deal more responsibility than the title of secretary would suggest. She stresses the importance of (**22**) .... fluent in Spanish because part of her job is dealing (**23**) .... customers from Latin America. (**24**) .... such clients come from abroad, she has to translate everything (**25**) .... say into English. She is given (**26**) .... time for preparation at all, so this aspect of her job is one of the (**27**) .... difficult.

It is important for Sarah to be up-to-date with changes (**28**) .... her own language, so she reads Spanish newspapers and books looking for new additions to (**29**) .... vocabulary. Sarah says she (**30**) .... not give up this job even if they offered her a better salary in another company.

For Questions **31–40**, complete the second sentence so that it has a similar meaning to the first sentence, using the word given. **Do not change the word given.** You must use between two and five words, including the word given. Here is an example (**0**).

Example: **0** All your lockers must be left completely empty at the end of term.

nothing

You must .... your lockers at the end of term.

The gap can be filled by the words 'leave nothing in' so you write:

0	leave nothing in

Write **only the missing words** on the separate answer sheet.

31 'Don't touch the cake, Toby, it's still hot,' said Mrs Smith.

not

Mrs Smith .... the cake because it was still hot.

32 Tamsin was the only student who hadn't done her homework.

apart

All the students .... done their homework.

33 I expect Lucy was pleased that she'd won the prize.

been

Lucy .... that she'd won the prize.

34 'I will only work extra hours if I get paid at a higher rate.'

unless

'I will .... I get paid at a higher rate.'

35 Max offered Gaby a lift to the station, but she didn't accept.

turned

Gaby .... offer of a lift to the station.

36 Valerie doesn't object to her photograph appearing in the magazine.

objection

Valerie .... her photograph appearing in the magazine.

37 There is no more petrol left in the car.

run

The car .... petrol.

38 'If you ask me, you should buy a new coat, Tracy,' said her mother.

advised

Tracy's mother .... a new coat.

39 People say that the famous couple are about to get married.

said

The famous couple .... about to get married.

40 You can borrow my camera, but you must be careful with it.

long

You can borrow my camera .... careful with it.

For Questions **41–55**, read the text below and look carefully at each line. Some of the lines are correct, and some have a word which should not be there.

If a line is correct, put a tick (✔) by the number **on the separate answer sheet**. If a line has a word which should not be there, write the word **on the separate answer sheet**. There are examples at the beginning (**0** and **00**).

Examples:	0	*it*
	00	✔

THIS IS MY HOBBY

0	....	If I had to say it what my hobby is, I suppose the answer would
00	....	have to be reading. It all started in early childhood when my
41	....	father used to enjoy much making up stories for my brother and
42	....	myself. This was a hugely popular every night at bedtime. As we
43	....	grew older, we turned to books and by the time I was ten, I had
44	....	a large collection of these children's literature. Ever since I can
45	....	remember, I have read about a book a week and I am get through
46	....	lots and lots of such magazines too. I especially enjoy reading in bed
47	....	and if I am really enjoying a book, I will stay up all night to finish it. But
48	....	I also tend to fill my spare up time with reading. You will often see
49	....	me reading on the bus, for example, or if I am waiting from in a queue.
50	....	I never go anywhere without have something to read. I actually
51	....	collect magazines and I have a room at home filled with them. I even
52	....	buy magazines written in languages that I don't know them, just for
53	....	the pleasure given of looking at the pictures and seeing the way
54	....	how they are designed. It will come as no great surprise, therefore,
55	....	if I will tell you that my main ambition in life is to become an editor.

For Questions **56–65**, read the text below. Use the word given in capitals at the end of each line to form a word that fits in the space in the same line. There is an example at the beginning (**0**). Write your answers **on the separate answer sheet**.

Example:	**0**	*interested*

THE TRAINING PROGRAMME

If you're (**0**) .*interested*. in getting fit, then what you need is a training	**INTEREST**
programme. Although aimed at improving physical (**56**) ...., this	**FIT**
programme can also be (**57**) .... in such a way that it helps in the	**DESIGN**
(**58**) .... of particular athletic skills. There is a range of different	**DEVELOP**
(**59**) .... to choose from and a growing amount of scientific	**ACTIVE**
(**60**) .... to explain the effects of each one.	**KNOW**
When you begin training, it is important to start (**61**) ...., raising	**GENTLE**
the (**62**) .... of the programme in a gradual way. Although it is	**INTENSE**
important to work sufficiently hard to make an (**63**) .... on your	**IMPRESS**
physical condition, the activities shouldn't be (**64**) .... It is	**PAIN**
(**65**) ...., therefore, to ignore warning symptoms such as sharp or	**WISE**
persistent pain in particular muscles.	

PAPER 4 Listening (40 minutes)

You will hear people talking in eight different situations. For Questions **1–8**, choose the best answer **A**, **B** or **C**.

---

1 You hear part of a play on the radio.
   Who is the woman talking to?
   A her boss
   B her mother
   C her doctor
   `[  ] 1`

2 You hear a man talking about a boat trip on a river.
   What made this river dangerous?
   A its depth
   B its speed
   C its rocks
   `[  ] 2`

3 You hear this advertisement on the radio.
   What is the advertisement for?
   A a TV programme
   B a shop
   C a book
   `[  ] 3`

4 You hear part of a play on the radio.
   How does the man feel?
   A guilty
   B nervous
   C bored
   `[  ] 4`

5 You are listening to the radio and hear this announcement.
   What is the purpose of the announcement?
   A to complain about something
   B to praise someone's house
   C to recommend something
   `[  ] 5`

6 You hear a man talking about the house where he lives.
   What caused him problems in his bedroom?
   A the view from the window
   B the space for storing things
   C the heating system
   `[  ] 6`

7 You hear a radio announcement about a future event.
   What is the aim of the event?
   A promoting understanding of wildlife
   B developing electronic machinery
   C protecting the natural environment
   `[  ] 7`

8 In a radio play, you hear this discussion about jigsaw puzzles.
   Why does the man like jigsaw puzzles?
   A They help him to concentrate.
   B They help him to relax.
   C They help him to pass the time.
   `[  ] 8`

You will hear someone welcoming students to an English School. For Questions **9–18**, complete the notes.

Tip Strip

Another task in Part 2 asks you to complete notes.

- Before you listen, read the questions. Think about the type of information which is missing.
- The words you need to write are on the tape.
- Write one to three words in each space.
- Check your spelling.

Question 9: Two places have the 'Guide to Activities' – the library and the reception. But only one of them has a copy available at the moment. Which is it?

Question 15: Two possible meeting places are mentioned, but where should students meet *this* Saturday?

Question 18: The teacher recommends one class, but recommends against another. Which one does she think students should do?

International English School

Guide to Activities: *available in* [_____ **9**]

Course content: *conversation classes* * [_____ **10**]

Problems with your course? *Go to* [_____ **11**]

Activities organised:

Friday morning [_____ **12**]

Friday afternoon [_____ **13**]

For Saturday trip:

remember to bring [_____ **14**]

meeting place [_____ **15**]

Sunday 6 p.m.:

go to [_____ **16**]

collect materials and [_____ **17**]

Recommended extra class: [_____ **18**]

You will hear five young swimmers talking about what's happened to them in the past year. For Questions **19–23**, choose from the list **A–F** what each speaker says. Use the letters only once. There is one extra letter which you do not need to use.

A   I took a break from swimming.

Speaker 1 [   ] **19**

B   I gave up my studies to swim.

Speaker 2 [   ] **20**

C   I went on a swimming tour abroad.

Speaker 3 [   ] **21**

D   I swam for my college team.

Speaker 4 [   ] **22**

E   I had a physical problem.

Speaker 5 [   ] **23**

F   I was a winner of competitions.

You will hear an interview with Ricky Foyles, a singer and songwriter. For Questions **24–30**, decide which of the statements are TRUE and which are FALSE and write T for **True** or F for **False** in the boxes provided.

24   Ricky's songs are about the lives of famous people.   [   ] **24**

25   The message in Ricky's songs is difficult to understand.   [   ] **25**

26   Ricky's popularity is on the increase.   [   ] **26**

27   Money is unimportant to Ricky.   [   ] **27**

28   Ricky has followed the advice of some of his fans.   [   ] **28**

29   Ricky thinks his fans are disappointed when they meet him.   [   ] **29**

30   Ricky is anxious about his new album.   [   ] **30**

Tip Strip

Another task in Part 4 asks you to mark statements true or false.
- Before you listen, underline key words in the statements. Verbs and adjectives are often important.
- Look out for prefixes, e.g. unimportant.
- The ideas in the statements will be mentioned on tape, but does the statement reflect what is said?

Question 25: Ricky says the words in the songs are easy to understand, but what does he say about the message?

Question 27: Ricky talks about his attitude to money in the past and present. Listen for how his attitude has changed.

Question 30: Ricky uses the word 'anxious' when talking about new songs. Does 'anxious' mean worried or not worried?

PAPER 5

Speaking (14 minutes)

Tip Strip

- Listen to the instructions. Make sure you do what is asked.
- Don't be afraid to ask your partner or the examiner to repeat something if you haven't understood.
- Listen to the questions the examiner asks your partner, and listen to what your partner says. The examiner may say 'And what about you?' or 'Do you agree?'.
- Don't give short answers. Say what you think and why.

PART 1 (3 minutes)

The examiner encourages you both to talk briefly about yourselves by answering questions such as:

Do you have any brothers and sisters?
What do the other members of your family do?
Tell us something about the place where you are living at the moment.
What type of house would you like to live in, in the future?

PART 2 (3 or 4 minutes)

You each talk for a minute without interruption in response to a visual prompt. You are encouraged to make a brief comment after your partner has spoken.

People painting (compare, contrast and speculate)

Turn to pictures 1 and 2 on page 154 which show people painting.

Candidate A, compare and contrast these photographs, and say why you think the people are painting. You have a minute to do this.

Candidate B, do you like painting?

People waiting (compare, contrast and speculate)

Turn to pictures 1 and 2 on page 155 which show people waiting in different situations.

Candidate B, compare and contrast these photographs, and say how you think the people are feeling about having to wait. You have a minute to do this.

Candidate A, do you get impatient waiting for things?

PART 3 (3 or 4 minutes)

You both discuss a decision-making / problem-solving task, illustrated by visual material, without interruption by the examiner.

Student advice centre (discuss and evaluate)

Turn to the pictures on page 156 which show ideas for an Advice Centre at an international college for students from abroad.

What kind of advice may students need in each area? Which three areas do you think are the most urgent?

PART 4 (3 or 4 minutes)

The examiner encourages you to develop the discussion in Part 3 by asking questions such as:

Where else might students get advice?
Have you ever asked for advice? When?
Do you think adults should give young people advice even if they don't ask for it?
How difficult is it to follow other people's advice?
How do people in your country feel about spending time abroad on their own?

PAPER 1   Reading (1 hour 15 minutes)

PART 1   You are going to read an extract from an article about space tourism. Choose from the list **A–H** the sentence which best summarises each part (**1–6**) of the extract. There is one extra sentence which you do not need to use. There is an example at the beginning (**0**).

Mark your answers **on the separate answer sheet**.

A	Careers can be planned in readiness for jobs in space tourism.	**E**	Financial planning is required now if you want to be a space tourist in the future.
B	We can look forward to a time of widespread space tourism.	**F**	There are good reasons for encouraging space tourism.
C	Individuals can contribute in various ways to making space tourism a reality.	**G**	In its initial phase, space tourism will offer only basic facilities.
D	The development of space tourism will depend on the level of commercial investment.	**H**	Space tourism is becoming the concern of private companies.

SPACE TOURISM

The idea of what's called Space Tourism, where ordinary members of the public queue up to buy tickets for travel into outer space and back, really stretches the imagination. According to Alan Grant, this distant dream could soon be a reality ...

0	H

On Earth, governments provide a number of services, such as defence, police and a legal system. But most activities are done by individuals and companies and it is going to be the same in space. Over the past few years a growing volume of work has been done on the subject and it is now clear that setting up commercial space tourism services is a realistic target for businesses today.

1	D/C

Many people still think that to get the chance to go to space you have got to try to become an astronaut. Unfortunately, the chances of succeeding are tiny, simply because there are so few astronauts – and there is no prospect of a lot more being employed. However, you need not despair because you will be able to go as a visitor. So for anyone, the first thing you should do if you want to go to space is save up because the demand is expected to be strong and, in the early stages, prices will be high.

2	B E

In order to stay longer in space, you could work in one of the businesses that will be set up in orbit. There will be opportunities in manufacturing – aerospace vehicle makers, orbital construction, electric power, extra-terrestrial mining, chemical engineering and other fields. So you can start university studies and try to get the sort of work experience that will ensure you are well-placed to apply for a job in any of these areas.

3	A

The general public are very interested in travelling to space. Apart from the interest factor, such tourism is the only way in which space activities can become profitable and the quickest way to start to use the limitless resources of space to solve our problems on Earth. And living in space involves every line of business, from construction to marketing, fashion, interior design and law.

4	D

It is possible to envisage a future when demand for space tourism travel will grow from thousands of passengers per year to hundreds of thousands per year. Tickets to orbit will cost less and flights will depart from many different airports. Orbital facilities will grow from just being prefabricated modules to large structures constructed for hundreds of guests.

5	B

But like any other business, space tourism will develop progressively. Starting as a relatively small-scale and relatively high-priced activity, customers will find that the service will be nearer to 'adventure travel' than to a luxury-style hotel. Orbital accommodation will be safe but rather simple. This will be a time for the pioneers who will not mind the lack of comfort.

6	G

Few projects are successfully completed without the help of people who believe in them. It is possible to take an active role in bringing space tourism about by asking airlines, hotels and travel companies if and when they intend to offer space travel. Others may prefer to lend a hand by doing research into one or more of the areas needing it, or by joining one of the many companies that are already working towards a future in space.

You are going to read a magazine article about a young sports person. For Questions **7–14**, choose the correct answer **A**, **B**, **C** or **D**.

Mark your answers **on the separate answer sheet**.

Wakeboarding

Knowing that Tom Finch, a junior champion in the relatively new sport of wakeboarding, had won so many competitions, I was more than a little taken aback to see how slight he was. Wakeboarding, you see, involves being pulled along at high speed behind a power boat, rather like in water skiing, then launching yourself into the air to perform a series of complicated tricks, as in skateboarding or snowboarding. Now, that is a feat you'd think required big bones and bulging muscles. But Tom is just 1.44m tall and weighs 38 kilos.

'It hurt my forearms at first, but now I guess I'm used to it,' Tom told me. At 14 years old, Tom has been practising the sport for just two years, but has already found competing in his age group almost too easy. He didn't say that, of course. Maybe because he didn't want to seem bigheaded, especially with his Dad sitting just a few metres away, or maybe because he just doesn't think it's important. 'I wakeboard because it's fun,' he told me with a smile, 'and scary!'

He knows he's good though and one look at his results confirms that this is justified. Yet when Tom started, the organisers tried to persuade him not to enter his first competition, thinking he'd be upset when he came last. Tom won by a mile and silenced them all. So, what makes him so good? Perhaps putting on a wetsuit, whatever the weather, and practising

for at least two hours everyday. For 42 **that** is what Tom does. He also buys and studies every new wakeboarding video and spends hours working on every new trick, finding new ways to twist and turn his small body.

He's also not afraid to take advice from people better than him. 'I wouldn't be where I am without my trainer,' Tom says. 'It takes so much longer to learn without him; he can spot what I'm doing wrong in a second and put me right. He gives me lots of tips on some of the real technical details too.'

Although the sport is still relatively unknown compared to surfing and snowboarding, which everyone's 59 heard of, Tom reckons it's **on the up**. 'Everyone at school is well aware of it, trying it and loving it,' he says. He's not wrong either. Even on the rainy, windy day that I met him, there's a queue of eager bodies in wetsuits getting into the freezing water at the watersports centre near London where Tom trains.

It will take a few years until the overall standard reaches that of the USA though. Tom told me that everything is twice as fast, twice as big there, which makes it really scary and dangerous. Tom knows no fear though and wants one day to be a professional. He might only be 1.44m tall, but let's not forget that the professionals were all fourteen-year-olds at one time too.

7 What surprised the writer most on first meeting Tom Finch?

    A his height
    B his strength
    C his skilfulness
    D his bravery

8 When asked about his success in competitions, Tom appeared to be

    A embarrassed.
    B proud.
    C modest.
    D nervous.

9 When Tom started entering competitions, people thought

    A he had not been trained.
    B he might hurt himself.
    C he was below the age limit.
    D he would be disappointed.

10 What does 'that' in line 42 refer to?

    A studying hard
    B practising daily
    C buying videos
    D working on new tricks

11 Tom is particularly grateful when his trainer

    A points out his mistakes.
    B makes him work hard.
    C stops him being afraid.
    D spends long hours with him.

12 What does Tom mean by the phrase 'on the up' in line 59?

    A becoming better understood
    B getting more practice
    C getting easier for people
    D becoming more popular

13 In the future, Tom hopes to

    A train others in his sport.
    B go and live in the USA.
    C get over his remaining fears.
    D make the sport his career.

14 In general, what does the writer think of Tom?

    A He's very determined.
    B He's easily persuaded.
    C He's overconfident.
    D He's underachieving.

You are going to read a magazine article about marathon running. Seven sentences have been removed from the article. Choose from the sentences **A–H** the one which fits each gap (**15–20**). There is one extra sentence which you do not need to use. There is an example at the beginning (**0**).

Mark your answers **on the separate answer sheet**.

MARATHON RUNNING – A RECIPE FOR HEALTH?

If ever there was living proof that marathon running keeps you fit, Jenny Wood Allen from Dundee is it.

0   *H*   She was 71 and she did not even have proper training shoes then.

At first she could only run to the end of her avenue, which is about three quarters of a mile. She had problems getting back and had to either take a bus or ask somebody for a lift. **15**

Scientifically speaking, human beings are perfectly tuned for jumping and running and walking long distances. **16** One of them, Professor Craig Sharp says that if you are reasonably fit, you can probably run for two hours at a medium pace and feel OK. At this point your muscles run out of glycogen – the best source of energy we have.

This means you start using fat for energy, and your body has to work harder to transform fat into energy. This happens at a time when you are starting to feel exhausted. **17** All this is proof – he believes – that the body isn't designed for long-distance running.

Other specialists have a very different opinion. Dr Percy Brown believes that if you train sensibly and prepare several months in advance, it could even help you live longer. **18**

He believes the only problem you may have when running a marathon is exhaustion or a small injury caused by falling or tripping over things. **19** Only 1 in 1,000 actually makes it to hospital.

Another problem may be post-race exhaustion. Surveys show most runners are much more likely to catch colds or develop chest infections in the week after running a race. **20** There is no evidence of lasting disease or an increased risk of illness.

At 87, Jenny Wood Allen will be doing the London marathon for the 13th time this Sunday. And she plans to go on taking part for many years to come.

A He argues that after 16–20 miles, you have to slow down and running gets really hard.

B After a quick top up of water and a rest, most go home and make a full recovery.

C When it comes to marathon running, however, the experts are divided.

D In spite of this, marathon running is bad for your health.

E But this weakening effect on the system is short-lived.

F Within a couple of months, however, she was managing two or three miles.

G This is because running halves your risk of getting heart disease.

H She started by running to the shops, wearing an anorak and carrying her shopping bag.

You are going to read an article about wildlife photographers. For Questions **21–35**, choose from the people (**A–D**). The people may be chosen more than once. There is an example at the beginning (**0**).

Mark your answers **on the separate answer sheet**.

A	George Fenns
B	Paul Sommer
C	Roger Miller
D	Nathan Ribbs

Who

defends a previous employer?	**0**	D
learnt to make something at an early age?	**21**	
does not mind working in low temperatures?	**22**	
earned money to buy equipment?	**23**	
needs long preparations before taking photos?	**24**	
completed a university course?	**25**	
likes to photograph what others can't see?	**26**	
would like to work in a milder climate?	**27**	
found his camera gave him confidence?	**28**	
admits his profession may be dangerous?	**29**	
has had something he wrote published?	**30**	
wants to save animals from extinction?	**31**	
turned down a well-paid job?	**32**	
made his own equipment?	**33**	
had an encouraging family?	**34**	
has seen his work used by writers?	**35**	

WILDLIFE PHOTOGRAPHERS

Wildlife photographer **George Fenns** is a man who loves his job. 'When I was three, a neighbour's kid taught me to climb our fence,' he recalls. 'I slipped away and brought back a snake I found on the road. I've been interested in wildlife ever since.' George's parents encouraged his enthusiasm for animals and also nurtured his appreciation of art, which led to photography. 'I sold turtles for two dollars each when I was sixteen,' he says. 'That money got me my first camera.' He now spends three months a year photographing life under water. In 1999 he braved the frigid Pacific Ocean to do a series of photos on salmon, and he also wrote an article about it for a wildlife magazine which won him an award as a journalist. His latest job was in the Arctic in freezing temperatures. 'I'd now like a job where it's warm and sunny,' he says. He never complains about the rigours of his job, but would like to have time to write articles and train young photographers who are starting out in this profession.

Photographer **Paul Sommer** is working in Siberia. 'On bad days it can be minus 20 degrees, with a strong wind,' he says. He protects his film from freezing by keeping it inside his gloves. 'You get used to it,' he says. Siberia is a far cry from his childhood in north Brazil. His years at college gave him no hint of future high adventure either: 'I worked two jobs – as a waiter and as a restaurant manager – to get money for college,' he says. And his efforts paid off when he finished his degree. He was offered a job as a journalist in an award-winning newspaper, but said no to it in order to concentrate on photography. His contract as photographer in Siberia does not pay as much as he would have got as a journalist. However, he has no regrets. 'My photos have been used by researchers who are studying animals here. They have been the basis for important pieces in scientific journals,' he says, 'so this is a very satisfying job.'

Freelance photographer **Roger Miller** is on a contract to take photos of volcanoes, of the lava that flows after an eruption and of the animal life around these areas. He is aware of the risks involved in his assignments, but takes it all in his stride. By age 11 Roger was building his own telescopes and photographing stars. 'I was a very shy kid. The camera made me comfortable around people,' he says. In 1970 a science instructor took Roger and his classmates to Mexico to view a total solar eclipse. It was this experience and the help of the science teacher that prompted him to take up photography as a career. 'My parents wanted me to become a writer,' he says, 'they have not lost hope.' His parents may have to wait a long time because Roger's newest challenge in his next assignment is teaching astronauts how to set up their equipment to photograph the activities around the space vehicle. After that he is planning to take a year off to complete a degree in geology which he started years ago.

Nathan Ribbs spends a lot of his time on a 30-metre-high platform that puts him at eye level with the nests of rare birds in the jungle. The platform is very small and the danger of falling off it is evident to everyone except Roger. 'It's like taking pictures from a hill,' he says. For each of his jobs, the steel structure for the platform often has to go on river canoes and along difficult forest trails. 'But it is very rewarding to see and photograph animals that few people will ever see. I do this work because I think these creatures have to be protected so they won't disappear altogether.' Nathan has no intention of returning to his previous job as a photographer of animals held in captivity. 'Zoos are undergoing very positive changes,' he says, 'they are now a leading method of educating about the natural world. But I've done my share of that kind of photography. This is so much more challenging.'

PAPER 2

Writing (1 hour 30 minutes)

You **must** answer this question.

1   You and a friend participated in your club's Sports Weekend a fortnight ago. Your friend has sent you a letter with a small article from a newspaper about the Sports Weekend. Read the letter and the article, together with the notes. Then write to the newspaper editor saying what your friend suggests and asking them to publish another article.

> Look at this article in the paper about our Sports Weekend! What they say is not true. I'm going on holiday today. Could you write a letter to the editor using the notes I've made?

Not true! —

sick —

rain —

The local Milton Club Sports Weekend did not come up to our expectations. The Milton team lost 3 to 1 against Rangers in a match which was very disappointing. The Milton team did not seem to have done enough preparation work and two of its best players simply did not turn up. There were unexplained delays throughout the day and some of the athletics events were cancelled. They will need to do better next year.

3 days a week training!

Write a **letter** of between **120** and **180** words in an appropriate style. Do not write any addresses.

Write an answer to **one** of the Questions **2–5** in this part. Write your answer in **120–180** words in an appropriate style.

2   This is part of a letter from an English friend who will be visiting your country next month.

> It'll be good to spend a week at your place. Any ideas as to what we might do? Should I bring any special clothes? Do let me know if there is anything I can get you from England.
>
> Gary

Write your **letter**, answering your friend's questions and giving relevant details. Do not write any addresses.

3   You have been asked to write a story for a magazine for young people. Your story must **end** like this:

Clara woke up with a shock. It had been only a dream.

Write your **story**.

4   You have just come back from a two-day study trip to a historic town. Your teacher has asked you to write a report about your visit, saying what you saw during the two days and whether you would recommend a similar visit for other students.

Write your **report**.

5   Answer **one** of the following two questions based on your reading of **one** of the set books.

Either (a) Write a **composition**, describing the good and bad qualities of one of the characters in the book you have read.

Or (b) 'It was very difficult to follow the plot of this story and at times I got lost.' With reference to the book you have read, write a **composition**, saying whether you agree or disagree with this statement and why.

PAPER 3

Use of English (1 hour 15 minutes)

For Questions **1–15**, read the text below and decide which answer **A**, **B**, **C** or **D** best fits each space. There is an example at the beginning (**0**).

Mark your answers **on the separate answer sheet**.

Example:

0   **A**   as well as   **B**   as long as   **C**   as soon as   **D**   as good as

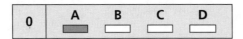

SINGING FOR A MUSICAL LIFE

According to a group called The Voices Foundation, everyone has a singing voice (**0**) ..... a speaking voice somewhere inside them. This, they say, should be encouraged from an early (**1**) ..... because it provides the best, and the cheapest, (**2**) ..... on which to build an understanding of music.

(**3**) ..... the Foundation's ideas, lies the teaching of the Hungarian composer Zoltan Kodaly. He observed that song can (**4**) ..... a key part of the relationship between mother and child almost from birth. This is especially (**5**) ..... of more traditional societies, like those of West Africa, where some small children are (**6**) ..... to sing literally hundreds of songs, all of which have been learnt by (**7**) ...... But many modern children first (**8**) ..... to an understanding of music when they learn to play an instrument, and (**9**) ..... some teaching of the theory of music is usually a part of this, their relationship with the music on the (**10**) ..... is often a mechanical one.

The (**11**) ..... of the Voices Foundation is that a natural (**12**) ..... for rhythm, harmony and musical structure, the very (**13**) ..... we appreciate in the greatest musicians, can only be achieved through the exploration of music with the voice from the start. The foundation has, therefore, (**14**) ..... itself the task of developing a singing-centred musical education programme that could (**15**) ..... junior pupils all over the world.

1	**A** start	**B** life	**C** time	**D** age
2	**A** ground	**B** basis	**C** root	**D** plot
3	**A** Behind	**B** Beneath	**C** Besides	**D** Between
4	**A** grow	**B** do	**C** form	**D** make
5	**A** fact	**B** true	**C** real	**D** actual
6	**A** able	**B** expert	**C** skilled	**D** fit
7	**A** repeat	**B** heart	**C** memory	**D** mind
8	**A** come	**B** reach	**C** go	**D** arrive
9	**A** however	**B** despite	**C** although	**D** whether
10	**A** lines	**B** notes	**C** book	**D** page
11	**A** rule	**B** certainty	**C** trust	**D** belief
12	**A** awareness	**B** touch	**C** grasp	**D** feeling
13	**A** degrees	**B** qualities	**C** measures	**D** practices
14	**A** let	**B** set	**C** put	**D** cut
15	**A** benefit	**B** favour	**C** gain	**D** profit

For Questions **16–30**, read the text below and think of the word which best fits each space. Use only **one** word in each space. There is an example at the beginning (**0**).

Write your answers **on the separate answer sheet**.

Example:

0	*was*

THE BIRTH OF THE T-SHIRT

The T-shirt, or at least the T-shirt as we know it, (**0**) .... born in the theatre. When Tennessee William's play *A Streetcar Named Desire* opened in New York in December 1947, a young actor (**16**) .... Marlon Brando went (**17**) .... stage wearing a (**18**) .... of blue jeans and a bright, white, capped-sleeve T-shirt. It was the first time the T-shirt (**19**) .... been seen publicly as anything (**20**) .... an item of underwear and it set a fashion trend that was to last through (**21**) .... the end of the century.

The idea for the T-shirt came (**22**) .... Brando himself. He had worn one at rehearsals for the play. The director was (**23**) .... impressed by the look that was created that he asked Brando to wear the shirt in the play itself. Brando may have seen the shirt being advertised by the American company Sears Roebuck. They had decided to market the shirt (**24**) .... a fashionable garment in its (**25**) .... right, rather than just something to be worn (**26**) .... warmth beneath a denim workshirt (**27**) .... an army uniform.

It was Brando, however, (**28**) .... popularised it, especially with (**29**) .... release of the film version of *Streetcar* in 1951. A short leather jacket completed the look that was to be adopted (**30**) .... teenage rebels in many countries for decades afterwards.

For Questions **31–40**, complete the second sentence so that it has a similar meaning to the first sentence, using the word given. **Do not change the word given.** You must use between two and five words, including the word given. Here is an example (**0**).

Example: **0** It was the most relaxing holiday I ever had.

   such

   I have never .... holiday.

The gap can be filled by the words 'had such a relaxing' so you write:

0	had such a relaxing

Write **only the missing words** on the separate answer sheet.

---

31 I find Robert's taste in music very hard to tolerate.

   put

   I find it hard .... Robert's taste in music.

32 I find waiting for buses very boring.

   get

   I .... waiting for buses.

33 It's very difficult to predict the weather here.

   tends

   The weather .... unpredictable here.

34 People say learning lists of words is not a good use of time.

   waste

   Learning lists of words is .... of time.

35 Christine complained formally when her course of study was cancelled.

   made

   Christine .... when her course of study was cancelled.

36 'I find all the advertisements on TV really irritating,' said John.

   nerves

   'All the advertisements on TV really ....,' said John.

37 Mark regretted selling his old motorbike.

   wished

   Mark .... his old motorbike.

38 'If you take my advice, Paul,' said Lynda, 'you should buy a personal computer.'

   advised

   Lynda .... a personal computer.

39 Pauline hadn't expected to see so many people at the concert.

   surprise

   It came .... to see so many people at the concert.

40 Golf is becoming increasingly popular in Britain.

   popularity

   The .... in Britain.

For Questions **41–55**, read the text below and look carefully at each line. Some of the lines are correct, and some have a word which should not be there.

If a line is correct, put a tick (✔) by the number **on the separate answer sheet**. If a line has a word which should not be there, write the word **on the separate answer sheet**. There are examples at the beginning (**0** and **00**).

Examples:	0	*in*
	00	✔

TV CRITIC

0	....	I am replying to the letter which you published in last week from
00	....	a girl called Jessica on the subject of television. I am not what you
41	....	would call a television addict, and I am agree that there are badly-
42	....	written programmes which they contain unnecessary bad language
43	....	and violence, but television does have its good points. Many of the
44	....	programmes which are broadcast on are educational and can help
45	....	with schoolwork. A good soap-opera or comedy it is a source of
46	....	the relaxation for many people. Television also provides jobs
47	....	for thousands of people, so that think how much unemployment there
48	....	would be without it. In general, therefore, I think that television is
49	....	a good thing. There is, however, one most thing I would like to
50	....	complain about, and that there is the amount of smoking in the films
51	....	that are shown on television. Adults are always lecturing up children
52	....	about how they shouldn't to smoke, and yet we see many smoking
53	....	scenes on television. What's more so, smoking is often shown as a
54	....	very 'cool' thing to do, making young people much more likely to
55	....	copy what they see and take up with smoking themselves.

For Questions **56–65**, read the text below. Use the word given in capitals at the end of each line to form a word, that fits in the space in the same line. There is an example at the beginning (**0**). Write your answers **on the separate answer sheet**.

Example:	**0**	*happiness*

HAPPY IS HEALTHY

Medical research has found that (**0**) .*happiness*. has a strongly   **HAPPY**
beneficial effect on health. The healing properties of (**56**) .... are   **LAUGH**
such that humour is now being used alongside more (**57**) ....   **TRADITION**
courses of (**58**) .... in some hospitals. In a London children's   **TREAT**
hospital, for example, two clowns are provided for the (**59**) .... of   **ENTERTAIN**
patients. Doctors say that these clowns are (**60**) .... in making the   **SUCCESS**
children feel better.

It seems that when we laugh, there can be a (**61**) .... in both   **REDUCE**
blood pressure and the amount of (**62**) .... in our muscles.   **TENSE**
Although it is (**63**) .... to prove it at the moment, this may also   **POSSIBLE**
mean that people who feel unhappy and who are, therefore,
(**64**) .... to laugh so much, suffer more often from physical   **LIKELY**
(**65**) ....   **ILL**

PAPER 4 Listening (40 minutes)

You will hear people talking in eight different situations. For Questions **1–8**, choose the best answer **A**, **B** or **C**.

---

1   On the radio you hear an announcement about a future programme. What type of programme is being discussed?
   A   a play
   B   an interview
   C   a music programme
          1

2   You hear a School Principal talking on the phone.
   Who is he talking to?
   A   a teacher
   B   an architect
   C   a secretary
          2

3   You hear a scientist talking about pollution on the radio.
   What do scientists need to know more about?
   A   the animals at risk
   B   the causes of the problem
   C   the effects on plants
          3

4   You hear part of a play about life in a school.
   Who is talking?
   A   one of the teachers
   B   the Head Teacher
   C   one of the students
          4

5   You hear a man talking about his tent.
   What does he like about it?
   A   It is easy to put up.
   B   It is large.
   C   It is waterproof.
          5

6   You hear part of nature programme on the radio.
   Why are kangaroos being studied?
   A   to help protect their environment
   B   to learn about fitness from them
   C   to make sure they are in good health
          6

7   You hear the weather forecast on the radio.
   What will the weather be like tomorrow afternoon?
   A   cloudier than in the morning
   B   warmer than in the morning
   C   windier than in the morning
          7

8   You hear a news report about a fire.
   Where did the fire take place?
   A   in a food storage area
   B   in a restaurant
   C   in agricultural buildings
          8

You will hear an archaeologist talking about her job. For Questions **9–18**, complete the sentences.

Anna first thought she'd like to be an archaeologist after she saw a

| | **9** |

Anna prefers archaeology to history because it is a | | **10** |

activity.

Recently Anna and her colleagues found a | | **11** | in

London.

Much of Anna's time is spent dealing with the | | **12** |

produced by other archaeologists.

One of Anna's responsibilities is to check that the

| *and* | **13** | of the excavation are in the right place.

After cleaning the piece she has found, Anna has to | | **14** |

it.

Anna finds it interesting to clean an old wall because she may learn

| *and* | **15** | it was built.

Anna particularly dislikes working in | | **16** | because they're

hot and dusty.

Archaeologists use scientific techniques to find out about the

| | **17** | of people in past centuries.

The Archaeology Service is often involved in helping

| | **18** | to understand the law.

You will hear five people saying why they became professional artists. For Questions **19–23**, choose from the list **A–F** what each speaker says. Use the letters only once. There is one extra letter which you do not need to use.

Why I became a professional artist

A I needed to earn a living.

B I had relatives who gave me support.

C I did not have other skills.

D I was offered an interesting job.

E I wanted to avoid academic studies.

F I was persuaded by somebody else.

Speaker 1 [ ] **19**

Speaker 2 [ ] **20**

Speaker 3 [ ] **21**

Speaker 4 [ ] **22**

Speaker 5 [ ] **23**

You will hear a conversation about three films, *Imitation*, *Midday Train*, and *Postman Gregg*. For Questions **24–30**, decide which of the following is said about each film. Write **I** for *Imitation*, **M** for *Midday Train* or **P** for *Postman Gregg*.

24   This film deals with unattractive characters. [ ] **24**

25   This film has some very good actors. [ ] **25**

26   This film is based on real-life events. [ ] **26**

27   This film ends in an unexpected way. [ ] **27**

28   This film has a plot that is difficult to follow. [ ] **28**

29   This film is about travelling adventures. [ ] **29**

30   This film shows interesting scenery. [ ] **30**

Tip Strip

Another task in Part 4 asks you to match statements to three different speakers or topics.
- Before you listen, underline the key words in the questions. Adjectives and nouns are often important.
- The films will be discussed altogether. Listen out for pronouns such as *it, that one, the other one*, etc. Which films do they refer to?

Question 24: The woman describes the characters in one film as 'unpleasant'. But which film is she talking about?
Question 30: This question talks about scenery. One of the films takes place mostly indoors, another doesn't show much of the countries it's based in. So which is the film with the wonderful views of hills, lakes, etc.?

PAPER 5

Speaking (14 minutes)

PART 1 (3 minutes)

Answer these questions:

Do you work or do you study?
Can you tell us something about the place where you study or work?
What type of work would you like to do in the future?
What qualifications do you think you'll need in the future?

PART 2 (3 or 4 minutes)

Working at home (compare, contrast and speculate)

Turn to pictures 1 and 2 on page 157 which show people who work at home.

Candidate A, compare and contrast these photographs, and say why you think the people have chosen to work at home. You have a minute to do this.

Candidate B, would you like to work at home?

On holiday (compare, contrast and speculate)

Turn to pictures 1 and 2 on page 158 which show people on holiday.

Candidate B, compare and contrast these photographs, and say why you think the people have chosen this type of holiday. You have a minute to do this.

Candidate A, do you like city holidays?

PART 3 (3 or 4 minutes)

Youth centre (discuss and evaluate)

Turn to the pictures on page 159 which show ideas for a Youth centre. A local council has got an old house they want to use for the centre. Look at the plan of the house and the suggestions for how each area could be used.

How popular would the various suggestions be with young people? How would you use the space available?

PART 4 (3 or 4 minutes)

Answer these questions:

Which of the activities would you choose to do in a Youth centre? Why?
How necessary is it to have spaces for young people only?
Which age groups do you think should be admitted to a Youth centre?
What spaces do young people have in your country?
How easy is it for young people to get on with older people?
Do you think life for young people is easier or more difficult than it was in the past?

TEST 4

PART 1

You are going to read an article about an island off the coast of south-west England. Choose the most suitable heading from the list **A–I** for each part (**1–7**) of the article. There is one extra heading which you do not need to use. There is an example at the beginning (**0**).

Mark your answers **on the separate answer sheet**.

A	A natural fortress	**D** A lack of variety	**G** A surprising impression
B	An unfortunate choice	**E** A chance to escape	**H** An unexpected development
C	An undeserved reputation	**F** A range of facilities	**I** A mystery solved

Across to Lundy Island

Andrew Osmond took a boat to Lundy – an island where the weather is no laughing matter

0   I

I had always been slightly puzzled as to why the boat trip to Lundy Island, eleven miles off the coast of Devon in south-west England, takes such a long time. The scheduled two-hour journey time seems excessive. Now, three hours into the voyage, the island felt no nearer than when I had boarded the ship. I began to understand something of Lundy's isolation, for this stretch of water, where the Atlantic Ocean meets the Bristol Channel can be very rough.

1   E

The captain's voice came over the loudspeaker, 'Would all day visitors please report to the main lounge area.' It was the only thing to make me smile during the whole voyage; the shocked expression on the faces of the day-trippers as they realised they'd have to spend the night on the island because the sea was too rough for the return crossing. Those of us who had pre-booked accommodation on the island could afford to look smug.

2   B/E H

My thoughts were already turning to the warm little stone house that was awaiting my arrival on dry land. And suddenly, we were there. Lundy presents a formidable face to seaborne arrivals. Its cliffs rise 400 feet, along the island's three-mile length, and fingers of rock jut out into the sea, making the water dance white with agitation. It is not surprising that the island has resisted all attempts at invasion over the centuries.

3   G

The tiny collection of stone buildings that make up the village of Lundy are situated at the southern end of the island, and here you find the only anchorage too. The clear blue water of the landing bay made me think we must have taken a wrong turn at sea and somehow found ourselves coming ashore on one of the Greek Islands. I had never seen such beautiful waters around the English coast.

4   B

Before leaving home, I had read that Lundy was famous for its diving and snorkelling, but I had laughed at the idea of swimming in these cold seas and had left my snorkel and face mask behind. Now, confronted with this brilliant-blue truth, I was almost beginning to regret my decision. I would certainly come to regret leaving behind my hooded waterproof jacket and my torch, in favour of a smart shirt for the evenings that was clearly not needed.

5   B F

The absence of any true native population on Lundy means that as a tourist, you don't feel that you are invading anyone's privacy. Most of the residents are people employed to look after the welfare of visitors. The rental accommodation is both imaginative and evocative of the island's past. There are 166 buildings for rent. You can choose between a 12-room castle, a fisherman's cottage or, like me, a modest lighthouse keeper's house.

6   G F

When I told people that I was going to Lundy, the most frequent remarks were, 'Won't you be bored and lonely?' and 'Isn't it only for bird-watchers?' What surprised me on arrival was just how diverse a range of activities my fellow travellers were planning. As well as divers, there were rock-climbers, artists, naturalists and, of course, some birdwatchers because Lundy is deservedly famous as a haven for all kinds of seabirds.

7   E C

But, should you be thinking of a trip to Lundy, remember that you don't have to take part in the outdoor pursuits. The most popular activity on Lundy these days must be doing very little. I went for rest and relaxation and found it in abundance. I suggest taking a good book and then finding a sheltered corner where you can enjoy the beautiful scenery and the incomparable tranquillity.

You are going to read a magazine article about a young mother whose house was burgled. For Questions **8–15**, choose the correct answer **A**, **B**, **C** or **D**.

Mark your answers **on the separate answer sheet**.

Lisa Tyler was weary after a long, hard day at the pottery factory where she works. But as she approached her home in the English city of Stoke-on-Trent, her heart lightened; soon she would be having a nice cup of tea, putting her feet up and watching *Friends*, her favourite TV series.
5 But first, she needed to change out of her work clothes and **pick up** her three-year-old son from his grandmother's house nearby.

As Lisa walked up her garden path, she noticed a light flashing on and off in an upstairs bedroom. A shiver went down her back. What if it was a burglar? Quietly, she crept round to the back of the house to see if there was any sign of a break-in. Sure enough, a window was open and someone's coat was hanging on the gatepost!

Well, 26-year-old Lisa didn't fancy coming face to face with a burglar, so she ran to a neighbour's house and rang the police. But as she sat waiting for the police to arrive, Lisa's curiosity got the better of her and she decided to go back and see what was going on. That's when she saw a leg coming out of the downstairs front window. It was a man climbing out. Lisa gasped in shock. The burglar was carrying her portable television!

18 At this point, **Lisa saw red**. She didn't have many possessions and she'd saved long and hard to buy that set. Besides, nobody was going to stop her watching *Friends*.

'Oh no you don't,' she muttered under her breath, as the fury swelled inside her. Without even stopping to think, she tore across the garden and started shouting at the burglar. 'Give me my TV – drop it now!' she screamed.

Ignoring her, the man fled across the garden. So Lisa threw herself at him and successfully rugby-tackled him to the ground. The burglar struggled to escape, but Lisa hung on like the best kind of guard dog despite being punched and kicked. As she looked up, she realised that she recognised the burglar's face. She was so surprised that she lost her grip and the burglar got away, leaving the TV behind in the garden.

By the time the police and her father arrived, Lisa was in tears. 'I can't believe you were so foolish, Lisa,' scolded her father. 'You could have been killed.'

'I know, but at least he didn't get my TV,' she replied.

Lisa later remembered the name of the burglar, who had been in the same year as her at school. He was later caught and jailed for 15 months after admitting burglary and assault. In May last year, Lisa was given a Certificate of Appreciation by Staffordshire Police, for her 'outstanding courage and public action'. But in the future she intends to leave household security to a new member of her family, Chan, who is a real guard dog.

8 How was Lisa feeling as she walked home from work?

    A tired ✓
    B anxious
    C depressed
    D relieved

9 What does 'pick up' mean in line 5?

    A contact
    B visit
    C collect ✓
    D check

10 What first led Lisa to think there was a burglar in her house?

    A Something had been broken.
    B Something had been left outside.
    C Something was in the wrong place.
    D Something was moving inside. ✓

11 Why didn't Lisa wait in her neighbour's house until the police arrived?

    A She was worried about losing her television.
    B She wanted to know what was happening. ✓
    C She noticed something from her neighbour's window.
    D She realised that the burglar was leaving.

12 What does 'Lisa saw red' (line 18) mean?

    A She got impatient.
    B She felt frightened.
    C She got angry. ✓
    D She felt brave.

13 What happened when Lisa shouted at the burglar?

    A He tried to explain why he was there.
    B He fell over as he ran towards her.
    C He pretended not to have heard her. ✓
    D He dropped the TV and attacked her.

14 What did Lisa's father do when he arrived?

    A He told her off.
    B Her comforted her.
    C He praised her.
    D He argued with her. ✓

15 How was the burglar caught?

    A Lisa was able to describe him.
    B He was found at another burglary.
    C Lisa realised she could identify him. ✓
    D He was already known to the police.

You are going to read a magazine article about herons. Seven sentences have been removed from the article. Choose from the sentences **A–H** the one which fits each gap (**16–21**). There is one extra sentence which you do not need to use. There is an example at the beginning (**0**).

Mark your answers **on the separate answer sheet**.

HERONS

Herons are beautiful birds. Years ago, as I walked to work in a fish factory in Aberdeen, herons would always bring a little bit of light to the dark winter mornings. Usually there would be a couple of them standing on the river's edge. **0** | *H*

This natural cautiousness is usual in herons. They prefer to spend the day in areas where they can hunt for fish in peace. They seldom allow close approach and are quick to take to the air when they sense humans are about. **16** | C⏋H

This cruel treatment is now on the decline and consequently the latest *Bird Atlas* estimates there are probably twice as many herons breeding in Britain today than in the late 1960s. **17** | D A This means herons can feed and survive in areas which were previously unavailable because they were either too cold or ruined by poisonous substances in the water.

Weather is probably the single most important factor in the improvement in the heron population. In effect, new areas of habitat have been opened up. **18** | ᵗZ The one of 1963 had a notable impact, but surprisingly there is little to suggest that the same happened in the freezing temperatures of 1979 and 1892.

19 | B G As well as the UK, similar increases have been recorded throughout Europe. By the early 1970s, the heron had become threatened in many parts of central Europe, but has since recovered dramatically. And if not persecuted, will even breed in city centres, such as happens in Amsterdam.

20 | D There are still numerous threats, mostly to do with habitat degradation, and which certainly affect populations on a local scale. Drainage of fields and excavation reduce food supplies. The planting of forests, while providing nesting sites, may also reduce the water flow in some water courses and hence fish availability.

The heron lives on fish. **21** | U On other occasions a different tactic is adopted, this time slowly stalking through the water, looking intently at any stirrings. If the need arises, the heron will wade deep until the body is afloat and it can even swim for a short distance. They are such a delight to watch, particularly in the morning when they go hunting in the frost-draped winter semi-darkness.

A Another reason for this increase can be found in the milder winters and the reduction in water pollution.

B Further north the bird is equally widespread, although it is absent from areas of high ground.

C Such nervousness is understandable, given that they have suffered from persecution from fish farmers.

D While heron numbers have increased, it is important not to be complacent.

E However, a hard winter will temporarily set numbers back.

F The commonest hunting technique is to stand still by the water's edge, with only the eyes twinkling as it carefully scans for fish.

G It appears, however, that all is well for the heron at the moment.

H But once dawn broke, the herons would move upstream to quieter stretches of the river.

You are going to read a magazine article about holidays abroad. For Questions **22–35**, choose from the people (**A–D**). The people may be chosen more than once. There is an example at the beginning (**0**).

Mark your answers **on the separate answer sheet**.

A	Graham Buckley
B	Tom Farley
C	Peter Sampson
D	Gordon Monts

Which of the people A–D

goes to a different place each time?	**0**	D
finds some written information inadequate?	**22**	
is careful to keep his money safe?	**23**	
is dissatisfied with airport staff?	**24**	B
prefers to take little equipment with him?	**25**	
gives advice on travel documents?	**26**	
believes he ruined somebody else's holiday?	**27**	
had a problem at an airport?	**28**	
thinks travellers should do some reading?	**29**	
is nervous before trips?	**30**	
informs travel agents about his walking skills?	**31**	
shows respect for local cultures?	**32**	
finds communicating in the local language helpful?	**33**	
asks mountain climbers for advice?	**34**	
is careless with his luggage?	**35**	B

TRICKS OF THE TRADE

Walking in a foreign country

If you're planning to go on your first walking holiday abroad, make sure it runs smoothly … Alan Barns gives us the opinions of four experienced travellers.

Graham Buckley has been climbing hills ever since he was eight. He books his walking holidays through travel agents. He believes there is plenty of choice when it comes to deciding where to go, with something to match everyone's abilities and aspirations. 'But matching your ability with what you find in a brochure isn't easy,' he says. 'What you find is an attractive description but the brochure won't give you a breakdown of the skills required.' His advice is to get information about the chosen area from the abundant printed material available, before starting off. 'It should not be forgotten that once you are in a foreign country, you may have trouble finding out information if your command of the language is shaky.' Graham is convinced that people usually pack last minute and as a result take too much gear. 'I find it's virtually impossible to take too little equipment,' he says, 'unless you forget to take your boots and passport, of course!'

Tom Farley likes to play safe when he books his walking holidays ever since he found himself struggling up a steep mountain that he was ill-prepared for. 'What I regret most about it is that I ruined the walking experience for the others because they had to keep waiting for me,' he says. He now asks the travel agents about the area he'll be covering and gives them details about the type of walking he normally does to allow them to match his ability to a suitable walking holiday. Tom is also very careful when it comes to packing his rucksack. 'If I am flying, I put the rucksack inside a large bag with a zip,' he says, 'the people who handle luggage at airports are often very careless and things could go very wrong if you find your rucksack's damaged.' What Tom likes best about his travelling experiences is the chance to use the languages he has learnt. 'Just a few words of the local language make all the difference to a trip,' he says. 'People will help you solve any problems you may have if you try and speak their language.'

Peter Sampson is also a seasoned traveller and believes that in order to enjoy a walking holiday abroad it is important to get the essential things right. 'Your trip of a lifetime could easily get off to a slow start if you don't arrive in time for the flight,' he says. 'Arriving just in time is risky, I did it once and found that someone else had already taken my seat.' No less important, he says, is working out a plan to carry your cash safely. 'It is not a good idea to just stuff it in your pocket,' he says. Peter usually gets on very well with the local inhabitants and makes an effort to respect their customs. 'Every country has its unique rules that local people live by,' he says, 'and you can appear rude if you, for example, wear the wrong sort of clothes. I don't speak any foreign languages, but I ask local people who speak English for advice in this respect.'

Gordon Monts goes on a mountain climbing holiday twice a year, and has so far never been to the same place twice. In spite of his experience, he admits to feeling uneasy when preparing for a trip. 'I've never had anything go wrong, but I know things can happen, and do happen.' Just in case things do go wrong, Gordon thinks it is a good idea to keep a record of his passport number and flight numbers, and makes copies of all the holiday papers the travel agent gives him. 'This is a good idea, particularly if you are as bad as I am at looking after your rucksack and things.' Once at his destination, he spends a day or two studying the mountain routes he has chosen. 'Even if you have done a lot of preparation beforehand, you need to look at your plan again. There are usually many other people who have already climbed in the area, so I talk to them and get lots of good tips.'

PAPER 2   Writing (1 hour 30 minutes)

PART 1

You **must** answer this question.

1   You are planning to do an English course in an English-speaking country with a friend who has sent you a letter with an advertisement. Read the letter and the advertisement together with the notes. Then write to the Seymour Travel Agency asking for the information which your friend suggests and adding any relevant questions of your own.

> I found this advertisement and thought they sounded serious and well-organised. I'm going to see my grandparents for a few days, so could you write to them asking for more details? I have made a few notes and maybe you can think of other points.
>
> Thanks. See you soon.

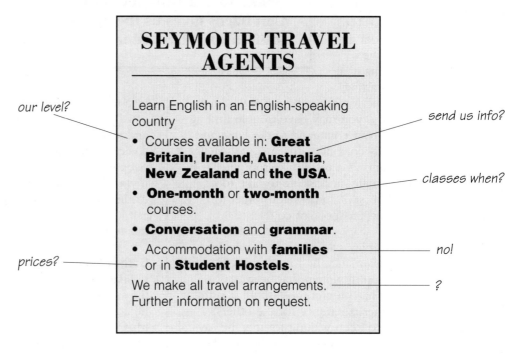

SEYMOUR TRAVEL AGENTS

our level?

Learn English in an English-speaking country

send us info?

- Courses available in: **Great Britain**, **Ireland**, **Australia**, **New Zealand** and **the USA**.

- **One-month** or **two-month** courses.

classes when?

- **Conversation** and **grammar**.

prices?

- Accommodation with **families** or in **Student Hostels**.

no!

We make all travel arrangements. Further information on request.

?

Write a **letter** of between **120** and **180** words in an appropriate style. Do not write any addresses.

Write an answer to **one** of the Questions **2–5** in this part. Write your answer in **120–180** words in an appropriate style.

2   This is part of a letter you received from an English friend:

> *When I saw you last summer you said you were going to join the new sports club in your area. How often do you go? What sports can you do? Do they organise competitions? Have you made any new friends there?*
>
> *Please write soon,*
>
> *Jack*

Write your **letter**, answering Jack's questions and giving relevant details. Do not write any addresses.

3   Your teacher has asked you to write a story for the school magazine. The story must begin like this:

Anna was walking home when the storm broke out. Where could she find shelter? There was a house only 50 metres away.

Write your **story**.

4   An international magazine has asked you to write an article describing your home town and saying what attractions it has for young visitors.

Write your **article**.

5   Answer **one** of the following two questions based on your reading of **one** of the set books.

Either (a) Which part of the story you read did you like the least? Write a **composition**, describing the part you liked least and explaining why.

Or (b) 'One of the characters in the story I have read is uninteresting and boring.' With reference to the book you have read, write a **composition**, saying whether you agree or disagree with this statement and why.

Use of English (1 hour 15 minutes)

For Questions **1–15**, read the text below and decide which answer **A**, **B**, **C** or **D** best fits each space. There is an example at the beginning (**0**).

Mark your answers **on the separate answer sheet**.

Example:

0	**A** answer	**B** reason	**C** explanation	**D** solution

0	A ▬	B ☐	C ☐	D ☐

WHALES

How far would you travel for a good meal? If you were a humpback whale, the (**0**) ..... would be five thousand miles. These large sea animals travel at least that far from their winter home off the (**1**) ..... of Columbia to their summer (**2**) ..... areas off Antarctica. The distance covered by some types of whale is amazing, especially when you (**3**) ..... their enormous size. The blue whale is the largest animal that has ever (**4**) ..... and it can weigh as much as thirty elephants. It (**5**) ..... as no surprise, therefore, to hear that ancient folk legends tell of sailors (**6**) ..... these creatures for islands.

The more we (**7**) ..... about whales, the more wonderful they seem. Some species can (**8**) ..... their breath for more than an hour and dive to a (**9**) ..... of over 2000 metres. They use a system of sounds (**10**) ..... as echo-location to find the fish they eat and they have further sounds to keep in (**11**) ..... with each other. The noises they (**12**) ..... can travel hundreds of miles under water. Some species seem to sing complicated songs which (**13**) ..... of a number of separate themes, sung in a specific order which can (**14**) ..... up to half an hour or more. If you ever get the (**15**) ..... to see one of these great creatures in the wild, you will understand why they have inspired so many legends.

1	**A** beach	**B** coast	**C** seaside	**D** ground
2	**A** feeding	**B** dining	**C** eating	**D** chewing
3	**A** view	**B** think	**C** consider	**D** believe
4	**A** been	**B** stayed	**C** born	**D** lived
5	**A** gets	**B** comes	**C** goes	**D** seems
6	**A** supposing	**B** mixing	**C** confusing	**D** mistaking
7	**A** find out	**B** look out	**C** show up	**D** turn up
8	**A** store	**B** keep	**C** hold	**D** save
9	**A** depth	**B** length	**C** width	**D** breadth
10	**A** called	**B** known	**C** referred	**D** named
11	**A** reach	**B** touch	**C** call	**D** range
12	**A** provide	**B** propose	**C** process	**D** produce
13	**A** consist	**B** compose	**C** include	**D** involve
14	**A** long	**B** last	**C** play	**D** give
15	**A** break	**B** choice	**C** chance	**D** luck

For Questions **16–30**, read the text below and think of the word which best fits each space. Use only **one** word in each space. There is an example at the beginning (**0**).

Write your answers **on the separate answer sheet**.

Example:

0	*how*

A PIANO AROUND THE HOUSE

Have you ever asked yourself (**0**) .... people passed the long evenings in the days before television? The answer is that those (**16**) .... could afford it used to play the piano, or (**17**) .... the very least tried to persuade their daughters to (**18**) .... so. Although there is less piano-playing nowadays, pianos are still (**19**) .... interest to collectors of antiques, both as instruments and as pieces of furniture.

As a result, it is once (**20**) .... very fashionable, amongst those (**21**) .... both money and space, to have a grand piano in the living room. Not (**22**) .... pianos, however, are equally fashionable. It would be a mistake to (**23**) .... too excited about the possible resale value of a modern piano bought ten years (**24**) ...., for example. Similarly, not every old piano is going to be a good investment.

Rather (**25**) .... television sets today, they were made (**26**) .... huge numbers in the early twentieth century. At that time, pianos became (**27**) .... popular that most sizeable towns had a local manufacturer. Newly-married couples frequently got (**28**) .... as a main wedding present. So nowadays, many pianos are (**29**) .... little more than the value of the materials they are made from, and end their days being chopped (**30**) .... for firewood.

For Questions **31–40**, complete the second sentence so that it has a similar meaning to the first sentence, using the word given. **Do not change the word given.** You must use between two and five words, including the word given. Here is an example (**0**).

Example: 0   It is said that gardening is very good exercise.

   supposed

   Gardening .... very good exercise.

The gap can be filled by the words 'is supposed to be' so you write:

0	*is supposed to be*

Write **only the missing words** on the separate answer sheet.

---

31   The new one-way system seems pointless to me.

   point

   I can't .... the new one-way system.

32   The old house will need a thorough redecoration before you can live in it.

   have

   The old house .... redecorated before you can live in it.

33   Unless you promise to get back in time for lunch, you can't borrow the car.

   long

   You can borrow the car .... to be back in time for lunch.

34   Paula never succeeded in getting her homework done on time.

   able

   Paula was .... her homework done on time.

35   Carrie doesn't run as fast as Sarah.

   runner

   Sarah is .... than Carrie.

36   It was necessary to follow the instructions exactly.

   had

   The instructions .... exactly.

37   It may be dark when you get back, so take a torch with you.

   case

   Take a torch with you .... dark when you get back.

38   This old car probably won't last for more than a year.

   unlikely

   This old car .... for more than one year.

39   It isn't easy for Daniel to get up before the sun rises.

   difficulty

   Daniel .... up before the sun rises.

40   David remembered to take everything except his front door key.

   forgot

   The only thing which .... his front door key.

For Questions **41–55**, read the text below and look carefully at each line. Some of the lines are correct, and some have a word which should not be there.

If a line is correct, put a tick (✔) by the number **on the separate answer sheet**. If a line has a word which should not be there, write the word **on the separate answer sheet**. There are examples at the beginning (**0** and **00**).

Examples:	0	*whose*
	00	✔

HOW TO BE ANIMAL FRIENDLY

0	....	I am writing to recommend a book whose called 'How to be Animal
00	....	Friendly', which I read recently. This is a book for young people
41	....	who are interested in animals but don't know how much about them.
42	....	It has great cartoons and photographs and is packed with them facts
43	....	about the relationship between people and animals. There are written
44	....	chapters on vegetarianism, wearing fur and leather and endangered
45	....	animals. It is written in such a way that it helps you for to see things
46	....	from the animals' viewpoint. In some of places, this book was
47	....	so much sad that I wanted to cry, but on the whole it is fun to read.
48	....	As well as facts about the animals mostly themselves, there is also
49	....	information about that what cruel people do to animals, and how
50	....	people use animals for different things in various parts of the world.
51	....	It also tells you how animals have been saved people's lives. For example,
52	....	I was amazed to read the such exciting story of how three wild bears
53	....	saved a five-year-old girl when she got lost in the woods. I thought
54	....	this book was excellent and would definitely recommend it as for anyone
55	....	over the seven years old who wants to know more about animals.

For Questions **56–65**, read the text below. Use the word given in capitals at the end of each line to form a word that fits in the space in the same line. There is an example at the beginning (**0**). Write your answers **on the separate answer sheet**.

Example:	0	*punctuality*

ON TIME

For many people, (**0**) .*punctuality*. is a big issue. Parents are often   **PUNCTUAL**
keen to impress upon their children the (**56**) .... of being   **IMPORTANT**
punctual because they see it as an aspect of (**57**) .... and   **POLITE**
consideration for others. It is also a quality that (**58**) ....   **EMPLOY**
regard as very positive, and those who are (**59**) .... unpunctual   **USUAL**
may end up being (**60**) .... in their careers as a result.   **SUCCESS**

It may be, however, that less punctual people have (**61**) ....   **CHOOSE**
a more (**62**) .... lifestyle than those who always arrive on time.   **RELAX**
They may find it (**63**) .... when so much emphasis is placed   **STRESS**
on timekeeping. Indeed, if others get (**64**) .... when   **PATIENCE**
they are late for appointments, this may not seem (**65**) ....   **REASON**
to them.

PAPER 4   Listening (40 minutes)

You will hear people talking in eight different situations. For Questions **1–8**, choose the best answer **A**, **B** or **C**.

---

1 You hear an announcement on the radio about a competition.
In the competition, what do you have to answer a question about?
A a film
B wildlife
C clothing

| 1 |

2 You hear an announcement on the radio.
What problem does the radio station have this morning?
A lack of information
B lack of staff
C lack of time

| 2 |

3 You hear an advertisement on the radio.
What is being advertised?
A an article of clothing
B a type of bag
C a piece of electronic equipment

| 3 |

4 You hear a man talking about a sub-tropical island.
How does he feel about the island?
A It should become a centre for research.
B There should be no human activity at all.
C It should be developed as a tourist resort.

| 4 |

5 You hear a woman talking about a rock music festival.
What does she like about the festival?
A the organisation
B the performances
C the atmosphere

| 5 |

6 You hear a news report about an outdoor market.
What is the advantage of the market to customers?
A The food costs less than elsewhere.
B There is more information about the food.
C There is a wider variety of food.

| 6 |

7 You hear a woman talking about an experience while travelling in
Africa. In her opinion, why did the hippopotamus go away?
A It lost interest in them.
B It was hurt by one of the oars.
C It was frightened by the noise.

| 7 |

8 You hear somebody complaining about plans to open a restaurant.
What does he say?
A The food will be unhealthy.
B The streets will be dangerous.
C The local shops will be affected.

| 8 |

You will hear an interview with a man who plays the traditional Australian musical instrument called the didgeridoo. For Questions **9–18**, complete the sentences.

Today's celebration of the didgeridoo is being held at a

| | **9** | in England.

Didgeridoos are made from wood that has been attacked by

| | **10** |

After making the instrument, the aborigine people use

| | **11** | to put traditional artwork on it.

Bob is keen to correct the interviewer when she describes him as an

| | **12** |

Bob was first attracted to the | | **13** | of the didgeridoo.

The earliest evidence of the didgeridoo comes from pictures found in

| | **14** | in Australia.

Didgeridoos are believed to have existed as long as | | **15** |

years ago.

When playing the didgeridoo, it's important not to | | **16** |

To keep a note going on the instrument, you have to be able to control your

| | **17** |

There will be displays of the | *and* | **18** | of aboriginal peoples at

today's event.

You will hear five writers giving advice to young people who want to start writing stories. For Questions **19–23**, choose from the list **A–F** what each speaker says. Use the letters only once. There is one extra letter which you do not need to use.

A Concentrate on your writing.

B Use simple language.

C Write about your own life.

D Write something original.

E Keep a personal diary.

F Do a lot of research.

Speaker 1		**19**
Speaker 2		**20**
Speaker 3		**21**
Speaker 4		**22**
Speaker 5		**23**

You will hear an interview with a young TV soap opera star, Jack Benton. For Questions **24–30**, choose the best answer **A**, **B** or **C**.

24 Jack got a role in the soap opera because
    A he had a certificate in drama studies.
    B one of his friends was a TV star.
    C a TV star had just resigned.   **24**

25 Jack finds the most difficult part of his job is
    A remembering his lines.
    B pretending to be a bad person.
    C working with famous people.   **25**

26 How does Jack avoid the bad effects of fame?
    A He reads about other actors' experiences.
    B He listens to his old friends.
    C He follows his mother's advice.   **26**

27 What does Jack say about the clothes he wears?
    A They are light-coloured.
    B They are expensive.
    C They are fashionable.   **27**

28 What does Jack value most in his friends.
    A They help him to relax.
    B They listen to his problems.
    C They protect him from his fans.   **28**

29 What is Jack's reason for not going to the gym?
    A He prefers team sports.
    B He is too busy.
    C He thinks it is unnecessary.   **29**

30 Jack's dream for the future is
    A to become a cinema actor.
    B to win a TV prize.
    C to become world-famous.   **30**

PAPER 5

Speaking (14 minutes)

PART 1 (3 minutes)

Answer these questions:

What do you enjoy doing in your free time?
Has your choice of freetime activities changed over the years?
Where do you like to go on holiday?
Is there a part of the world you would particularly like to visit? Why?

PART 2 (3 or 4 minutes)

Responsible jobs (compare, contrast and speculate)

Turn to pictures 1 and 2 on page 160 which show people doing responsible jobs.

Candidate A, compare and contrast these photographs, and say what type of person you need to be to do those jobs. You have a minute to do this.

Candidate B, could you do either of these jobs?

Making things (compare and contrast)

Turn to pictures 1 and 2 on page 161 which show people making things.

Candidate B, compare and contrast these photographs, and say how difficult these things are to make. You have a minute to do this.

Candidate A, are you good at making things?

PART 3 (3 or 4 minutes)

Discussion group (discuss and evaluate)

Turn to the pictures on page 162 which show ideas for a discussion group at your college. Students will have the opportunity to participate in a discussion with guest speakers who will be invited once a month. Look at the suggested discussion topics for the first three months.

What kind of advice may students need in each area? Which three areas do you think are the most urgent? How popular will these subjects be with students? What type of questions might students ask the speakers?

PART 4 (3 or 4 minutes)

Answer these questions:

What discussion subject interests you the most?
How difficult can it be to discuss these subjects with adults?
Why is it important to discuss these subjects?
What well-known personality would you invite to a discussion group?
How could you organise a discussion group?

TEST 5

PART 1

You are going to read an article about a man who went on a training course for rangers in a wildlife reserve in Africa. Choose from the list **A–I** the sentence which best summarises each part (**1–7**) of the article. There is one extra sentence which you do not need to use. There is an example at the beginning (**0**).

Mark your answers **on the separate answer sheet**.

A This is the situation the professionals fear.

B This is a realistic assessment of the situation.

C This was a good opportunity to sample certain conditions.

D This was a chance to share the experiences of others.

E This was an opportunity to see the wider picture.

F This was an unexpected achievement.

G This is why it's important to keep your distance.

H This was a mistake not to be repeated.

I This was an essential skill to master.

RANGER TRAINING

Mark Thompson went to one of Africa's top wildlife reserves to take part in a training course for park rangers.

0 | **I**

As the buffalo charged towards me, I raised the rifle to my shoulder, tried to steady my arm, took aim and fired. The bullet hit it square in the chest, saving us from the dangerous attack, or least it would have done if this had been for real. The hole in the paper target was proof of that. I was in Africa to learn some of the skills that a park ranger requires and, although I have no love of guns, knowing how and when to shoot is a must.

1

We were practising using real guns and bullets in the safety of a dried-up river bed, under the instruction of a real park ranger called Rick. 'Animals have a flight zone and a fight zone,' he explained. 'Get up close to them and they will run away, but at a certain point, if you get too close, they will turn and fight.'

2

Apparently the danger when travelling is that you might suddenly come across an animal unexpectedly and surprise it, and buffaloes are the ones that scare the rangers most. 'Elephants usually stop short when they charge, but the buffalo just keeps on going, you have to shoot,' Rick warned us.

3

Rick gave out such pieces of useful, common-sense advice at regular intervals. 'Don't stray too far from the camp,' he warned us. I looked around at the four large tents and ring of stones that marked the campfire under a great marula tree. Whilst all the holidaymakers in the safari lodge enjoyed hotel-style comforts, we had oil lamps and showered under a

bucket which was suspended from a tree. But I wasn't tempted to swap the simplicity of the camp for a hotel room, because in the camp I really felt a part of the bush.

4

'One night a pride of lions came into the camp after we had gone to bed,' Michael from Chicago told me. He was one of a party from the USA who were making a return visit to the camp. The four of us on the ranger training course listened avidly to their tales from the wild side. 'The cubs were playing with the tent ropes.' As he continued, I made a mental note to sleep with my gun next to me.

5

Soon I was in the mood for some adventures of my own. The days ahead were divided between lessons in ranger skills, and excursions into the bush. These tours, made either on foot or by four-wheel drive vehicle, began at the crack of dawn. They provided an opportunity not only to take in the wide variety of wildlife on the reserve, but also to gain an understanding of the whole ecosystem and the role of the ranger in that.

6

Although I doubt if I'll ever be ready for a lone stroll across lion country, the course has at least increased my chances of survival. One afternoon, Rick let me take the wheel of the jeep and use my usually dreadful sense of direction to find our way back to camp. To my great astonishment I managed it, and realised that I was starting to make some sense of the landscape that had at first all looked the same.

7

I had also learned that only a handful of dedicated and skilled individuals can really make it as a true professional in this business. What was called a ranger training course was really a lesson in ranger appreciation. There was no way that any of us would ever come close to being ready to take on any of their duties for real.

PART 2   You are going to read a article about a group of engineering students. For Questions **8–14**, choose the correct answer **A**, **B**, **C** or **D**.

Mark your answers **on the separate answer sheet**.

Fast-track Studies

Students at Birmingham University have found the drive to succeed – by building their own racing car.

Formula one motor racing is very much an international sport. Many of the leading formula one racing teams choose to base their operations in Britain, however. This is surprising because Britain no longer has a car manufacturing industry of any great significance. So why do the formula one teams choose to work there? In part the answer lies in the long tradition of mechanical engineering in British universities which continue to turn out highly-skilled graduates in the subject.

At Birmingham University, for example, the engineering department has specialised in preparing students for a career in the motor-racing industry. Students at the University have designed and built a single-seater racing car as part of their course. Each third-year student took sole responsibility for a section of the car, for example, the engine, bodywork or brakes, and the work was assessed as part of the students' final degree mark. Even more exciting for the students is the fact that the team building the car also gets to race it against teams from other universities.

This October, Martin Corsham, the student responsible for the engine on last year's course, is starting work as a trainee with one of the world's leading formula one teams. It is a dream job that makes every other mechanical engineering student in the country feel more than slightly envious. More significantly, it's a job that 21-year-old Corsham is

30 **adamant** he would not have got without the hands-on experience he gained at Birmingham.

'I've worked on cars since I was a kid,' he says, 'but this was the first engine that I'd worked on completely on my own. I took what was basically a motorcycle engine and turned it into an engine for the racing car.'

Corsham is clearly a true obsessive. He worked on the engine for at least three hours a day throughout his final year at university. The project finally came to a head the day before the car's official test run on April 22nd. Until that day, the engine had never actually run in the car itself. They eventually got it going at dawn after a desperate all-night session. 'But what a night!' Corsham says. 'I don't think I've got words to describe what it felt like, that feeling of great pride when it actually started. The most satisfying thing though was actually getting to drive the car. I was the first person who got the chance to drive the car with my engine in it, it was wonderful.'

Ian Stewart, who was responsible for the bodywork on the car, also found the whole experience very valuable, if a little frustrating. 'It's difficult relying on other people finalising their part before you can do yours,' he remembers. Stewart spent his whole Christmas holidays producing a model of the bodywork at home. He returned to college to find a few crucial details on other parts of the car had been changed and he had to start again.

The idea for the racing car programme originally came from the students themselves. Reading about an annual competition for racing-car builders in Detroit, USA, students on the course decided that they too would be capable of designing and building their own car. The university was quick to see the value of the idea and gave its backing.

Last May, the team took the car they had built to Detroit. Although the team was new to the competition, and had received relatively little funding compared to their rivals, their car impressed the judges. The university now plans to make the 71 project a regular feature of the course. **It** has proved very successful, not only as a practical demonstration of the students' theoretical studies, but also in allowing them to get their hands dirty and impress future employers.

8 On the Birmingham University course, each of the students

    A builds a complete racing car.
    B works with professional racing drivers.
    C is expected to be successful in races.
    D has a separate area of responsibility.

9 How do other students view Martin's new job?

    A They are jealous of him.
    B They are encouraged by it.
    C They are proud of him.
    D They are surprised by it.

10 'adamant' in line 30 describes a feeling of

    A certainty.
    B gratitude.
    C satisfaction.
    D modesty.

11 Which part of the project did Martin find most rewarding?

    A working without assistance
    B the last-minute preparations
    C the moment the engine started
    D driving the finished car

12 What did Ian Stewart find most difficult about the project?

    A working in the holidays
    B being dependent on other people
    C producing a model of the car
    D getting the details right

13 Where did the idea of the racing-car project come from?

    A racing-car builders in Detroit
    B staff at the university
    C students on the course
    D local employers

14 What does 'it' refer to in line 71?

    A the car
    B the course
    C the project
    D the university

You are going to read an extract from a book about a biking adventure. Seven paragraphs have been removed from the extract. Choose the most suitable paragraph from the list **A–H** for each gap (**15–20**). There is one extra paragraph which you do not need to use. There is an example at the beginning (**0**).

Mark your answers **on the separate answer sheet**.

Bikes on Kilimanjaro

We had succeeded in reaching the top of the mountain with our bikes still in working order. The next challenge was going to be coming down. We melted enough snow to provide us with water for the descent.

0	*H*

Then the whole lot was dropped into the top of my rucksack. The tent was plastered with ice, which added to the weight.

15	

And we had the bikes on top of that. When we pulled our bikes out of the snow to make our conclusive exit from the mountain, the sun was dropping down with increasing speed towards the black cliffs of Uhuru Peak and there was total silence.

16	

Nevertheless, our immediate objective had been fulfilled: that of cycling to Uhuru Peak. Unfortunately, much excitement and experimentation with the bicycles had to be abandoned.

17	

But principally, we had not done everything we had planned with our bikes because of the constraints of time in the modern society 3,000 miles away to which we were bound. Before starting the descent, we sat down to consider what we had gained from this experience.

18	

And only by living under stress with others can we form true bonds. It was certainly sad to leave Kibo summit, but we were in no doubt that there would be other adventures. Setting off down a mountain towards warmth and safety normally encourages a spring in the step.

19	

The combined weight of rider, bike and rucksack was over 130 kilograms; a lot for a pair of brakes to hold in normal conditions. I was sitting as far back as possible on the bike seat, keeping the weight as far rearwards as possible on the steep slope. I could just reach the handlebars with outstretched fingers.

20	

After that incident we experimented with other varying modes of downhill travel. Most ended with wild, uncontrollable slides and somersaults. But with every metre descended we felt better. Until we suddenly realised that our adventures on the mountain side were being observed from below. A crowd of mountain climbers had been following our every fall through binoculars!

A Part of the reason for this had been our physical state. We had suffered a number of minor injuries on the way up, which had delayed our ascent. Getting to the top had left us with little energy for any extra bicycle riding.

B However, that afternoon I was barely capable of lifting one foot above the other. In the first section of our descent there were many large rocks, so we were carrying our bikes down. At this point, I decided to try to ride the bike down, something that ended in disaster.

C It was so quiet and calm that I could almost hear the creak of ice in the northern glacier. It was sad to say goodbye to the peak because we were leaving the adventure before we had really got started on the more exciting bits.

D What I didn't realise until the whole ensemble was travelling at high speed, was that I couldn't see where I was going. The rucksack I was wearing on my chest had been pushed upwards into my face, leaving me totally sightless.

E Instead of that, the bike turned over and the large rucksack took off down the slope in a series of giant hops. Picking up the bike, I wondered whether I'd ever recover the sack.

F When we'd got everything packed up, we found we had the biggest and heaviest loads we'd ever seen. Each of us had one of the huge expedition rucksacks to carry, stuffed to the brim.

G In spite of the sadness we felt, we knew that we had learnt a little more about ourselves and a drop more about other people. It is only by pushing ourselves to our limits that we get to explore ourselves.

H This added up to several pints of valuable liquid in plastic containers, which weighed a ton. Sleeping bags, assorted socks and spare layers of clothing were packed away.

You are going to read a magazine article about successful young people. For Questions **21–35**, choose from the people (**A–D**). The people may be chosen more than once. There is an example at the beginning (**0**).

Mark your answers **on the separate answer sheet**.

A	**Justin Weston**
B	**Tom Hall**
C	**Adam Huntley**
D	**Josh Rendell**

Who

has been successful at writing?	**0**	*B*
thinks criticism has a positive effect on him?	**21**	
found a job was easier than expected?	**22**	
has seen his income increase?	**23**	
is grateful to a teacher?	**24**	
was influenced by the area where he lived?	**25**	
wants to change the responsibilities of a job?	**26**	
considers experience more important than qualifications?	**27**	
always had a clear sense of purpose?	**28**	
does not want to be a role model?	**29**	
is worried about leaving others in charge?	**30**	
did not accept a job he was offered?	**31**	
thinks his success may have a positive effect on others?	**32**	
is unhappy about the calls he receives?	**33**	
is not liked by some fellow workers?	**34**	
is in contact with young people in his area?	**35**	

Justin Weston is one of the most hotly discussed young British artists. After a childhood in the south of England, he discovered his passion for art while at secondary school in Scotland, where the whole family had moved when he was fifteen. 'I owe my success to the arts instructor who pushed me all the way to Arts College,' he says. The move from England to Scotland also brought him into direct contact with the landscape that was to become his main subject matter. Mr Weston looks set to become one of his generation's great painters, but his style is not universally popular, as a number of negative comments from colleagues has shown. 'Such comments only give me more courage to do new and exciting things and to paint more effectively,' he says.

Tom Hall is a political correspondent. He has built up a glittering career in television journalism since graduating from London University in 1993. Even at university, he knew where he was going. While fellow history students enjoyed an active social life, Tom performed in plays and edited the student newspaper. When he graduated, he turned down job offers from the national papers for the exciting performance aspects of television reporting. He found the work much less demanding than he had thought it would be. 'I was able to turn my attention to writing as well,' he says. Days after publication, his thriller, *Shadows*, has won critical acclaim. The only thing Tom Hall dislikes about his job is finding an average of thirty messages on his answering machine every day. 'Mostly from newspaper editors asking my opinion,' he says.

MEET THE RISING TALENTS

WITH CAREERS VARYING FROM FARMING TO POLITICS, THESE YOUNG ACHIEVERS – MOST STILL IN THEIR TWENTIES – ARE OUR TIPS FOR THE MOVERS OF TOMORROW …

Adam Huntley is a gardener. It is refreshing to meet a successful young person who is not happy at the thought of being seen as a leader of a generation. 'I don't like that at all,' he says. But the facts speak for themselves. At the age of 26, Adam has just become Head Gardener at Cromart, one of the most renowned gardens in England. 'My approach as Head Gardener will be different from what has gone on so far,' he says, 'the modern Head Gardener also has to be involved in attracting visitors.' Adam has been awarded a grant for a trip to the Caribbean, where he hopes to find a number of plants to enrich the Cromart garden. 'I am pleased at the prospect of travelling,' he says, 'but I'm also nervous about letting somebody else take over my job.'

Josh Rendell is a farmer. Owner and manager of a large dairy and arable crop farm, 29-year-old Josh finds he is the youngest of all farmers in the area. In 1991, he and his three brothers inherited the land from their father. Since then, he has reduced costs and increased efficiency to such an extent that his profits have doubled. Josh has a geography degree from Exeter University and a degree in business management, but most of what he has learnt, he says, came from his day-to-day work on the job. His recreations include organising visits to the farm for children in local schools, but his central role is running the farm well. 'If your business is healthy,' he says, 'it can benefit the local community.'

PAPER 2

Writing (1 hour 30 minutes)

You **must** answer this question.

1 You are planning a camping holiday with a friend who has sent you a letter with a Camping Site advertisement. Read the letter and the advertisement together with the notes. Then write to Willows Camping Site asking for the information which your friend suggests and adding any relevant questions of your own.

This would be a good place for our holiday but we need to find out more! I'm busy helping in my parent's shop. Could you write for more details using my notes? May be we won't need to take our tents. Can you think of anything else we need to ask?

See you soon.

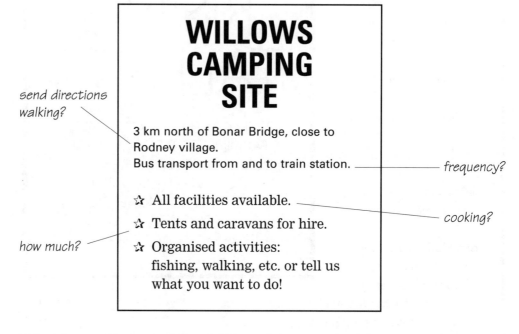

Write a **letter** of between **120** and **180** words in an appropriate. Do not write any addresses.

Write an answer to **one** of the Questions **2–5** in this part. Write your answer in **120–180** words in an appropriate style.

2   You see this announcement in an international magazine for young people learning English.

> **Take my advice ...**
>
> Write an article telling other students the things that have worked for you in learning English.
>
> You should describe any method, books or people who have helped you and explain how these could help other students.

Write your **article**.

3   You have decided to enter a short story competition. The competition rules say that the story must **begin** with these words:

It all began when the phone rang.

Write your **story**.

4   This is part of a letter you have received from a friend in another country.

> *We're doing a project at school about how computers are changing people's lives in different countries. Please could you write me a short report about your country, saying how computers are changing things and how people feel about it? I can then include this in my project.*

Write your **report**.

5   Answer **one** of the following two questions based on your reading of **one** of the set books.

Either   (a) Which character in the book or one of the short stories you have read did you like least? Write a **composition**, explaining which character you have chosen and why.

Or   (b) A magazine for young people has a page where readers can give their opinions about books they have read. Write a short **article** for the magazine, saying what type of young people would enjoy the book and why.

Use of English (1 hour 15 minutes)

For Questions **1–15**, read the text below and decide which answer **A**, **B**, **C** or **D** best fits each space. There is an example at the beginning (**0**).

Mark your answers **on the separate answer sheet**.

Example:

| 0 | **A** origin | **B** age | **C** spring | **D** growth |

| 0 | **A** ▆ | **B** ☐ | **C** ☐ | **D** ☐ |

MUSIC

Nobody knows for certain what the (**0**) ..... of music was. Music is certainly older than poetry and painting but as early man had no way of (**1**) ..... it, we can only (**2**) ..... what it sounded like. Watching a child (**3**) ..... on a drum with its hands or a (**4**) ..... of wood, it is easy to see that this is the simplest of instruments. It does not (**5**) ..... much effort to produce a rhythm on it.

Wall paintings show what some of the first instruments (**6**) ..... like. Early civilisations had already discovered the three basic (**7**) ..... of producing music: blowing into a tube, striking an object, and scraping a string. We know that western music comes from the (**8**) ..... Greeks. The musical scales we use now are (**9**) ..... on certain sequences of notes which the Greeks used to create a particular (**10**) ......

Until the sixteenth century, most players of instruments were (**11**) ..... performers, but as music became more (**12**) ....., orchestras and musical groups began to (**13**) ...... This (**14**) ..... about the writing of music to be played by several musicians at one time. This can certainly be (**15**) ..... the birth of modern music.

1	**A** recording	**B** playing	**C** producing	**D** performing
2	**A** think	**B** reckon	**C** guess	**D** realise
3	**A** hitting	**B** knocking	**C** crashing	**D** banging
4	**A** slice	**B** point	**C** piece	**D** shape
5	**A** make	**B** call	**C** take	**D** do
6	**A** looked	**B** appeared	**C** felt	**D** sounded
7	**A** forms	**B** manners	**C** systems	**D** ways
8	**A** ancient	**B** old	**C** aged	**D** antique
9	**A** raised	**B** based	**C** established	**D** supported
10	**A** spirit	**B** temper	**C** mood	**D** humour
11	**A** separate	**B** lonely	**C** unique	**D** single
12	**A** widespread	**B** enlarged	**C** expanded	**D** extended
13	**A** turn	**B** appear	**C** spring	**D** be
14	**A** produced	**B** affected	**C** caused	**D** brought
15	**A** appointed	**B** called	**C** decided	**D** named

For Questions **16–30**, read the text below and think of the word which best fits each space. Use only **one** word in each space. There is an example at the beginning (**0**).

Write your answers **on the separate answer sheet**.

Example:	**0**	*one*

RUNNING

Running is (**0**) .... of the cheapest and most effective forms of exercise. When you first (**16**) .... up the sport, it is important to build up your strength slowly. You should, however, plan to go out for (**17**) .... least thirty minutes, running for a minute and walking for a minute. (**18**) .... this seems like a long time, you should try running (**19**) .... a partner as this will help you to (**20**) .... going.

It is a good idea to run on grass rather (**21**) .... hard surfaces. This will help you to avoid injury to your muscles which may not be (**22**) .... to this kind of exercise. You (**23**) .... to wear clothes that are both waterproof and lightweight and you should take care over your choice of footwear. This is (**24**) .... the right kind of shoes are absolutely essential for running.

Make (**25**) .... you buy them from a shop (**26**) .... the staff are trained to help you to match the shoe to things (**27**) .... the weight and shape of your foot. Don't be influenced (**28**) .... brand names, but look for comfort. You should allow a centimetre (**29**) .... the tip of your big toe and the end of the shoe. The average shoe is good for 200–300 miles, so you should be prepared to buy a new (**30**) .... regularly.

For Questions **31–40**, complete the second sentence so that it has a similar meaning to the first sentence, using the word given. **Do not change the word given.** You must use between two and five words, including the word given. Here is an example (**0**).

Example: **0** You should book their ticket today to be sure of getting a seat.

had

To be sure of getting a seat, ... your ticket today.

The gap can be filled by the words 'you had better book' so you write:

0	*you had better book*

Write **only the missing words** on the separate answer sheet.

---

31 If Amy had arrived a moment later, she would have missed the start of the film.

time

Amy arrived just .... the start of the film.

32 Guests are asked to say if they prefer tea or coffee with their breakfast.

rather

Guests are asked to say if .... tea or coffee with their breakfast.

33 Mrs Parker expressed her thanks for all the help she'd received.

grateful

Mrs Parker said that .... all the help she'd received.

34 People say that there are bears living in these mountains.

said

Bears .... in these mountains.

35 Not many people read magazines about stamp collecting these days.

widely

Magazines about stamp collecting .... these days.

36 John will only answer if you ring the doorbell twice.

unless

John .... you ring the doorbell twice.

37 Too tired to continue, Phil stopped walking.

carry

Phil couldn't .... he was too tired.

38 Trevor decided to wait and only book his flight at the last minute.

put

Trevor decided .... his flight until the last minute.

39 You must not waste any time in applying for a visa.

soon

You must apply for a visa .... possibly can.

40 We'll only eat indoors if it rains.

long

As .... rain, we'll eat outdoors.

For Questions **41–55**, read the text below and look carefully at each line. Some of the lines are correct, and some have a word which should not be there.

If a line is correct, put a tick (✔) by the number **on the separate answer sheet**. If a line has a word which should not be there, write the word **on the separate answer sheet**. There are examples at the beginning (**0** and **00**).

Examples:	0	*to*
	00	✔

STUDENT'S WEEK

0	....	In my town, students like to celebrating Students' Week,
00	....	which begins with a party on the first day of spring.
41	....	There is a whole week of activities which organised by all
42	....	the schools in the area, and students like to invite them
43	....	their parents and teachers to the party so that everyone
44	....	can have a really good time and enjoy of the celebrations.
45	....	First, I am going to tell you something about the preparations
46	....	made up in advance. Students build stands, which are
47	....	large tables where they can be put all the food
48	....	for the party. Music is very important, so that the students
49	....	who can play instruments get together with to practise the
50	....	songs they are going to play. Everyone looks forward to
51	....	Students' Week because it is such a fun for the young and
52	....	also for the old. Even so, when it rains, the celebrations are
53	....	not spoilt as it is always possible to move into the tents
54	....	which students put up just in the case they are needed.
55	....	If you think ever visit my town in spring, come and join us.

For Questions **56–65**, read the text below. Use the word given in capitals at the end of each line to form a word that fits in the space in the same line. There is an example at the beginning (**0**). Write your answers **on the separate answer sheet**.

Example: | **0** | *visitors* |

RULES FOR WILDLIFE WATCHERS

There are a few rules that all (**0**) ....*visitors*.... to the wildlife reserves   **VISIT**

should observe. (**56**) .... these rules is necessary   **FOLLOW**

if people want to enjoy themselves and have an (**57**) ....   **FORGET**

experience. First of all, it is (**58**) .... to leave your car   **ADVISE**

in the car park so as to cause as little (**59**) .... as possible   **DISTURB**

to the varied wildlife. The animals can be easily (**60**) ....   **FRIGHT**

by unexpected noises, (**61**) .... those made by   **PARTICULAR**

machines. Secondly, people need to be (**62**) .... if they   **PATIENCE**

want to see the animals in their natural (**63**) ....   **SURROUND**

This often means that people have to put up with (**64**) ....   **PLEASANT**

weather conditions and (**65**) .... insects.   **ANNOY**

Listening (40 minutes)

You will hear people talking in eight different situations. For Questions **1–8**, choose the best answer **A**, **B** or **C**.

1 You hear a man talking about a new public building.
   What does the building contain?
   A a museum
   B a library
   C a leisure centre

   [ ] 1

2 You overhear a man talking.
   What is the man doing?
   A giving advice
   B telling a story
   C asking someone to do something

   [ ] 2

3 You hear a man talking about a mountain.
   Why did he advise his friend not to climb it?
   A The walk would be too long.
   B His friend was not fit enough.
   C The mountain paths were rough.

   [ ] 3

4 You hear a man talking about a meal he had.
   What was unexpected about the meal?
   A the amount of food
   B the quality of the cooking
   C the price he had to pay

   [ ] 4

5 You hear a woman who works for a dance company.
   What is her role in the company?
   A She trains the dancers.
   B She selects new dancers.
   C She organises the tours.

   [ ] 5

6 You hear a manager talking about her employees.
   What does she expect them to do?
   A check their own work
   B work a fixed number of hours
   C keep their skills up to date

   [ ] 6

7 You hear an advertisement for a boat trip.
   What will customers get if they don't get to see dolphins?
   A another trip on a boat
   B their money back
   C a free meal

   [ ] 7

8 You hear a man talking about his job.
   What does he do now?
   A He is a writer.
   B He is an actor.
   C He is a teacher.

   [ ] 8

You will hear part of a radio programme about restaurants. For Questions **9–18**, complete the notes.

The Blue Restaurant

Best place to sit: [_____ **9**]

What you can see: *The River Thames*

[_____ **10**]

Best thing to eat: [_____ **11**]

Apple pie

Tamsin's Restaurant

Best place to sit: [_____ **12**]

What you can see: *Shopping street*

[_____ **13**]

Best thing to eat: [_____ **14**]

Mushroom soup

The River Restaurant

Best place to sit: [_____ **15**]

What you can see: *The park*

[_____ **16**]

Best thing to eat: [_____ **17**]

[_____ **18**]

PART 3

You will hear five tour guides saying why tourists value their work. For Questions **19–23**, choose from the list **A–F** what each speaker says. Use the letters only once. There is one extra letter which you do not need to use.

Why tourists value my work

A   I speak several foreign languages.

B   I am a specialist on local museums.

C   I organise the tour myself.

D   I adapt my services to different age groups.

E   I offer tourists advice on entertainment.

F   I know the history of this area well.

Speaker 1		19
Speaker 2		20
Speaker 3		21
Speaker 4		22
Speaker 5		23

PART 4

You will hear a radio interview with Ella Webster, a fashion photographer. For Questions **24–30**, decide which of the statements are TRUE and which are FALSE and write T for **True** or F for **False** in the boxes provided.

24   Ella thinks travelling is an unpleasant part of her job. | | 24 |

25   Ella's problems are often caused by insensitive editors. | | 25 |

26   In Mauritius, Ella had no time to take all the planned photos. | | 26 |

27   A problem at the airport prevented the plane from landing at Nairobi. | | 27 |

28   After the landing in Uganda some of the luggage was lost. | | 28 |

29   The experience at Nairobi made Ella change some of her opinions. | | 29 |

30   At present, Ella is thinking about whether to change jobs. | | 30 |

Speaking (14 minutes)

PART 1 (3 minutes)

Answer these questions:

Tell us something about your reasons for studying English.
Tell us where and how you've learnt English.
Do you know any other foreign languages?
Which other language do you think will be most useful for you to learn?

PART 2 (3 or 4 minutes)

Taxis (compare, contrast and speculate)

Turn to pictures 1 and 2 on page 163 which show people who have chosen to travel by taxi.

Candidate A, compare and contrast these photographs, and say why you think the people have chosen to travel by taxi. You have a minute to do this.

Candidate B, do you often travel by taxi?

People and animals (compare, contrast and speculate)

Turn to pictures 1 and 2 on page 164 which show people and animals.

Candidate B, compare and contrast these photographs, and say how you think the people are feeling about the animals. You have a minute to do this.

Candidate A, do you like animals?

PART 3 (3 or 4 minutes)

Weekend activities (discuss and evaluate)

Turn to the pictures on page 165 which show ideas for special weekend activities at a college. The activities are designed to encourage young people to play and work in teams.

What team skills might students learn in each activity? Which activity do you think would encourage team spirit best?

PART 4 (3 or 4 minutes)

Answer these questions:

How much do you like working in teams?
What happens when a team member is not really making an effort?
When is it better to work individually instead of in a team?
Who is better at playing in teams, teenagers or children?
How do people study in your country, in groups or individually?
What team sports are popular in your country?

TEST 6

PAPER 1   Reading (1 hour 15 minutes)

PART 1 You are going to read an extract from an article about rowing. Choose the most suitable heading from the list **A–I** for each part (**1–7**) of the extract. There is one extra heading which you do not need to use. There is an example at the beginning (**0**).

Mark your answers **on the separate answer sheet**.

A	The challenge of middle-age	**F**	Childhood impressions
B	A record broken	**G**	Learning to accept danger
C	A priority: understanding oneself	**H**	Wanted: an almost impossible challenge
D	The earliest successes	**I**	A decision taken
E	Unexpected success stories		

0   *I*

Planning what to do for one's birthday becomes increasingly difficult as one gets older, but I know how I will celebrate on October 9th next year. I intend to row the 2,900 miles from Tenerife to Barbados.

1

Many people have tried to row across the Atlantic and quite a few have managed it. It is clear from accounts of survivors that it is an exhausting test of endurance. Soldiers, sailors, housewives, Olympic rowers: the triumphant emerge from surprisingly varied quarters.

2

What is apparent, however, is that the main struggle takes place not in the muscles but in the mind. So, before fussing over such preliminaries as finding a crewmate and sponsorship to the tune of £50,000, I realised that first I had to explore my own mind and try to answer the obvious question of why I wanted to do something that most people would find frightening and painful.

3

When we are young we can afford to dream; as we grow older the gap widens between what we would like to do and what we actually can do. We come to the realisation that we either have to act now or dream on. After the age of forty, people respond to that realisation

in varying ways, and rowing across the Atlantic is one of them.

4

I have sailed, climbed, explored the Amazon and run marathons, but what I am looking for now is an endeavour that scares me and may not be within my capabilities. Such as racing across the Atlantic in a rowing boat.

5

Two Norwegian sailors were the first to row the Atlantic in 1896. They took 60 days and their achievement was unequalled until 1966, when two soldiers, John Ridgway and Chay Blyth, made it in 91 days.

6

It wasn't until the first Atlantic Rowing Race, in 1997, that New Zealanders Rob Hamill and Phil Stubbs shot across to Barbados in an incredible 41 days. This was less than half the time Ridgway and Blyth had taken.

7

As a schoolboy I had read about Blyth and Ridgway and about the innumerable hardships and setbacks they suffered. It was horrifying, and I concluded they were mad. Looking back at the book now, I see they thought so too. When people asked them why they had undertaken such a dangerous journey, they replied that every person had secret ambitions.

You are going to read a passage written by a zoologist. For Questions **8–14**, choose the correct answer **A**, **B**, **C** or **D**.

Mark your answers **on the separate answer sheet**.

Most children at the tender age of six or so are full of the most impractical schemes for becoming policemen, firemen or train drivers when they grow up. But when I was that age, I could not be bothered with such mundane ambitions. I knew exactly what I wanted to do, I was going to have my own zoo. At the time, this did not seem to me, and still does not seem, a very unreasonable idea. My friends and relatives, who had long found me strange because I showed little interest in anything that did not have fur or feathers, accepted this as just another manifestation of my strangeness. They felt that, if they ignored my often-repeated remarks about owning my own zoo, I would eventually grow out of it.

11 As the years passed, however, to the **bewilderment** of those friends and relatives, my resolve to have my own zoo grew greater and greater, and eventually, after going on a number of expeditions to bring back animals for other zoos, I felt the time was ripe to acquire my own.

From my latest trip to West Africa, I had brought back a considerable collection of animals which were living, temporarily I assured her, in my sister's suburban garden in Bournemouth. But after a number of unsuccessful attempts to convince local councils in various areas to support my plans, I began to investigate the possibility of starting my zoo on the island of Jersey in the English Channel.

I was given an introduction to a man named Hugh Fraser who, I was told, was a broad-minded, kindly soul. He would show me around the island and point out suitable sites. So, I flew to Jersey and was met by Hugh Fraser who drove us to his family home, probably one of the most beautiful old houses on the island. There was a huge walled garden with lots of outbuildings all built in the beautiful local stone which was the colour of autumn leaves glowing in the sunshine. Turning to my wife, I said: 'What a marvellous place for a zoo.'

If my host had promptly fainted on the spot, I could not have blamed him. The thought of creating the average person's idea of a zoo, with all the grey cement and iron bars, in such a lovely spot was horrible. To my astonishment, however, Hugh Fraser did not faint, but merely cocked an enquiring eyebrow at me and asked whether I really meant what I said. Slightly embarrassed, I replied that I had meant it, but added hastily that I realised that it was impossible. Hugh said he did not think it was as impossible as all that.

He went on to explain that the house and grounds were too big for him to keep up as a private individual, and so he wanted to move to a smaller place in England. Would I care to consider renting the property for the purpose of establishing my zoo? I could not imagine more attractive surroundings for my purpose, and by the time lunch was over, the bargain had been sealed.

The alarm displayed by all who knew me when this was announced can be imagined. The only exception to the general chorus of disapproval was my sister. Although she thought it a mad scheme, at least it would rid her back garden of the assorted jungle creatures who were beginning to put a great strain on her relationship with her neighbours.

8 How did the writer's friends and family react to his childhood ambition?

    A They took no notice of it.
    B They encouraged him in it.
    C They tried to talk him out of it.
    D They tried to interest him in other things.

9 What does the word 'bewilderment' in line 11 tell us about the attitude of friends and relatives to the writer as he grew up?

    A They were pleasantly surprised by him.
    B They became increasingly angry with him.
    C They were shown to be right about his ideas.
    D They didn't really understand his ambitions.

10 Why didn't the writer start a zoo in England?

    A He had too many animals.
    B His sister was against it.
    C Nobody wanted to help him.
    D He couldn't get permission.

11 Why was the writer introduced to Hugh Fraser?

    A Hugh knew a lot about zoos.
    B Hugh owned a number of houses.
    C Hugh knew the island very well.
    D Hugh had offered land for rent.

12 What was Hugh's initial reaction to the writer's comment about the walled garden?

    A He was horrified at the prospect.
    B He was surprised by the suggestion.
    C He was too embarrassed to reply.
    D He was interested in the idea.

13 What did the writer particularly like about the place he chose for his zoo?

    A its size
    B its price
    C its setting
    D its facilities

14 How did the writer's sister feel about the establishment of the zoo in Jersey?

    A alarmed
    B relieved
    C supportive
    D disappointed

You are going to read a magazine article about a woman who makes mirrors decorated with seashells. Six sentences have been removed from the article. Choose from the sentences **A–I** the one which fits each gap (**15–21**). There is one extra sentence which you do not need to use. There is an example at the beginning (**0**).

Mark your answers **on the separate answer sheet**.

MAKING MIRRORS

Viv Thomas used her exotic shell collection to embark on a new career making the decorated mirrors which she now sells all over the world.

Viv Thomas, together with her husband Clive, returned to Britain after nearly 30 years of living abroad with wonderful memories. **0** | **I**

Determined to use them rather than just keep them in a box or throw them out, Viv made a shell mirror for her bathroom. This was very much admired by friends and neighbours who came to visit her. **15**

That was two years ago. Viv now runs her own small mirror-making business. She buys shells from all over the world through a wholesale company and has converted a spare bedroom in her house into an office-cum-studio. **16**

A local carpenter makes frames for her and a glazier then fits the glass inside. Viv does everything else herself; the design, the initial painting of the frame and then the final making up. **17**

Clive is a banker and was able to advise Viv on deciding how much money should be invested when she decided to set up the business. Around £3000 was spent on shells alone. **18** Viv's main problem was knowing how to market her work more widely.

Local shops could only sell a small number because once they had added their profit margin, the mirrors became rather expensive. However, Viv has now made contact with another company that makes and sells mirrors of a different type. **19** At such events, the right sort of people get to see the mirrors and can order them directly.

Venturing into other areas, Viv plans to approach restaurants and hotels directly as she thinks her mirrors might be attractive to them. She has also taken a website on the Internet. **20** It means Viv doesn't have the expense of travelling around with her range of mirrors in the back of the car.

Viv reckons it will take another year before her business starts to make money. **21** She would like to employ someone to help her with the administration and preparation of the frames, for example, which would allow her to devote more time to the artistic side.

A Together they can afford to take stands at specialist exhibitions and craft fairs.

B This represents about one week's work and each mirror brings in anything between £100 and £400 for the business.

C As Viv discovered, it's a good idea to find a company willing to sell goods on your behalf.

D Before long, she was being asked to make mirrors for other people.

E But it didn't end there, Viv also had to think about equipment such as the heavy-duty boxes needed to send the mirrors abroad.

F She works there, surrounded by shells of every shape and colour and the other materials needed to make the mirrors.

G Once this happens, she feels she will be able to concentrate on the side of the business she enjoys.

H This is a very economical way of selling.

I She also brought back a huge collection of sea shells collected from beaches around the Indian Ocean.

You are going to read an article about student accommodation in which four college students talk about the place they live. For Questions **22–35**, choose from the people (**A–D**). The people may be chosen more than once. There is an example at the beginning (**0**).

Mark your answers **on the separate answer sheet**.

Which student says …?

My accommodation seems quite expensive.	**0**	A
I have plenty of storage space.	**22**	
I have reason to regret a decision.	**23**	
My college doesn't provide accommodation.	**24**	
My room is maintained to a high standard.	**25**	
I have washing facilities in my room.	**26**	
I would like to have more independence.	**27**	
I had to buy some extra electrical equipment.	**28**	
I would like to have more private space.	**29**	
It's easy to keep in touch with people here.	**30**	
My room is not very well-furnished.	**31**	
I'm expected to do my share of the housework.	**32**	
This is the only place where I can afford to live.	**33**	
I save money by doing my own cooking.	**34**	
There are good recreational facilities nearby.	**35**	

A	Matthew Wren

I live in what's called a hall of residence where I get full board as well as a room. It's not exactly what you call cheap, though. I pay £87 per week for my single room and three meals a day. This also includes the use of a washing machine and ironing board. But I can't complain because my room has just been re-carpeted, the furniture's new and the cleaner comes in daily. The main drawback is sharing the bathroom with nine other students and we don't have any kitchen facilities. The first thing I did when I arrived was buy myself a mini-fridge, so I could have cool drinks whenever I wanted. But, we're on the university network, so I have access to the Internet and free e-mail from my room, and we get room phones so I can ring friends around the campus for nothing.

B	Kerry Dunnock

The city where I study is appalling for cheap accommodation, and the college has nothing of its own to offer you, but I was lucky. I found a room in a nice little terraced house with central heating which I share with three other girls. I have a yearly contract with a private landlady and I pay £220 a month for my study bedroom. This is not bad as it also has a large walk-in wardrobe where I put all my stuff. I share the bathroom, kitchen and a small living room with the other girls, and we split all the bills between us. We tried to make a rota for the washing up, cleaning and putting out the rubbish, but it's not always strictly followed. Cooking your own food is much cheaper than eating at college, and I like it because I have what I want when I want it.

C	Becky Martin

I live in a college-owned self-catering block. There's not much luxury, but I get value for money. For my £38 per week rent, I get a reasonably-sized room with an old wardrobe, a tiny desk, one shelf, a rather stained carpet and a sink. When I first moved in, I probably spent more on decoration than I did on food. My only real complaint, though, was that I had to buy a new pillow because the one I was provided with felt like a plastic bag full of old towels. I share the kitchen and bathroom with six other girls. One of them has a TV in her room, but she is a bit possessive about it. The fridge is not huge, so you're always trying to squeeze your food into the last remaining inch of space. I twice set off the fire alarm by burning my dinner, so tended to give up on cooking after that. We eat a lot of take-aways. In the next block, there's a games room where we hang out which has things like table football and satellite TV if you need a break from studying.

D	Karl Yorat

I made the big mistake of going to a college fairly near my home. It isn't so much the course that I don't like, but the fact that I'm stuck at my parents' house so I don't feel in touch with what's going on at campus. In some ways I'm lucky because I'm not paying out all the money for food and rent that other people have to find, and I have someone to do my washing, but I don't have the same amount of freedom or privacy as the people who're living away from home. I even have to share a room with my younger brother. When I told my parents I wanted to move out and go into college accommodation, they said they'd stop supporting me financially. So, in the end, I had to give up the idea, that hasn't made any of us very happy.

Writing (1 hour 30 minutes)

You **must** answer this question.

1 You are planning to do a computer course with a friend who has sent you a letter with a school advertisement. Read the letter and the advertisement together with the notes. Then write to the school asking for the information which your friend suggests and adding any relevant questions of your own.

> I think this may be just the kind of course we want. Could you write to the school for more details? I've made some notes and maybe you can think of other points.
>
> See you when I come back from holiday!

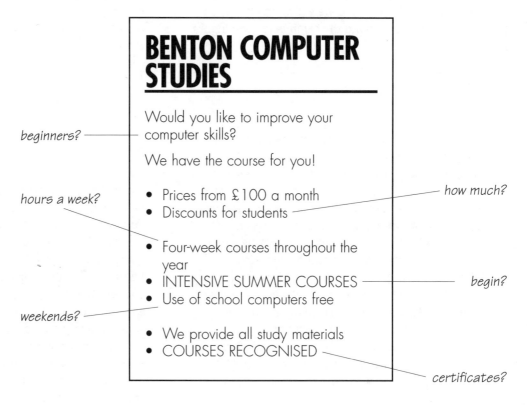

Write a **letter** of between **120** and **180** words in an appropriate style. Do not write any addresses.

Write an answer to **one** of the Questions **2–5** in this part. Write your answer in **120–180** words in an appropriate style.

2   An international magazine for English learners of your age is organising a writing competition. The rules of the competition say you must write a composition with this title about a musical or theatrical performance you have seen.

A live performance I will never forget

Write your **composition**.

3   A small town in your country is hoping to attract foreign tourists. You have been asked to write an article for an international travel magazine describing the town briefly and explaining what tourists can see and do there.

Write your **article**.

4   You see this advertisement in an international newspaper. You are interested in applying for the job.

> An English language newspaper needs reporters in all countries to write about local events in the areas of sport, fashion or the arts. If you are interested, please write to us explaining why you would be a good person to do this job and what you could write about.

Write your **letter of application**. Do not include any addresses.

5   Answer **one** of the following two questions based on your reading of **one** of the set books.

Either   (a)   A television company is planning to turn the book you have read into a television serial aimed at teenagers. You have been asked to write a report saying whether you think this is a good idea and what changes might be necessary to the plot, the setting or the characters.

Write your **report**.

Or   (b)   An Internet magazine has a page where people can recommend books they have read to others. Write an article for the magazine saying what you liked and disliked about the book you have read and what type of people you think might enjoy it.

Write your **article**.

Use of English (1 hour 15 minutes)

For Questions **1–15**, read the text below and decide which answer **A**, **B**, **C** or **D** best fits each space. There is an example at the beginning (**0**).

Mark your answers **on the separate answer sheet**.

Example:

0	**A** further	**B** older	**C** greater	**D** more

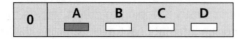

0	A	B	C	D
	▪	▫	▫	▫

TEDDY BEARS

The history of the teddy bear goes back no (**0**) ..... than 1903. In that year, a cartoon (**1**) ..... in an American newspaper showing President Theodore (Teddy) Roosevelt (**2**) ..... to shoot a bear cub on a hunting expedition. Soon after this, an enterprising toy shop owner in New York made some toy bears and (**3**) ..... them in his shop window with a sign that (**4**) ..... 'Teddy's bear'. These bears proved to be so popular that they soon sold (**5**) ....., and it wasn't long before a factory was established to (**6**) ..... advantage of the great (**7**) ..... for these new toys.

At about the same time, the Steiff toy factory in Germany had introduced a (**8**) ..... of soft toys, made (**9**) ..... mohair and wood shavings, with movable heads and limbs. (**10**) ..... the popularity of teddy bears in the USA, Steiff decided to (**11**) ..... making these as well and they were modelled (**12**) ..... the real bears in Stuttgart zoo. It is these early Steiff bears that are now most eagerly sought (**13**) ..... by collectors.

These days, teddy bears are a good investment for people who want to sell them years later at a much (**14**) ..... price. However, it's obvious that most teddy bear lovers collect them for (**15**) ..... rather than profit.

1	**A** remarked	**B** approached	**C** appeared	**D** reported
2	**A** defending	**B** reversing	**C** denying	**D** refusing
3	**A** displayed	**B** published	**C** introduced	**D** demonstrated
4	**A** said	**B** wrote	**C** spoke	**D** named
5	**A** out	**B** up	**C** off	**D** away
6	**A** take	**B** find	**C** make	**D** get
7	**A** claim	**B** order	**C** demand	**D** request
8	**A** grade	**B** chain	**C** kind	**D** range
9	**A** along with	**B** down from	**C** up for	**D** out of
10	**A** Given	**B** As	**C** Although	**D** Since
11	**A** enter	**B** put	**C** set	**D** begin
12	**A** on	**B** at	**C** with	**D** in
13	**A** through	**B** to	**C** after	**D** for
14	**A** hotter	**B** harder	**C** heavier	**D** higher
15	**A** charm	**B** purpose	**C** choice	**D** pleasure

For Questions **16–30**, read the text below and think of the word which best fits each space. Use only **one** word in each space. There is an example at the beginning (**0**).

Write your answers **on the separate answer sheet**.

Example:

0	*have*

HOLIDAY READING

Tourists in the British holiday resort of Blackpool (**0**) .... no excuse to be without a book to read on the beach this summer, (**16**) .... to the launch of the UK's first mobile seafront library. For the two months of high season, two local students will be pushing a multicoloured barrow (**17**) .... the deckchairs and sunshades on the beach, handing (**18**) .... novels and reading advice to some of the resort's sixteen million visitors.

The scheme, (**19**) .... has been launched by the local council's library and information service, relies (**20**) .... second-hand books, specially donated (**21**) .... the people of the town. This means that borrowers can either keep, return (**22**) .... swap the books. In (**23**) .... event of poor weather the two students, Catherine and Melanie, will be offering indoor storytelling sessions for children instead.

Both women have been selected for (**24**) .... combination of good humour, love of books and fitness. They will be trying to persuade people sitting on the beach to (**25**) .... down their newspapers and (**26**) .... into a book instead. Holiday reading, they insist, isn't just to (**27**) .... with relaxation, it's a chance to read things you (**28**) .... not otherwise have time to try. The only problem that Catherine and Melanie foresee is that they might (**29**) .... out of books. (**30**) .... the idea is a success, other resorts could soon be following Blackpool's example.

For Questions **31–40**, complete the second sentence so that it has a similar meaning to the first sentence, using the word given. **Do not change the word given.** You must use between two and five words, including the word given. Here is an example (**0**).

Example: **0** It was difficult for Angela to understand why Peter had gone away.

> **found**

> Angela .... why Peter had gone away.

The gap can be filled by the words 'found it difficult to understand' so you write:

0	*found it difficult to understand*

Write **only the missing words** on the separate answer sheet.

---

31 The police were there to make sure that the crowd did not invade the football pitch.

prevent

The police were there to .... the football pitch.

32 During the storm, they did not let the children leave the school building.

allowed

During the storm, the children .... the school building

33 The heavy summer rainfall has caused severe floods.

brought

Severe floods .... the heavy summer rainfalls.

34 It is not advisable for Jane to request a bank loan at the moment.

ought

Jane .... a bank loan at the moment.

35 Paul did not visit the Smiths because he didn't know where they lived.

if

Paul would have visited the Smiths .... where they lived.

36 Mary made mistakes because she refused to listen to advice.

resulted

Mary's mistakes .... refusal to listen to advice.

37 They say the government is considering the introduction of a new tax on fuel.

said

The government .... the introduction of a new tax on fuel.

38 George's health is better than I had been led to believe.

as

George's health .... I had been led to believe.

39 Although Tom eats large amounts of chocolate, he never puts on weight.

spite

Tom never puts on weight .... large amounts of chocolate.

40 My grandmother had to sell her house in order to pay off all her debts.

that

My grandmother had to sell her house .... pay off all her debts.

For Questions **41–55**, read the text below and look carefully at each line. Some of the lines are correct, and some have a word which should not be there.

If a line is correct, put a tick (✔) by the number **on the separate answer sheet**. If a line has a word which should not be there, write the word **on the separate answer sheet**. There are examples at the beginning (**0** and **00**).

Examples:	0	✔
	00	*to*

0	....	I am writing to tell you what happened when I
00	....	visited to you last week. You will remember that I
41	....	left off your house at about eight as I wanted
42	....	to catch the ten o'clock time train back home. Instead
43	....	of following your advice for to take a bus, I walked to the
44	....	station. I had been walking for twenty minutes when then
45	....	I realised I would not catch the train if I didn't
46	....	hurry up. I started walking more faster and kept looking
47	....	back in case of a bus came. But there wasn't a single
48	....	bus to be seen on the road. Then I did something
49	....	that was so much silly: I decided to go a quicker
50	....	way by cutting myself across the fields, something I
51	....	am used to be doing when I go on holiday. By the time
52	....	I reached the station, the train had been gone, however.
53	....	What is the worse, I had to sleep on a hard bench
54	....	because there wasn't going another train till the following
55	....	day. Some people never follow good advice!

For Questions **56–65**, read the text below. Use the word given in capitals at the end of each line to form a word that fits in the space in the same line. There is an example at the beginning (**0**). Write your answers **on the separate answer sheet**.

Example:	0	*ambitious*

MUSIC IN SCHOOLS

Primary schools in London are trying out an (**0**) .*ambitious*. plan **AMBITION**

through which young children get an (**56**) .... to serious music. **INTRODUCE**

The idea comes from a group of famous (**57**) .... who are **MUSIC**

concerned about the (**58**) .... of certain types of classical **SURVIVE**

music. They see the plan as one possible (**59**) .... to the **SOLVE**

problem of declining audiences at classical concerts.

Their (**60**) .... is that an interest in classical music should be **ARGUE**

developed in early (**61**) .... They reject the idea that children **CHILD**

are (**62**) .... in serious music or necessarily find it boring. The **INTEREST**

group goes into a school and gives a live (**63**) .... of a short **PERFORM**

classical piece and then this is followed by an (**64**) .... of how **EXPLAIN**

the instruments work. These sessions have proved so (**65**) .... **SUCCESS**

that they have now become a regular feature in some schools.

PAPER 4   Listening (40 minutes)

PART 1   You will hear people talking in eight different situations. For Questions **1–8**, choose the best answer **A**, **B** or **C**.

1   You hear part of a play on the radio.
    Where is the scene taking place?
    A   in a station
    B   in a shop
    C   in a restaurant

    | | 1 |

2   You hear a man talking on the telephone.
    Who is he talking to?
    A   his boss
    B   his doctor
    C   his teacher

    | | 2 |

3   You hear a man talking about a car he has hired.
    What is his opinion of the car?
    A   It is too old.
    B   It is too slow.
    C   It is too small.

    | | 3 |

4   You hear a man talking to a friend about a broken vase.
    Who does he blame for breaking it?
    A   himself
    B   his friend
    C   a third person

    | | 4 |

5   You hear a woman talking about something she saw when she was driving.
    How did she feel about what she saw?
    A   amused
    B   anxious
    C   angry

    | | 5 |

6   You hear a woman recommending a hotel.
    Why does she recommend the Dorian Hotel?
    A   It is close to tourist attractions.
    B   There are good views to enjoy.
    C   The rooms are very comfortable.

    | | 6 |

7   You hear the beginning of a radio programme.
    What is the radio programme going to be about?
    A   flowers which you can eat
    B   how to grow your own food
    C   becoming a vegetarian

    | | 7 |

8   You hear a woman talking about a college.
    What is her connection with the college?
    A   She is a student there.
    B   She is one of the teachers.
    C   She works as a secretary there.

    | | 8 |

You will hear part of a wildlife programme which is about birds called waxwings. For Questions **9–18**, complete the sentences.

The interview takes place in a [_____ **9**] in a small town.

The main part of the waxwing's body is [____ *and* ____ **10**] in colour.

The black marks on the bird's [_____ **11**] are particularly beautiful.

Waxwings usually live in the [_____ **12**] of Europe.

The birds have probably come to England as a result of

[_____ **13**] in their home area.

The time of year when these birds normally come to England is

[_____ **14**]

The food that the birds most like to eat is [_____ **15**]

Many people in the area have reported seeing waxwings in their

[_____ **16**]

One good way of attracting waxwings is to hang [_____ **17**] from a tree.

The call of a waxwing is said to sound like the noise made by

[_____ **18**]

You will hear five people saying why they like reading novels. For Questions **19–23**, choose from the list **A–F** what each speaker says. Use the letters only once. There is one extra letter which you do not need to use.

Why do you like reading novels?

A   Novels are good for improving language skills.

B   Novels make me forget my problems.

C   Novels add some adventure to my life.

D   Novels are a good subject of conversation.

E   Novels teach me how to act in certain situations.

F   Novels increase my knowledge of other cultures.

Speaker 1   [   ] **19**

Speaker 2   [   ] **20**

Speaker 3   [   ] **21**

Speaker 4   [   ] **22**

Speaker 5   [   ] **23**

You will hear two people talking about holidays. For Questions **24–30**, decide which of the views are expressed by either of the speakers and which are not. In the boxes provided, write **YES** next to those views which are expressed and **NO** next to those views which are not expressed.

24   I generally prefer not to travel abroad on holiday.   [   ] **24**

25   My recent holiday came at an inconvenient moment.   [   ] **25**

26   I once went on a free holiday as a result of my job.   [   ] **26**

27   On holiday, I prefer to choose the activities I take part in.   [   ] **27**

28   Sitting on a beach is enjoyable if you go well-prepared.   [   ] **28**

29   I begin to feel restless if I sit alone in the sun for too long.   [   ] **29**

30   If I have a good book to read, I don't mind where I sit.   [   ] **30**

PAPER 5   Speaking (14 minutes)

Answer these questions:

What type of things do you like to read?
Do you prefer to read a novel or see the film? Why?
Which film actor or actress do you like most? Why?
Do you prefer going to the cinema or watching a video at home? Why?

P A R T   2   (3 or 4 minutes)

Getting away from it all (compare, contrast and speculate)

Turn to pictures 1 and 2 on page 166 which show people enjoying a break from city life.

Candidate A, compare and contrast these photographs, and say why you think the people have chosen to travel in this way. You have a minute to do this.

Candidate B, do you like to get away from it all sometimes?

Clothes (compare, contrast and speculate)

Turn to pictures 1 and 2 on page 167 which show people wearing special clothes.

Candidate B, compare and contrast these photographs, and say why you think the people are wearing these clothes. You have a minute to do this.

Candidate A, are you interested in clothes?

P A R T   3   (3 or 4 minutes)

Electricity (discuss and evaluate)

Turn to the pictures on page 168 which show the different uses of electricity. Imagine that you have to give a talk to young children about the importance of electricity in our lives.

How important is electricity for each of these activities? Which examples would you talk about with a group of young children?

P A R T   4   (3 or 4 minutes)

Answer these questions:

Would you be able to live without electricity? What would you miss most?
Are there any alternatives to the use of electricity?
Which do you think is the best way of making electricity?
How important is it for young children to understand about the environment?
Do the electrical goods we use in the home make us lazy?
How can we help young children to understand what life was like in the past?

TEST 7

PAPER 1   Reading (1 hour 15 minutes)

PART 1 You are going to read an article about a couple who run a business from their farm in the north of England. Choose the most suitable heading from the list **A–I** for each part (**1–7**) of the article. There is one extra heading which you do not need to use. There is an example at the beginning (**0**).

Mark your answers **on the separate answer sheet**.

A	Professional skills are exploited	**F**	Continuing investment in high standards
B	Ensuring that nothing gets wasted	**G**	Professional recognition is obtained
C	No shortage of ideas to come	**H**	Filling a gap in the market
D	A necessary alternative to farming	**I**	The idea that began it all
E	Time well spent is rewarded		

Waste Not, Want Not

A farming couple who hated to waste misshapen vegetables, have found a profitable way to put them to good use.

0   *I*

Bob and Clara Darlington, who own and run a farm in the North of England have always looked for new ways of making money out of the produce they grow. Their success began when they established a shop on their farm, so that people could come and buy fresh vegetables directly from them.

1   *G*

The business was an immediate success, and soon scored top marks in a competition set up by the Farm Retail Association to find the best farm shop in the country. The Association's inspectors found the Darlingtons' shop offered excellent service and value for money as well as quality fruit and vegetables.

2   *A*

Clara Darlington is a trained chef and, in addition to a range of home-grown foods and other local produce, she began offering a variety of prepared meals which she had made herself in the farmhouse kitchen. A small cafe alongside the farm shop was soon added, with everything that visitors could taste on the menu also being for sale in the shop.

3   *F*

Clara admits that starting the business was expensive, and she has worked very hard, but maintains that if the product is good, the public recognise this and buy it. 'I aim to offer the highest quality to our customers, whether they come in for a loaf of bread, or take a whole dinner-party menu. I take it as a compliment if people take home one of my dishes to serve to their family and friends and get away with pretending they made it themselves.'

4   *B*

So it was that the couple realised that they had a surplus of misshapen or damaged vegetables grown on the farm which were unsuitable for selling in the shop. Clara, not wishing to see them get thrown away, decided to turn them into soup.

5   *H*

The soup met with the immediate approval of customers to the shop and Clara now produces ten ten different varieties. She spent much of the summer travelling up and down to London by rail, doing presentations of the soups. As a result, they are now served in first-class railway restaurant cars belonging to three companies as well as being stocked by a number of high-class London stores.

6   *E*

'I realised there was a huge untapped demand in London and other big cities,' says Clara. 'Because people coming home late from the office find a tub of fresh soup and a slice of bread a quick and tasty easy-to-prepare meal, much healthier than a take-away.'

7   *C*

Clara's next idea is to produce a range of pasta sauces handmade to the same standards using natural ingredients and flavours. These she thinks she might be able to sell effectively through mail order. One thing you can be sure of at the Darlingtons' farm, there's always something new going on.

You are going to read an article about a man who has broken a long-distance windsurfing record. For Questions **8–14**, choose the correct answer **A**, **B**, **C** or **D**.

Mark your answers **on the separate answer sheet**.

Windsurfing around Britain

Kevin Cookson, a 23-year-old engineering student, has been keen on windsurfing for many years. Recently, he set a new record for travelling all the way round the coast of Great Britain on a windsurf board.

'I don't really know why I did it,' says Kevin, 'just for the fun of it, I suppose. It was there to be done, that was all.' Despite lacking both the obsessive ambition and the funds that normally go with attempts to break records, Kevin made the journey in eight weeks and six days, knocking one week off the previous record set in 1984.

Leaving from Exmouth in the south-west of England, Kevin travelled up the west coast of England and Wales, before going round the top of Scotland and then coming back down the other side. The journey officially covered 2,896 kilometres, although given the changes of direction to find the right wind paths, the actual distance Kevin travelled is probably closer to 4,000 kilometres.

Kevin fitted his fitness training in around his final year university examinations. 'I didn't have that much time to prepare,' he explains. 'But I went running often and supplemented that with trips to the gym to do weight training. I found I got a lot better during the trip itself actually. At the start, I was tired and needed a rest after four hours, but by the end I found I could do ten hours in a row no trouble.'

Kevin had a budget of £7,000 to cover the whole expedition. The previous record had been set with a budget twice that size, while a recent unsuccessful attempt had cost £40,000. Budgets have to meet the cost of fuel, food and accommodation for the support team, as well as the windsurfer's own equipment and expenses.

Previous contenders had been accompanied by a boat on which they slept at night, as well as a fleet of vehicles on land to carry their supplies. Kevin made do with an inflatable rubber boat and an old van manned by four friends who followed his progress. Overnight arrangements had to be found along the way. Apart from the odd occasion when they enjoyed the hospitality of friends, the team made use of the camping equipment carried in the van, and slept on the beach.

When asked if his athlete's diet was a closely kept secret, Kevin replied that he ate a lot of pasta and added the odd tin of tuna to keep up his energy. 'Basically, we had anything that was on special offer in the nearest supermarket,' he confided.

65 Such a prolonged period of **gruelling** windsurfing made relaxation important however, and for this, Kevin favoured the pub method. This also provided social opportunities. 'The people we met were really encouraging,' he recalls. 'They thought what we were doing was really great. It was hard work, but we had a lot of fun along the way.'

Kevin has been windsurfing since he was thirteen years old and is also a highly-ranked competitor at national level. 'I don't know where I'm ranked now,' he says, 'because I've missed a lot of important competitions this year. But what I did has more than made up for that and I'll be doing my best to be up there amongst the winners once I get back into the competitive sport next season.' Given his unique achievement this year, Kevin seems well-placed to take on the world's top windsurfers.

8 Why did Kevin decide to try and break the record?

    A He enjoyed the challenge.
    B It had always been his ambition.
    C It was a way of making money.
    D He was invited to do it by others.

9 Before making the trip, Kevin

    A spent a lot of time practising on water.
    B could already windsurf all day without a break.
    C had only a limited amount of time for training.
    D spent most of his time working out in a gym.

10 How was Kevin's trip unlike earlier attempts at the record?

    A He had no support team.
    B He used better equipment.
    C Only one vehicle was used.
    D It took less time to organise.

11 Where did Kevin sleep most of the time?

    A on a boat
    B in a tent
    C in the van
    D in friends' houses

12 What does Kevin say about his diet?

    A He didn't keep to his plan.
    B Variety was important.
    C Certain foods were essential.
    D It was largely left to chance.

13 What does 'gruelling' (line 65) mean?

    A extremely fast
    B quite lonely
    C very tiring
    D highly uncomfortable

14 How does Kevin feel about regular windsurfing competitions?

    A They no longer interest him.
    B He's sure he can do well in them.
    C He regrets missing them.
    D He has no plans to enter any.

You are going to read a newspaper article about a man who went on a holiday in Canada. Six paragraphs have been removed from the article. Choose from the paragraphs **A–H** the one which fits each gap (**15–20**). There is one extra paragraph which you do not need to use. There is an example at the beginning (**0**).

Mark your answers **on the separate answer sheet**.

All I had to protect me was a leaflet

It was just a leaflet, but it seriously affected my holiday. I had picked it up while innocently looking through a rack of tourist information in Jasper, a city in the Rocky Mountains of Canada.

0	*H*

Bears hadn't really figured in my traveller's dreams, but they did that night. 'If you meet a bear, stay calm, talk quietly, don't run,' the leaflet continued. If it was a black bear, all I had to do was play dead, whereas if it was a grizzly, then it was essential that I didn't play dead.

15	

To find out which of these was best, I asked around. 'I always hum *You are my sunshine*', said a jolly American. 'I just jangle my keys at the corners,' said a local. Many walkers appear to take strap-on bells but these, I was warned, may not be loud enough to do the trick.

16	

Within ten minutes, in fact, the mighty pine trees were blocking out the daylight, making civilisation seem a distant memory. Somewhere out there, I knew, there were bears. Although I didn't feel that brave, I walked on.

17	

Yet here I was in a Niagara of sweat as I walked deeper into the forest. There were strange rustlings everywhere. I knew it was time to start singing. I tried some Neil Young. Wasn't he Canadian?

18	

'The last one was in 1992,' explained a local guide I bumped into. 'It was a guy who went camping up in the backwoods.' And then he added: 'He was British too.'

19	

'Of course, it's the elks that are really dangerous at this time of year,' he let slip. 'What you mean the ones wandering all over town?' I replied. 'Sure you've got to keep well away from them when they're calving, they've got hooves like razors.'

20	

But don't be discouraged from visiting Jasper. The mountains are lovely and you get a great view from the Tour bus, or the local tramway that climbs up to 8200 feet. And neither of these attractions is patronised by bears!

A I had experienced similar fears on walking safaris in Africa. Except that there you do it in the company of a trained guide with a big gun. All you get for protection in Canada is a leaflet. Canada, I complained to the lonely trees, is supposed to be safe and calm, that's why people go there.

B Fortunately, May is one of the best months to see bears, I was informed. This was confirmed by a list of that week's sightings posted to the notice board in the park's Information Centre.

C Well, I'm glad to say I completed my hike without being attacked by either animal. But I can't say that I enjoyed it, I was too terrified for that.

D The thing is, and this is no joke, people do, very very rarely, get attacked by bears. As many as five visitors have died from bear-related incidents since the park opened in 1907.

E So I decided to trust to my own voice. Armed with nothing but a map, an apple, and a bottle of water, I set off on a three-hour hike. It was only a few kilometres out of the city, but to a timid townsperson like myself, it seemed wild enough.

F All of a sudden, the prospect of walking alone in the Canadian woods didn't seem so attractive. At breakfast, I reread the leaflet very carefully. It was important not to surprise a bear. To avoid this one should whistle, talk, sing or carry a noise maker.

G This comment really made my day. But he went on to tell me that only five percent of visitors to the Jasper National Park ever get to see a bear.

H 'You're in wild bear country,' it warned, and there were graphic pictures of both black bears and grizzly bears. I had come to Jasper to go walking in the mountains. I had a vision of enjoying the snowy peaks, mystic forests, and soothing lakes.

You are going to read a magazine article in which four men talk about the clothes they like to wear. For Questions **21–35**, choose from the people (**A–D**). The people may be chosen more than once. There is an example at the beginning (**0**).

Mark your answers **on the separate answer sheet**.

Which of the men

sometimes tries to surprise people through the clothes he wears?	**0**	*D*
admits that his clothes are generally untidy?	**21**	
buys clothes which last a long time?	**22**	
is used to being criticised for the clothes he chooses?	**23**	
likes to get a good deal when buying clothes?	**24**	
needs help with clothes for less formal occasions?	**25**	
needs to have the right clothes to get work?	**26**	
needs help in choosing his clothes?	**27**	
needs different clothes for different types of work?	**28**	
admits he doesn't look after his clothes very well?	**29**	
prefers to take his time when choosing clothes?	**30**	
relies on personal judgement when choosing what to wear?	**31**	
tends to avoid clothes in bright colours?	**32**	
used to work in a job where clothes were provided?	**33**	
wants to change his appearance completely?	**34**	
wants to buy clothes which are suitable for his age?	**35**	

You are what you wear

Four men talk about what they wear and why

A Alan Upshire

I would like to be taller. I have a long body and short legs, but I have no problems in dressing for work – smart suits, shirts and ties are the order of the day, and I do invest in good quality suits that keep going for years. My appearance is important for the work I do and I now know what labels to buy for suits that are going to fit well. What I have trouble with is casual wear for weekends – you know, the right sort of informal look for supper with friends, or taking the kids out. I'd like to find the perfect casual jacket, but I hate ties and wouldn't wear one out of work. I want to look casual and stylish even though I'm in my forties. I don't like to see older men wearing trainers, but I don't know what type of casual shoes to buy, for example.

B Barry Sheldon

Being an actor, the way I look can affect my opportunities and the parts I get. I've got used to wearing my hair long, but I know it's time for a change now. But how short do I go, and what style should I choose? That's the problem because I want it to look dramatic, I want a new look. My style of dressing is simple and stylish, especially for rehearsals when I'll go in jeans and T-shirt. But I also work part-time at a film-sales company and, although I work mostly on the telephone, I have to look smarter. I don't mind shopping for clothes, but I'm not very good if I have anyone with me because I like to browse at my own pace, you know, try lots of things on. I find I buy a lot of things in black and white. It's simple and stylish and easy to put together.

C Chris Theydon

I hate shopping for clothes and will only do so when it's absolutely necessary – about once every six months. My girlfriend usually comes with me because she has better taste than I do! I'd describe my style of dress as very casual, perhaps bordering on scruffy. I try to avoid wearing smart clothes, and this may be something to do with the fact that I'm hopeless at keeping things smart. Ironing's a skill I've never really mastered, for example. Also, as I was in uniform for about twelve years when I was in the army, I never really had to think about all this somehow. I know I should be smarter for work, but it's a pretty relaxed office and so jeans and T-shirt is the norm. It's very rare for me to wear a suit, but as I've got about three friends' weddings coming up, perhaps I ought to think about a new one.

D Des Waltham

I would describe my style of dressing as individual. I know what I like and I know what will suit a particular occasion. I'm very worried about the effect clothes have on the way other people react to you. I'll wear a suit if I think it will make a meeting more productive or my oldest jeans if I want to shock people. I like shopping and I like clothes, but I don't like shopping for clothes. Where I shop depends on where I am and as I travel abroad a lot, I'm also looking for bargains in the sales wherever I go. One problem is that my wife is a fashion designer and so I always get a reaction to the things I buy, although she's long since given up trying to influence me.

PART 1   You **must** answer this question.

1   You have seen an advertisement for volunteers in an Environmental Improvement
     Project in your area. You want to offer your help during the summer holidays but you
     need to know more. Using the notes you have made, write to the Environmental
     Improvement Project giving relevant details **and** asking for further information.

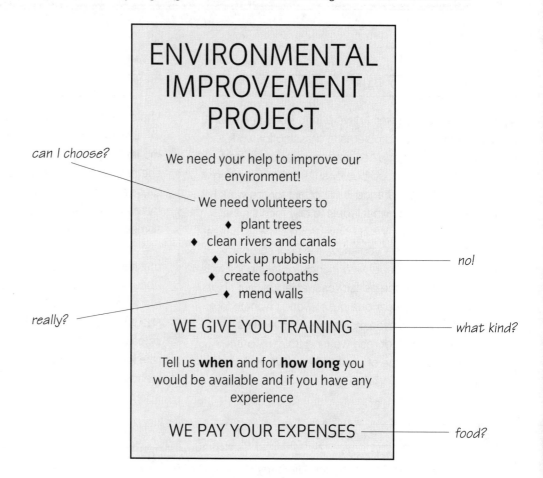

can I choose?

ENVIRONMENTAL IMPROVEMENT PROJECT

We need your help to improve our environment!

We need volunteers to

- ♦ plant trees
- ♦ clean rivers and canals
- ♦ pick up rubbish   — no!
- ♦ create footpaths
- ♦ mend walls

really?

WE GIVE YOU TRAINING   — what kind?

Tell us **when** and for **how long** you would be available and if you have any experience

WE PAY YOUR EXPENSES   — food?

Write a **letter** of between **120** and **180** words in an appropriate style. Do not write
any addresses.

Write an answer to **one** of the Questions **2–5** in this part. Write your answer in **120–180** words in an appropriate style.

2   Your class recently had a discussion about the importance of exercise and sport for keeping fit. Your teacher has now asked you to write a composition giving your opinion on the subject. This is the title of the composition.

Which is the best way for young people to keep fit; working out in a gym or playing a team sport?

Write your **composition**.

3   You have decided to enter a short story competition organised by an international magazine. The short story should begin with these words:

It was the last day of the summer holidays and I wasn't expecting much to happen …

Write your **story**.

4   Your school is planning to start a video club showing films in English. As a member of the committee, you have been asked to write a report suggesting the different types of film the club should show to appeal to as many students in the school as possible.

Write your **report**.

5   Answer **one** of the following two questions based on your reading of **one** of the set books.

Either   (a)   A penfriend in another country who also studies English has asked you to recommend a book to read in the summer holidays. Write to your friend saying whether the book you have read would be a good choice.

Write your **letter**. Do not include any addresses.

Or   (b)   Your teacher wants to read a short passage from the book you have read to a class of younger students. She aims to give them an idea of what the book is like and encourage them to read it. She has asked you to write a report saying which passage from the book would be most suitable and why.

Write your **report**.

Use of English (1 hour 15 minutes)

For Questions **1–15**, read the text below and decide which answer **A**, **B**, **C** or **D** best fits each space. There is an example at the beginning (**0**).

Mark your answers **on the separate answer sheet**.

Example:

| 0 | A | took | B | made | C | went | D | left |

0	A	B	C	D
	▬	☐	☐	☐

THE FLYING AUNTIES

Few passengers on the British Airways flight to Hong Kong which (**0**) ..... off from London Airport on Saturday 7th August, were (**1**) ..... that their flight was setting a record for the company. In fact their plane was carrying 112 'unaccompanied minors' – the largest (**2**) ..... of children travelling without parents or guardians ever to have flown on a (**3**) ..... flight. Most of these children, aged from six (**4**) ....., were returning to Hong Kong after taking three-week English (**5**) ..... at various language schools as (**6**) ..... an exchange scheme.

The children were not left to their own devices, (**7**) ...... Airline rules say that children under twelve can only fly if accompanied (**8**) ..... an adult. So, a group of three 'aunties' and one 'uncle' flew with them to (**9**) ..... them entertained and (**10**) ..... with any problems that might arise. They are part of a British Airways team known as the 'flying aunties'. These are BA employees who volunteer, in their own time, to (**11**) ..... an escorted service for unaccompanied minors to both European and long-haul (**12**) ...... Once in the air, there is a range of activities available to the youngsters (**13**) ..... computer games, colouring books and soft drinks on tap. In (**14**) ....., the children have the 'aunties' all to themselves – for such members of (**15**) ..... do not take on other duties.

1	A	realised	B	thought	C	aware	D	known
2	A	count	B	amount	C	number	D	quantity
3	A	unique	B	solo	C	single	D	lone
4	A	upwards	B	forwards	C	afterwards	D	backwards
5	A	classes	B	courses	C	studies	D	lessons
6	A	linked to	B	long as	C	part of	D	along with
7	A	however	B	although	C	altogether	D	moreover
8	A	from	B	by	C	with	D	at
9	A	hold	B	get	C	help	D	keep
10	A	manage	B	deal	C	solve	D	bother
11	A	provide	B	produce	C	pretend	D	present
12	A	departures	B	routes	C	destinations	D	arrivals
13	A	regarding	B	composing	C	containing	D	including
14	A	further	B	addition	C	extra	D	plus
15	A	staff	B	crew	C	team	D	group

For Questions **16–30**, read the text below and think of the word which best fits each space. Use only **one** word in each space. There is an example at the beginning (**0**).

Write your answers **on the separate answer sheet**.

Example:	**0**	*one*

LIQUORICE ALLSORTS

Bassett's Liquorice Allsorts have been (**0**) .... of Britain's favourite sweets for more (**16**) .... a hundred years. Each box contains a selection of the eight different liquorice sweets, each of (**17**) .... has a name. On the box itself is a picture of Bertie Bassett, a figure (**18**) .... body is made entirely from Allsorts. Over forty million Allsorts are now produced every week at the company's plant (**19**) .... the city of Sheffield and these are exported all (**20**) .... the world.

Yet the idea for the product was the result (**21**) .... an accident. In June 1899, Bassett's was already selling the individual liquorice sweets separately, when company employee, Charlie Thompson, dropped a tray full of them (**22**) .... a presentation to the owner of a sweet shop. Seeing (**23**) .... good they looked all mixed (**24**) .... on the floor, the shop owner said he (**25**) .... like to sell the sweets, (**26**) .... only if they could be sold as a mixture.

A new brand (**27**) .... thus created which soon became very popular. It has been in production (**28**) .... since. For something created purely (**29**) .... chance, the success of the product has been incredible. (**30**) .... its rather old-fashioned image, it is one of those brands which continues to grow, according to reports issued by the sweet industry.

For Questions **31–40**, complete the second sentence so that it has a similar meaning to the first sentence, using the word given. **Do not change the word given.** You must use between two and five words, including the word given. Here is an example (**0**).

Example: **0** Clara started to understand mathematics better after she'd changed school.

understanding

Clara's .... to improve after she'd changed school.

The gap can be filled by the words 'understanding of mathematics started' so you write:

| 0 | *understanding of mathematics started* |

Write **only the missing words** on the separate answer sheet.

---

31 Nigel asked if Ann could lend him her hairdryer for a while.

borrow

Nigel asked .... hairdryer for a while.

32 Chris is hungry because the last time he ate anything was Thursday evening.

not

Chris is hungry because he .... Thursday evening.

33 We will not be able to solve this difficult problem.

impossible

It will be .... a solution to this difficult problem.

34 Peter is angry because Joanna did not accept his invitation.

turned

If Joanna .... his invitation, Peter wouldn't be angry.

35 I don't think I can manage if Sheila doesn't help me.

do

I think I can't .... help.

36 'Have you finished your homework yet?' Mr Brown asked his daughter.

if

Mr Brown asked his daughter .... homework yet.

37 'Do we have to pay for our own tickets?' I asked my friend.

expected

I asked my friend .... pay for our own tickets.

38 The strong winds caused the tower to fall over.

knocked

It was the strong winds .... over.

39 The bus driver stopped frequently to allow the tourists to see the sights.

that

The bus driver stopped frequently .... see the sights.

40 Martha held George's hand and prevented him from falling over.

had

George would have fallen over .... his hand.

For Questions **41–55**, read the text below and look carefully at each line. Some of the lines are correct, and some have a word which should not be there.

If a line is correct, put a tick (✔) by the number **on the separate answer sheet**. If a line has a word which should not be there, write the word **on the separate answer sheet**. There are examples at the beginning (**0** and **00**).

Examples:	0	*for*
	00	✔

0	....	As you were not able to come to London for to see
00	....	the open-air concert, I am sure you are looking
41	....	forward to be hearing all about it from me.
42	....	I am sorry that to have to disappoint you, but the truth
43	....	is that I did also watched it on television. As you
44	....	know, I bought my ticket months ago because
45	....	I knew they would be sold out of very quickly.
46	....	Let me tell you what has happened that day. I wanted
47	....	to be one of the first person to arrive at the concert hall
48	....	to get a good seat right in front, near from the stage,
49	....	so I took up an early train. But when I got there, I realised
50	....	that I had left my ticket at home. So I had to go all the way
51	....	back to get it, which it took at least an hour. But then,
52	....	believe it or not, the organisers would not let me in because
53	....	the concert had already started! I was so much angry with
54	....	them. They simply refused to listen to my explanations.
55	....	In the end, I went back to home and switched on the TV!

For Questions **56–65**, read the text below. Use the word given in capitals at the end of each line to form a word that fits in the space in the same line. There is an example at the beginning (**0**). Write your answers **on the separate answer sheet**.

Example:	**0**	*fascination*

THE WILD WEST

In the USA, people have a (**0**) *fascination* for everything connected   **FASCINATE**
with the 'wild west' of the cowboy era. This has led to (**56**) ....   **VARY**
activities which are of interest to (**57**) .... who are travelling   **TOUR**
around the western states. There are (**58**) .... of wild west painting,   **EXHIBIT**
concerts of cowboy music and, most (**59**) .... of all, live rodeo   **EXCITE**
shows to watch.

Rodeos, where cowboys take part in horse-riding (**60**) .... for big   **COMPETE**
money prizes, are (**61**) .... popular. There are 739 each year, held   **EXTREME**
in giant (**62**) .... arenas as well as open-air show grounds across   **DOOR**
the west. Most of the riders are professional (**63**) ...., but most of   **PERFORM**
the events were (**64**) .... based on the cowboys' everyday working   **ORIGIN**
tasks. Despite some concerns over possible (**65**) .... to horses,   **CRUEL**
most people are thrilled by the display of skill and daring to be seen at a
rodeo.

PAPER 4   Listening (40 minutes)

You will hear people talking in eight different situations. For Questions **1–8**, choose the best answer **A**, **B** or **C**.

---

1   You hear part of a news report about complaints against railway companies.
What does David Driver think about the situation?
   A   The railway companies are doing their best.
   B   The situation has improved slightly.
   C   The complaints are exaggerated.

[ ] 1

2   On a phone-in consumer programme, you hear a call from à listener.
What is she doing when she speaks?
   A   explaining why a mistake occurred
   B   justifying her behaviour
   C   asking for advice

[ ] 2

3   You hear a man talking about a campaign he has been organising.
What is the aim of the campaign?
   A   to influence a decision that will be taken
   B   to support a decision that has been taken
   C   to prevent a decision being taken at the moment

[ ] 3

4   You hear part of an interview with a woman who used to run an agency for photographic models. Why did she give up the business?
   A   It became too big.
   B   She wanted to sell it.
   C   It no longer interested her.

[ ] 4

5   You hear an announcement about library services.
How are the services going to change?
   A   the number of staff employed
   B   the way money is collected
   C   the times when they are available

[ ] 5

6   You hear part of an interview with a famous writer.
What is his attitude towards ideas?
   A   Old ideas can always be recycled.
   B   Unused ideas may be useful one day.
   C   There is no such thing as a new idea.

[ ] 6

7   You hear a woman talking about an artist.
What is her opinion of the artist?
   A   She admires his courage.
   B   She respects his commitment.
   C   She appreciates his difficulties.

[ ] 7

8   You hear part of a radio phone-in programme.
What type of advice is the caller asking for?
   A   how to repair something
   B   how to find something he needs
   C   how to change the appearance of something

[ ] 8

You will hear part of a wildlife programme about a snake which comes from a group of islands in the Caribbean. For Questions **9–18**, complete the sentences.

The racer snake is one of the [_____ **9**] snakes in the world.

It is thought that around [_____ **10**] wild racer snakes are living in the Caribbean area.

Martin describes the news about racer snakes as [_____ **11**]

By last autumn, [_____ **12**] had been produced at the Wildlife Trust in Britain.

Martin describes baby racer snakes as too [_and_ **13**] to handle.

There are plans to set up a [_____ **14**] on an island in the Caribbean.

A group has been formed on the island to educate both

[_and_ **15**] about the wildlife.

A leading researcher now has the job of [_____ **16**] the racer snakes on the island.

Racer snakes on the island were being attacked by both

[_____ **17**] and the mongoose.

You can tell when a racer snake has been attacked because of the

[_____ **18**] marks on its body.

You will hear five students who want a summer job in an office saying why they are suitable for the job. For Questions **19–23**, choose from the list **A–F** what each speaker says. Use the letters only once. There is one extra letter which you do not need to use.

A   I have had work experience.

B   I have worked on projects.

C   I work well in teams.

D   I have a good grasp of written language.

E   I pay attention to detail.

F   I know the company well.

Speaker 1		19
Speaker 2		20
Speaker 3		21
Speaker 4		22
Speaker 5		23

You will hear a radio interview with Dominic Austin, a science-fiction writer. For Questions **24–30**, choose the best answer **A**, **B** or **C**.

24   What reason did one firm of publishers give for not accepting Dominic's first book?
   A   its subject
   B   its style
   C   its length

24

25   Dominic wanted the characters in his books
   A   to be as realistic as possible.
   B   to change as the story developed.
   C   to be likeable people.

25

26   What happens when Dominic writes a good series of books?
   A   Readers want more of the same.
   B   He gets tired of receiving letters.
   C   Many publishers offer him contracts.

26

27   What is Dominic's ambition at the moment?
   A   to win an award in the science-fiction field
   B   to get more people to read his novels
   C   to improve his story-telling skills

27

28   Dominic says that he accepted a film offer because
   A   he was too proud to reject it.
   B   he was promised high earnings.
   C   he wanted a rest from writing.

28

29   As a young child Dominic enjoyed reading
   A   poems.
   B   fictional stories.
   C   books about history.

29

30   What does Dominic say readers should do before buying a book?
   A   read reviews of the book
   B   read a small section of it
   C   find out about the author

30

PAPER 5

Speaking (14 minutes)

PART 1

(3 minutes)

Answer these questions:

Tell us about the type of food you like to eat.
Do you prefer eating at home or eating out?
Who cooks most of the food you eat?
Do you prefer formal meals or informal snacks?

PART 2 (3 or 4 minutes)

Classrooms (compare and contrast)

Turn to pictures 1 and 2 on page 169 which show different classrooms.

Candidate A, compare and contrast these photographs, and say which of the classrooms is better organised. You have a minute to do this.

Candidate B, which of these classrooms do you prefer?

Food shops (compare and contrast)

Turn to pictures 1 and 2 on page 170 which show different kinds of shops where you can buy food.

Candidate B, compare and contrast these photographs, and say which type of shop provides a better service. You have a minute to do this.

Candidate A, which of these shops would you rather buy food from?

PART 3 (3 or 4 minutes)

A long weekend (discuss and evaluate)

Turn to the pictures on page 171 which show different weekend activities. Imagine that a group of students from another country is coming to spend a long weekend in your area to learn about the local culture.

What type of places should they visit? Which activities should they do? Plan their weekend timetable.

PART 4 (3 or 4 minutes)

Answer these questions:

How important is it to understand the culture of other countries?
Which country would you choose to visit if you could?
Apart from exchange visits, how else can we share our culture with others?
How difficult do you think it would be to live in another country?

TEST 8

PART 1

You are going to read an extract from an article about a businesswoman. Choose from the list **A–I** the sentence which best summarises each part (**1–7**) of the extract. There is one extra sentence which you do not need to use. There is an example at the beginning (**0**).

Mark your answers **on the separate answer sheet**.

A	An up-market product	**F**	Personal taste influences a decision
B	Attracted to her latest interests	**G**	Building on previous success
C	Facing up to competition	**H**	The thinking behind a decision
D	Building a range of colours	**I**	An unusual combination of interests
E	Initial involvement pays off		

THE LADY WITH BLUE NAILS

Sandy Lerner is founder of an unusual range of nail-polish colours

0   **I**

The links between computers and cosmetics are not obvious, but one of the most successful self-made businesswomen in the USA, Sandy Lerner, has made her fortune in both.

1

With her long purple hair and taste for blue nail polish, it is not surprising that Sandy got fed up with not being able to find make-up she liked. After a brief spell of mixing her own colours, Sandy decided to set up her own company.

2

Since its launch in 1996, her company has taken the USA, Asia and Europe by storm. 'At the time everyone was still heavily into pinks and reds,' says Sandy, 'and I thought that given other developments going on in the fashion world, the time was ripe for an alternative.'

3

It's one thing to like blue nail polish yourself, but quite another to set up a company making it, however. 'The more money you have, the easier that decision is to make,' she admits. And she has plenty. Sandy made her fortune in a former career as a computer specialist. She set up a company in 1984 after designing a piece of technology which is now used in 80% of connections on the Internet.

4

The new company is proving to be a nice little earner too. As founder and chief executive of the company, Sandy was personally responsible for designing the eye-catching advertising campaigns that helped at the beginning, although she now tends to leave the day-to-day business to her partners.

5

But establishing the business was not easy, particularly when the large cosmetics companies realised there was a market for alternative colours and started selling them too. 'As an alternative, we're never going to threaten the main market of the big companies,' says Sandy, 'and although they now do similar colours, they only do a few of them. So people who want intense and complicated colours will still come to us.'

6

Although shades of blue, purple, yellow and green sound like just the thing for teenage girls and punks, the company actually aims its products at career women in their thirties and forties. Sandy thinks make-up is about a state of mind, 'It's for self-confident people who are not afraid of something you can wash off.' Indeed, the unusual colours and successful marketing campaigns, make the company's products a hit amongst Hollywood celebrities.

7

Although she keeps a close eye on the company, Sandy admits that she quickly loses interest once a project is up and running. She is now turning her attention to her current projects; a large country house in England, her farm in Virginia where she keeps horses and a new project for promoting nineteenth-century literature on the Internet.

You are going to read an article about an actor. For Questions **8–14**, choose the correct answer **A**, **B**, **C** or **D**.

Mark your answers **on the separate answer sheet**.

Thirty-five years ago, Malcolm Burwell was a very successful young actor appearing in a number of series on British television. He was lucky, he'd made it to the top quite quickly and had plenty of work. Hollywood directors had even begun to suggest that he might like to think of making his fortune across the Atlantic. But two things made Malcolm think twice about these offers. He didn't want to move his young family to the USA, and a mystery illness was beginning to throw his whole future into doubt.

Malcolm had a problem with his voice. It began to grow steadily weaker and weaker until hospital treatment became
19 necessary. Before **this** finally took effect, however, he found he could hardly talk. As he remembers, 'When you are in danger of losing something central to your career, it makes you think very hard. I have to say I learnt a lot from the experience.'

'My voice recovered, but it taught me the importance of getting the best out of what you've got. As it got better and stronger, I started doing things like public readings of poetry and pieces of literature, just to use it professionally again.' This turned out to be the start of a whole new direction for his career. So popular have these readings become, that Malcolm is now extremely familiar to people as the voice on a number of readings of best-selling books which have been recorded on to tape. Instantly recognisable, his voice is now a much
41 **sought-after** commodity.

Malcolm first approached publishers with the idea of selling books on tape all those years ago. At first, they said that only blind people listened to books on tape. But times were changing and when he did eventually convince one of them to try it, instant success followed. Now the market for such tapes in Britain is worth £25 million a year.

Although Malcolm continues to work in television and theatre, it is his readings of literature that have really made his name. When he is recording Malcolm uses his voice to give an impression of the different characters. 'I don't try to convince the audience that I am an 11-year-old boy at one moment and his grandfather the next,' he says, 'but I use my voice to try and make the listener believe that I've really got a story to tell them rather than just a book to read out.'

Malcolm carefully does his homework on any book he has agreed to record, although he knows that some actors do not. He tells the story of one well-known British actor whose enthusiastic producer commented on what a great thriller it was they were about to record. 'Is it?' said the actor, opening the script for the first time. 'Oh good.' All very well, says Malcolm, until you discover on page two hundred that the character you've given a Scottish accent to is supposed to come from Wales!

8 Why did Malcolm not go to the USA thirty-five years ago?

    A His family opposed it.
    B The offers weren't good enough.
    C He was in poor health.
    D He already had work in Britain.

9 What does 'this' in line 19 refer to?

    A the treatment he received
    B the effects of losing his voice
    C the hospital he went to
    D the weakness of his voice

10 How did Malcolm's illness affect his career?

    A He could no longer do certain types of work.
    B He had to be very careful when using his voice.
    C It made him appreciate his voice more.
    D It forced him to look for new areas of work.

11 What does 'sought-after' (line 41) mean?

    A makes a lot of money
    B everyone knows it
    C it cannot be copied
    D everyone wants it

12 How did publishers react initially to the idea of books on tape?

    A They thought the market was limited.
    B They thought nobody would buy them.
    C They were keen to open up a new market.
    D They realised it was a good idea.

13 When recording, Malcolm is keen to convince his listeners that

    A different people are reading the story.
    B he is actually telling them a story.
    C the events are really happening.
    D they are sitting in the theatre.

14 Malcolm relates the story about the other actor in order to show how

    A good he is.
    B difficult the job is.
    C important it is to prepare.
    D different approaches can work.

You are going to read a magazine article about a man who studies mountain lions in the USA. Seven sentences have been removed from the article. Choose from the sentences **A–I** the one which fits each gap (**15–21**). There is one extra sentence which you do not need to use. There is an example at the beginning (**0**).

Mark your answers **on the separate answer sheet**.

FACE-TO-FACE WITH A MOUNTAIN LION

Something was watching me. I stopped. Not a leaf moved, not a bird called. Then, less than a hundred metres away amongst the trees, I saw him. Just his face, eyes the colour of amber, whiskers glistening in the late afternoon sun.

Felis concolor, or the cat of one colour was the ghost of North America. It has a variety of names such as cougar and puma, but is most commonly known simply as the mountain lion. It was 1965. I was just beginning my life's work of trying to understand these secretive and elusive cats. **0** | **I**

A few years earlier, following five years of doing research into the habits of grizzly bears with my brother, also a wildlife biologist, I had sought a project of my own. **15**

Mountain lions seemed not only challenging but also romantic. Once they were found across the entire continent. But after centuries of ruthless hunting, they had been confined to a few wild spots. In the early 1960s, mountain lions were still considered as the enemy. Farmers, ranchers and hunters were trying to rid the world of these great cats. **16**

Many colleagues tried to discourage me. The lions moved across hundreds of miles of territory. I would never be able to keep track of them for long enough to study them. Moreover, as most mountain lions live in difficult country, they are best tracked in snow. That meant living in tents in winter and tracking with dogs in the intense cold before trapping them in a tree so that they could be captured and marked. **17**

By capturing and recapturing, and each time making very careful observations, I hoped to build a fund of information about these mysterious animals.

I began in January 1963, marking sixteen lions within a hundred miles of Missoula, Montana. **18** So I moved, next season, as far from civilisation as I could get in the USA, to the Idaho Primitive Area, a roadless wilderness in Salmon River Country.

I hired Wilbur Wiles, the best professional wildcat tracker in Idaho. Still, that winter we could not find enough lions for a valid study. **19** A meaningful study of mountain lions might be impossible. I decided to expand the study area. In the summer of 1965, I backpacked into the wilderness, into new territory.

Then, at the mouth of a small valley, I noticed some footprints. I forced my way through the undergrowth up the narrow valley and suddenly broke into a beautiful mountain meadow ringed by trees. **20**

I don't know how long we stared at each other. It was a wonderful moment. Every other mountain lion I had seen had been up a tree, cornered by the dogs below, or drugged by the tranquillisers we used to mark them in safety. Eventually this lion broke our gaze, turned his head slowly, and with majestic grace, leapt into full view. **21** I can still see his eyes. I've often thought he brought me good luck because that was indeed a turning point. The next winter's work went extremely well.

A I was beginning to think maybe my colleagues were right.

B But I was willing to give all that a try.

C He encouraged me to tackle something tough.

D It was then that I felt those eyes.

E Then he was gone.

F And yet we knew almost nothing about them.

G These animals are territorial and limit their own numbers.

H But by the spring, most of those had been shot by hunters.

I The effort had not been going well.

You are going to read a magazine article in which different people talk about letter writing. For Questions **22–35**, choose from the people (**A–F**). Some of the people may be chosen more than once. When more than one answer is required, these may be given in any order. There is an example at the beginning (**0**).

Mark your answers **on the separate answer sheet**.

A	**Amanda Littleport**
B	**Barbara Lynn**
C	**Charles Downham**
D	**Derek Watlington**
E	**Elizabeth Brandon**
F	**Fiona Stretham**

Which of the people

chooses to write letters for health reasons?	**0**	*B*
thinks some letters should not be posted?	**22**	
describes a regular letter-writing routine?	**23**	
has help with the letters he/she has to write?	**24**	
compares letter-writing with another activity?	**25**	
is expected to write letters as part of a job?	**26**	**27**
has made a point of keeping letters?	**28**	**29**
is aware of expressing his/her feeling more freely in letters?	**30**	
feels that electronic aids make letter writing less personal?	**31**	**32**
writes letters designed to amuse the reader?	**33**	
takes care over the appearance of their letters?	**34**	**35**

Just a few lines ...

E-mails are easy and faxes are fast – so is the old-fashioned letter really a thing of the past? According to a recent survey, 10% of the 18 billion letters delivered annually in Britain are private ones, so there must be people out there who are sitting down and putting pen to paper in the old-fashioned way.

For example, there's novelist **Amanda Littleport** who says, 'It's a very personal way of keeping in touch. I find I include things in letters that I might not mention in conversation, such as things I don't like about other people for example. But something nice, said in a letter becomes much more special. That's why love letters are so important.' Amanda always writes with a fountain pen. 'What looks best is black ink on pure white paper. A letter is like a gift you give someone, it's upsetting to see a lovely letter on horrible paper.'

The actress **Barbara Lynn**, if she's at home in London, writes at least three letters each morning at a desk in an upstairs bedroom that has become her 'writing room'. 'I find it an enjoyable experience, as important as talking to people. As I am deaf in one ear, I find the telephone difficult, and I don't have e-mail. Letters written by hand are an exchange of energy between people. It's like the energy that passes between an actor and audience in the theatre, which doesn't happen on film or television in the same way.'

Unlike Amanda and Barbara, playwright, **Charles Downham** confesses that he finds letter writing increasingly difficult. 'I never seem to get the time these days. I like receiving them though. I've got a cardboard box of them stored in the attic, so that I can reread them in my old age.' He also chooses his notepaper with care. 'I love wandering around stationery shops. It's something to do with the feel of the quality product. The matching envelope is an absolute must.'

Television Presenter, **Derek Watlington** is a well-known letter writer. He has carried on a 30-year correspondence with his actress wife whenever their work has kept them apart. Fortunately, both parties have held on to the letters, allowing them to be published last year, minus the 'silliest bits'. One of them begins, 'I do miss your letters when we're together ...' and the tone is light-hearted and amusing throughout, even when the subject matter is serious. 'I always hand-write my letters,' he says. 'Even though a word-processor means you can go back and improve things, there's something about the machine that brings out the more formal side of my character, so letters written on one are never quite so intimate.'

Politicians like **Elizabeth Brandon** have headed notepaper provided for them once they get elected to the Houses of Parliament, and there are special desks with old-fashioned dip pens and supplies of real ink for them to use for letter writing. Barbara is a shameless lover of gadgets, however, and prefers to reply to people by dictating letters into a cassette recorder so that her secretary can type them up and fax them. 'But I also write long chatty e-mails to my husband and daughter when I am away,' she says.

Don't even think of mentioning e-mails to **Fiona Stretham**, a journalist who is the 'agony aunt' for a top weekly magazine. Her problem page attracts hundreds of letters, all of which receive a personal reply. She thinks the handwriting is often a real clue to the personality and sincerity of the writer. 'I can't stand e-mail,' she says. 'They're so cold and concise.' She laments the general decline in letter writing as a way of letting off steam. 'Lots of people will remember heartfelt complaints or declarations of love that never got as far as the postbox. The act of just telling someone how you feel makes you feel better, even if they never get to read it!'

So it seems, the letter is not dead. But the thing to remember is that it's a two-way process. As a friend of Groucho Marx once wrote: 'Dear Groucho, I would have answered your letter sooner, but you didn't send one.'

You **must** answer this question.

1 You and a group of friends want to spend two days in a new Wildlife Learning and Leisure Centre outside your town. You have a leaflet with details about the centre but you need to know more. Using the notes you have made, write to the centre asking for more information and giving them relevant details.

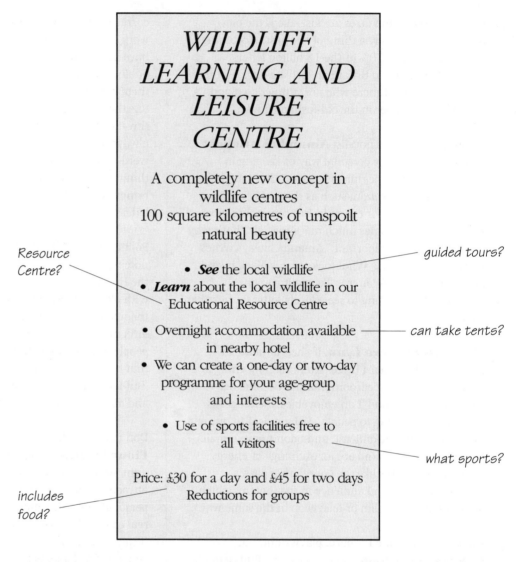

Resource Centre?

guided tours?

can take tents?

what sports?

includes food?

Write a **letter** of between **120** and **180** words in an appropriate style. Do not write any addresses.

Write an answer to **one** of the Questions 2–5 in this part. Write your answer in **120–180** words in an appropriate style.

2   You have decided to enter a short-story writing competition. The rules of the competition say that the story must begin with these words:

Looking back on that day, we all agreed it was our greatest victory.

Write your **story**.

3   You have received this letter from an English-speaking penfriend.

> *We're doing a project at college on the fashion industry in different countries. It would be nice to include a first-hand report from someone living abroad. The report should describe how fashions for young people have changed in recent years. Can you help?*

Write your **report**.

4   Following a class discussion on the environment, your teacher has asked you to write a composition with this title:

Some people think the recycling of used glass and paper is a waste of time. Do you agree?

Write your **composition**.

5   Answer **one** of the following two questions based on your reading of **one** of the set books.

Either   (a)   You have seen this announcement in an international magazine for young people.

> *Have you read a good book lately?*
> *We're offering a prize of £200 for the best article recommending a good book to our readers.*

Write your **article**.

Or   (b)   In a review of the book you have read you have seen this comment.

> *'It's difficult to believe in the characters in this story as real people.'*

Your teacher has asked you to write a composition giving your reasons for either agreeing or disagreeing with this comment.

Write your **composition**.

Use of English (1 hour 15 minutes)

For Questions **1–15**, read the text below and decide which answer **A**, **B**, **C** or **D** best fits each space. There is an example at the beginning (**0**).

Mark your answers **on the separate answer sheet**.

Example:

0	**A** up	**B** to	**C** off	**D** with

| 0 | A ▭ | B ▢ | C ▢ | D ▢ |

THE EARTH GALLERIES

To many people the word 'geology' conjures (**0**) ..... rather dull images of lumps of rock in glass cases. People (**1**) ..... to regard geology as an academic subject that you don't need to know about (**2**) ..... you have to study it at school. If you visit the Earth Galleries at London's Natural History Museum, however, you'll (**3**) ..... that this image couldn't be (**4**) ..... from the truth.

The (**5**) ..... of the exhibition is not to produce future geologists, but rather to inspire interest in a subject which is (**6**) ..... to everyday life. The Earth Galleries turn the traditional idea of the geological museum (**7**) ....., literally because you begin at the top. The central space in the museum is a glass-topped atrium. As you enter, you (**8**) ..... up to the top of this by escalator. On the (**9**) ....., the escalator passes through a massive revolving globe, measuring eleven metres (**10**) ..... diameter. This represents a planet, not necessarily the Earth. (**11**) ..... at the top, you work your way down through the six different exhibitions that (**12**) ..... the museum.

The individual exhibitions explain natural phenomena (**13**) ..... earthquakes and volcanoes as well as looking at the Earth's energy (**14**) ..... and where our most common building (**15**) ..... come from. These exhibitions allow everyone to appreciate the fascination of geology.

1	**A** pick	**B** know	**C** bound	**D** tend
2	**A** despite	**B** owing	**C** unless	**D** whether
3	**A** catch	**B** found	**C** discover	**D** convince
4	**A** further	**B** greater	**C** wider	**D** nearer
5	**A** ambition	**B** aim	**C** reason	**D** topic
6	**A** part	**B** relevant	**C** joined	**D** referred
7	**A** head to toe	**B** inside out	**C** back to front	**D** upside down
8	**A** drive	**B** ride	**C** run	**D** steer
9	**A** way	**B** route	**C** trip	**D** path
10	**A** on	**B** around	**C** across	**D** in
11	**A** From	**B** Once	**C** Got	**D** Yet
12	**A** bring together	**B** consist of	**C** make up	**D** show off
13	**A** not only	**B** such as	**C** so that	**D** in order
14	**A** resources	**B** talents	**C** treasures	**D** reservations
15	**A** ingredients	**B** substances	**C** contents	**D** materials

For Questions **16–30**, read the text below and think of the word which best fits each space. Use only **one** word in each space. There is an example at the beginning (**0**).

Write your answers **on the separate answer sheet**.

Example:

0	*was*

FADING MEMORIES

The instamatic camera (**0**) .... invented in 1963 and the mass marketing of colour film followed shortly after. Until then, almost (**16**) .... photographs had been in black and white. (**17**) .... the early 1970s, sales of colour film had overtaken those for black and white and today colour accounts (**18**) .... all but a tiny percentage of the 96 million films sold in Britain every year.

But those early colour photographs are already showing (**19**) .... of age. Millions of snapshots (**20**) .... since 1963 are changing colour because of their chemical make (**21**) .... These chemicals change over time. The deterioration of photographs is nothing new, of course. We tend (**22**) .... view the late nineteenth century in delicate shades of brown thanks to the chemicals used at the time. But (**23**) .... is a fair chance that future generations will (**24**) .... back at the late twentieth century as the era of   purple grass and pink skies. Because, (**25**) .... the fading is only gradual, the different colours change (**26**) .... different rates.

Keeping photographs in a dark drawer, (**27**) .... even in the fridge, will certainly (**28**) .... them last longer, but none of (**29**) .... will keep forever. Our grandparents' old-fashioned black and white photographs from earlier in the twentieth century will (**30**) .... the test of time better, in fact.

For Questions **31–40**, complete the second sentence so that it has a similar meaning to the first sentence, using the word given. **Do not change the word given.** You must use between two and five words, including the word given. Here is an example (**0**).

Example: **0** 'A bad headache made it impossible for me to attend school,' Alan said to his teacher.

missed

Alan told his teacher that he .... a bad headache.

The gap can be filled by the words 'had missed school because of' so you write:

0	*had missed school because of*

Write **only the missing words** on the separate answer sheet.

---

31 I am not strong enough to climb that steep path without a walking stick.

too

That path is .... climb without a walking stick.

32 That man stole a valuable picture but he was never punished.

got

That man .... a valuable picture.

33 Hitch-hiking is less popular now than ten years ago.

not

Hitch-hiking is .... was ten years ago.

34 'Why did you cancel the party, Lucy?' Martin asked.

called

Martin asked Lucy .... the party.

35 'We shall tell your parents that you are often absent from school,' Mrs Clerk said.

would

Mrs Clerk said to me that my parents .... my frequent absences from school.

36 'Do not leave your belongings unattended,' the group leader said to the tourists.

to

The group leader told the tourists .... belongings unattended.

37 Mrs Butler didn't buy her son a bicycle because she didn't have enough money.

afford

Mrs Butler .... her son a bicycle.

38 Sally will not buy that pony because she is no longer interested.

lost

Sally .... buying that pony.

39 Although it looks easy, that dance is actually quite difficult.

not

That dance is .... looks.

40 Take your mobile phone because the car might break down.

case

Take your mobile phone .... down.

For Questions **41–55**, read the text below and look carefully at each line. Some of the lines are correct, and some have a word which should not be there.

If a line is correct, put a tick (✔) by the number **on the separate answer sheet**. If a line has a word which should not be there, write the word **on the separate answer sheet**. There are examples at the beginning (**0** and **00**).

Examples:	0	*or*
	00	✔

0	....	I had a wonderful experience or last weekend and I
00	....	would like to tell you about it. Once a month I spend a
41	....	weekend away with two friends. We usually prefer sleep in
42	....	our tents, but sometimes when we feel like to having
43	....	a real rest, we book a room in a hotel. On Thursday evening,
44	....	I suggested them that we should go on a 'mystery weekend'
45	....	and they agreed with at once. On Saturday morning, we got into
46	....	my father's car, one which I had borrowed for the weekend.
47	....	No-one else knew for how long the drive would be. I was
48	....	the only one who knew it where we were going. I had been
49	....	busy on the telephone that morning making all the hotel
50	....	arrangements. Where do you think I took them off?
51	....	To the Bond Marina Hotel, on the banks of the River Dart,
52	....	where a boat was got ready to take us all on a trip up
53	....	the river. It was such a lovely day that we sat on the seats
54	....	on deck and enjoyed ourselves the sunshine. When we got
55	....	home on Sunday, everyone wanted another 'mystery weekend'!

For Questions **56–65**, read the text below. Use the word given in capitals at the end of each line to form a word that fits in the space in the same line. There is an example at the beginning (**0**). Write your answers **on the separate answer sheet**.

Example:	**0**	*flightless*

Penguins are (**0**) ..*flightless*.. birds which live south of the Equator. As their **FLIGHT**
legs are short, they (**56**) .... stand upright and walk when they are **USUAL**
on land. When they find it (**57**) .... to travel at greater speed, they **NEED**
often drop on to their stomachs and slide along. But it is at sea,
(**58**) .... when diving, that penguins really move fast, the **SPECIAL**
(**59**) .... of their streamlined bodies allowing them to reach a **WEIGH**
(**60**) .... of up to 265 metres in some cases. **DEEP**

The sixteen species of penguin tend to look rather (**61**) .... **LIKE**
with black or dark blue backs and white fronts. But (**62**) .... **VARY**
in size and head patterns allow them to be (**63**) .... The **IDENTIFY**
fact that a number of species spend their whole life in Antarctica
where there is little (**64**) .... from the world's least **PROTECT**
(**65**) .... weather conditions, makes their continued survival one **WELCOME**
of the wonders of the nature.

PAPER 4   Listening (40 minutes)

You will hear people talking in eight different situations. For Questions **1–8**, choose the best answer **A**, **B** or **C**.

---

1 You hear a man and a woman talking about something they bought in a shop.
What is the man going to complain about?
   A   faulty goods
   B   poor value for money | 1 |
   C   lack of information about goods

2 You hear a woman talking to a friend.
What is she talking about?
   A   travelling by public transport
   B   waiting in queues | 2 |
   C   joining a social club

3 You hear a man talking about wearing hats.
Why didn't he like wearing a hat at the wedding?
   A   It was the wrong size.
   B   People laughed at him. | 3 |
   C   He felt uncomfortable in it.

4 You hear someone comparing life in the town with life in the country.
What is his view of the country?
   A   He never wants to go there again.
   B   He can understand why people go there. | 4 |
   C   He wonders what people find to do there.

5 You hear a mother talking about her young son.
How does she feel when she watches him in class?
   A   ashamed of herself
   B   disappointed in him | 5 |
   C   curious about his teacher

6 You hear an announcement on the radio.
Why should listeners call the programme?
   A   to find out about science fiction
   B   to ask questions about an author | 6 |
   C   to get ideas about how to be a writer

7 You hear the beginning of a radio programme about the food at tourist attractions.
What point is being made about the attractions?
   A   People have little choice of food there.
   B   People like the kind of food served there. | 7 |
   C   People choose the unhealthiest food there.

8 You turn on the radio in the middle of something.
What are you listening to?
   A   travel news
   B   weather forecast | 8 |
   C   cookery feature

You will hear an interview with the actor Alex Beringer. For Questions **9–18**, complete the sentences.

Alex was at the [_____ **9**] when he was invited to be in a film.

For his first film, Alex had to get rid of his [_____ **10**]

Alex was paid little for his first film because the [_____ **11**] was small.

When he was younger, Alex's mother used to read [_____ **12**] to him.

Alex's father wanted him to be a [_____ **13**]

Alex changed his hair colour to [_____ **14**]

Alex is now playing the role of a [_____ **15**]

Alex says he prefers to play [_____ **16**] characters.

Alex says that many famous stars are [_____ **17**] people.

In the future, Alex would like to [_____ **18**]

You will hear five students saying what makes them successful in their studies. For Questions **19–23**, choose from the list **A–F** what each speaker says. Use the letters only once. There is one extra letter which you do not need to use.

What makes you successful in your studies?

A	I can study long hours.
B	I am helped by others.
C	I pay attention.
D	I read extra materials.
E	I study only what is important.
F	I have a good memory.

Speaker 1		**19**
Speaker 2		**20**
Speaker 3		**21**
Speaker 4		**22**
Speaker 5		**23**

You will hear a radio interview with Dave Salter, a deep-sea diving instructor. For Questions **24–30**, choose the best answer **A**, **B** or **C**.

24 Why did Dave consider a full-time career as a diving instructor?
    A He had always liked teaching.
    B His trainees were pleased with him.
    C It was a chance to earn more money.   **24**

25 David says instructors must
    A understand weather conditions.
    B know the best diving areas.
    C be patient with their trainees.   **25**

26 When does Dave become nervous?
    A When students become agressive.
    B When his students leave the group.
    C When other divers get close to his group.   **26**

27 What mistake did the girl called Elaine make?
    A She did not get on well with her group.
    B She mistook Dave for somebody else.
    C She went off alone.   **27**

28 How did David feel after the conversation with Mr and Mrs Jones?
    A embarrassed
    B upset
    C impatient   **28**

29 What does Dave find boring in his job?
    A allowing students time for photos
    B repeating instructions for students
    C following the same routine   **29**

30 What would Dave like to be in the future?
    A a photographer
    B a secretary
    C a manager   **30**

PAPER 5　Speaking (14 minutes)

PART 1　(3 minutes)

Answer these questions:

What is your favourite type of music?
Has your taste in music changed over the years? Why / Why not?
Where do you like to listen to music?
What effect do different types of music have on you?

PART 2　(3 or 4 minutes)

Workplaces (compare, contrast and speculate)

Turn to pictures 1 and 2 on page 172 which show people in their workplaces.

Candidate A, compare and contrast these photographs, and say how you think the people feel about the place where they work. You have a minute to do this.

Candidate B, do you like a tidy place to work or study?

Dancing (compare, contrast and speculate)

Turn to pictures 1 and 2 on page 173 which show people dancing.

Candidate B, compare and contrast these photographs, and say how you think the people feel about dancing. You have a minute to do this.

Candidate A, are you a good dancer?

PART 3　(3 or 4 minutes)

Summer courses (discuss and evaluate)

Turn to the pictures on page 174 which show different ideas for a leaflet about summer courses for young people at a British language school. Imagine you have to choose which pictures will appear in the leaflet.

How successful would each picture be in showing life at the school? Which three pictures do you think should appear in the leaflet?

PART 4　(3 or 4 minutes)

Answer these questions:

Do you think a summer course is a good way to learn a language?
What are the advantages of studying a language in the country where it is spoken?
Do you like to do things on holiday, or would you rather just relax?
How many languages do you think children should study in school?

VISUALS for Paper 5

Candidate A

Useful phrases

Well, there are people reading newspapers *in both photos. In the first photo*, it's a boy in a library, *in the second*, a man, maybe in an office.

The boy seems to be reading the sports page. *Perhaps* he's having a rest between lessons.

I get the impression that the man is not very comfortable sitting on the table.

He looks like he's …

Candidate B

Useful phrases

The young people in these photos are showing very different feelings, the boy is not happy at all while the girl is having a very good time.

In this photo, I think the mother is telling him that he is not allowed to go out.

Perhaps he has homework to do. Or maybe he is being punished for breaking something.

I think the mother probably reads to her daughter every evening and they both look forward to it.

Candidates A and B

Useful phrases

Most young people would love to work in a television company, *don't you think*?

In my opinion, some of these jobs require training and may be very difficult for somebody without the necessary skills. *Would you agree with that?*

Yes, that's a good point.

In this job they can learn how to communicate effectively, and that's a very useful skill.

Now, in which two jobs would they learn the most useful skills? *What do you think?*

My first choice would be …

I'm not sure I agree with that. Don't you think …

Candidate A

Candidate B

Candidates A and B

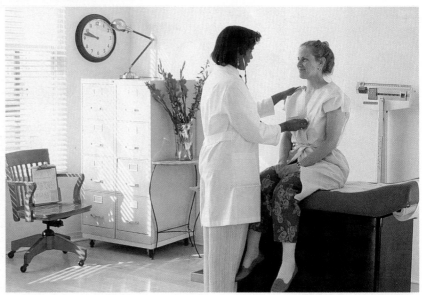

Candidate A

Candidate B

VISUALS

Candidates A and B

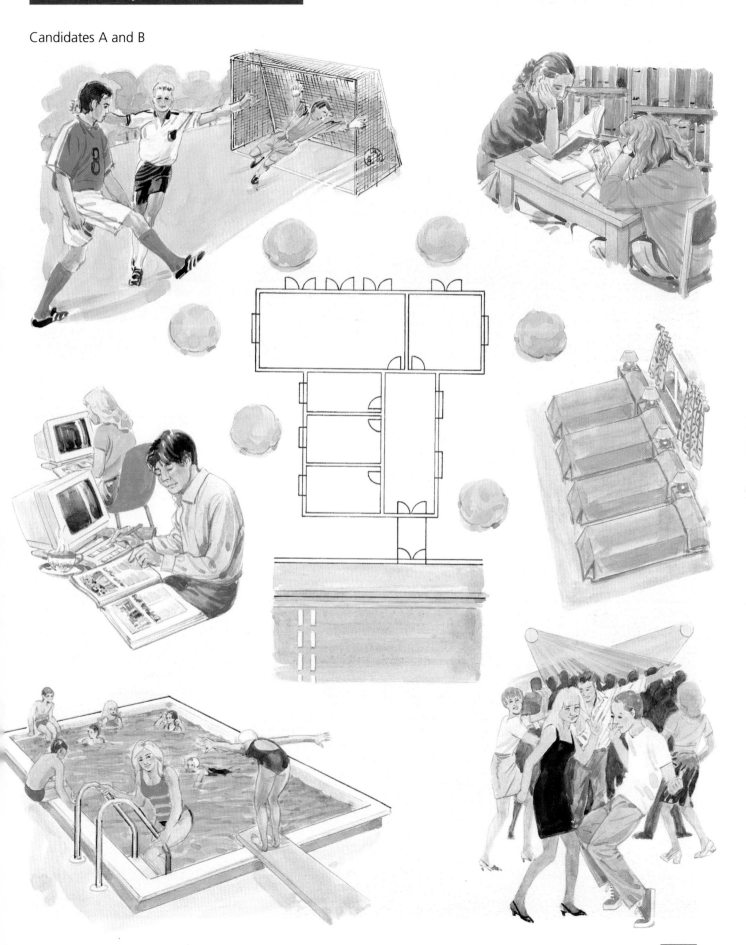

Candidate A

Candidate B

Candidates A and B

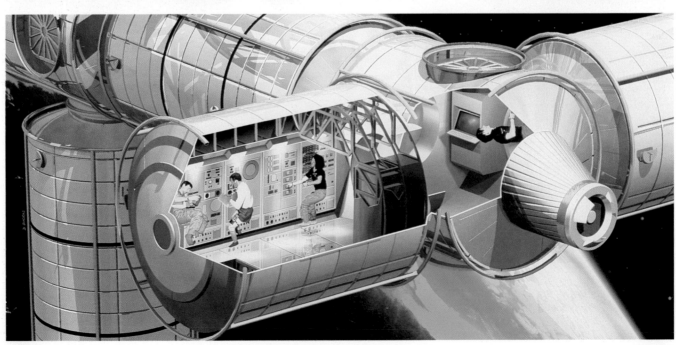

Candidate A

Candidate B

Candidates A and B

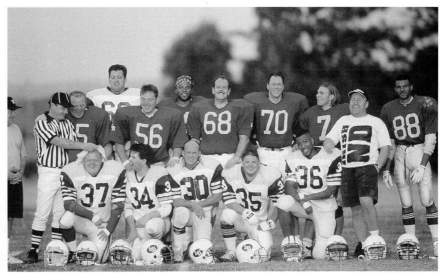

Candidate A

Candidate B

Candidates A and B

Candidate A

Candidate B

Candidates A and B

Timetable

Friday	pm	_____
Saturday	am	_____
Saturday	pm	_____
Sunday	am	_____
Sunday	pm	_____

Candidate A

Candidate B

Candidates A and B

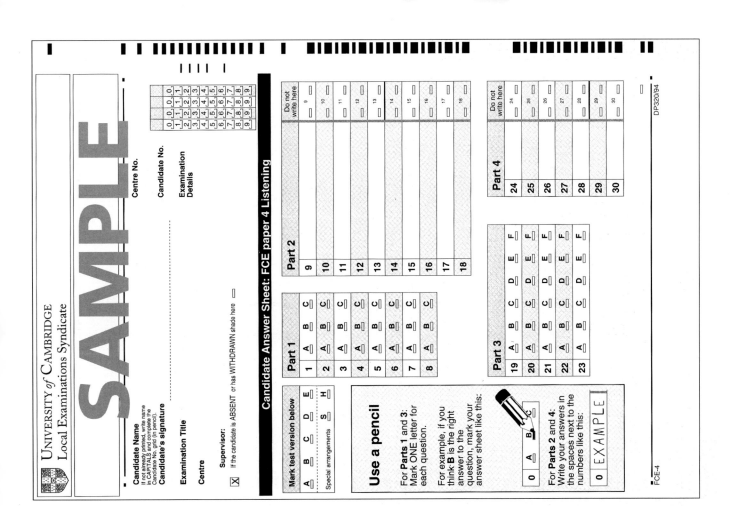

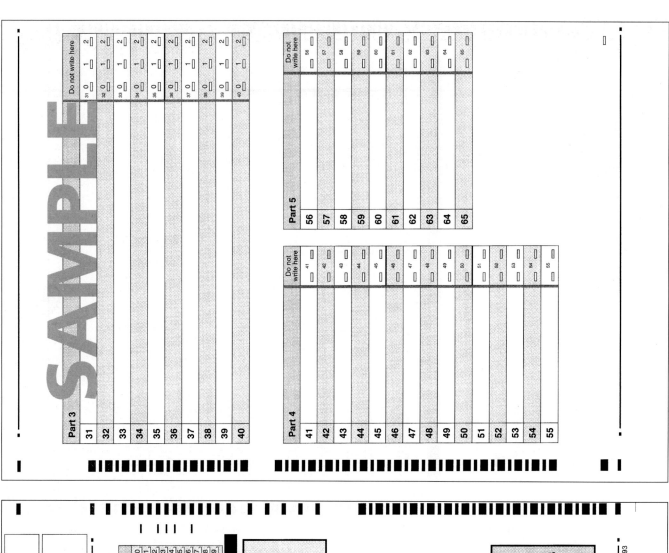

Part 3

	Do not write here
31	0 1 2
32	0 1 2
33	0 1 2
34	0 1 2
35	0 1 2
36	0 1 2
37	0 1 2
38	0 1 2
39	0 1 2
40	0 1 2

Part 5

	Do not write here
56	56
57	57
58	58
59	59
60	60
61	61
62	62
63	63
64	64
65	65

Part 4

	Do not write here
41	41
42	42
43	43
44	44
45	45
46	46
47	47
48	48
49	49
50	50
51	51
52	52
53	53
54	54
55	55

UNIVERSITY of CAMBRIDGE
Local Examinations Syndicate

Centre No.

Candidate No.

Examination Details

Candidate Name
If not already printed, write name
in CAPITALS and complete the
Candidate No. grid (in pencil).

Candidate's signature

Examination Title

Centre

Supervisor:
If the candidate is ABSENT or has WITHDRAWN shade here ☒

Candidate Answer Sheet: FCE paper 3 Use of English

Use a pencil

For **Part 1**: Mark ONE letter for each question.

For example, if you think **C** is the right answer to the question, mark your answer sheet like this:

0 [A] [B] [C] [D]

For **Parts 2, 3, 4** and **5**: Write your answers in the spaces next to the numbers like this:

0 | 0 |

Part 1

	A	B	C	D
1	A	B	C	D
2	A	B	C	D
3	A	B	C	D
4	A	B	C	D
5	A	B	C	D
6	A	B	C	D
7	A	B	C	D
8	A	B	C	D
9	A	B	C	D
10	A	B	C	D
11	A	B	C	D
12	A	B	C	D
13	A	B	C	D
14	A	B	C	D
15	A	B	C	D

Part 2

	Do not write here
16	16
17	17
18	18
19	19
20	20
21	21
22	22
23	23
24	24
25	25
26	26
27	27
28	28
29	29
30	30

Turn over for Parts 3 - 5 →

DP319/93

FCE-3

KEY

Test 1

Part 1: It's up, up and away

1 H: Modern balloons are a lot more sophisticated
2 D: Celebrations are high on the list … Birthdays, anniversaries
3 F: … twelve the maximum number allowed … have to be at least
4 A: You are invited to take an active part.
5 E: Most people are very happy that they have done it
6 B: To get a licence … Then you have to take written exams
7 G: You will need a trailer … You may need … permission

Part 2: Inline Skating

8 A: Correct. The key words are 'slight unease'.
8 B: Incorrect. She does not say or imply she was confident.
8 C: Incorrect. She was only *slightly* uneasy.
8 D: Incorrect. She does not say or imply it.
9 B: Correct. 'Not good for the sort of skating …'
9 A, C: Incorrect. The quality and fit of the skates are not mentioned.
9 D: Incorrect. The problem with the skates is not that they do not work.
10 C: Correct. '… which she wants to see all retailers use.'
10 A: Incorrect. It is future buyers she is thinking of.
10 B: Incorrect. The guidelines are for retailers to use.
10 D: Incorrect. She does not mention her students.
11 D: Correct. 'Tick off' means to reprimand.
11 A: Incorrect. You 'tick' items on a list to show they have been checked.
11 B: Incorrect. 'Tick away' is used to refer to passing time.
11 C: Incorrect. This is not the meaning of 'tick off'.
12 C: Correct. Tracy tells her to keep her 'hands out'.
12 A: Incorrect. Simple skating does not help her break a fall.
12 B: Incorrect. 'This' does not refer to how often the instructions are repeated.
12 D: Incorrect. Keeping her hands out will help her break a fall.
13 D: Correct. 'You don't look at the ground when you're riding a bike.'
13 A, B, C: Incorrect. Fear, the need to learn how to fall and the need to relax are all mentioned but they are not compared to cycling.
14 C: Correct. 'Wearing protective clothing'.
14 A: Incorrect. Older people are not mentioned.
14 B: Incorrect. The text does not say she disapproves of recreational skating.
14 D: Incorrect. A 'National Association' already exists.
15 D: Correct. 'I know how she feels' refers to 'It makes me feel good'.
15 A: Incorrect. This is not what Tracy says.
15 B: Incorrect. Tracy 'never tires of the sport'.
15 C: Incorrect. Tracy does not say it is hard to teach.

Part 3: Britain's Wildest Place

16 D: Link between 'a group of islands' and 'the waters around them'. Link between 'dolphins, whales …' and 'such marine animals'.

17 A: Link between 'you need to be on a boat' and 'companies offering such trips'.
18 B: Link between size of archipelago, 'stretches nearly …' and small number of inhabitants. 'However' indicates the contrast. Link between 'only … are permanently inhabited' and 'This relative lack of people'.
19 G: Link between 'freedom from pollution' and 'Despite being relatively unspoilt'. Link between 'facing many pressures' and 'Some of the islands are under threat …'.
20 C: Link between 'climate is wet and windy' and 'This is more than enough …'. Link between 'This is more than enough …' and 'Another discouraging factor'.
21 E: Link between '… the Hebrides can be hard on visitors' and 'But … you'll think they are paradise.'

Part 4: Jobs in Cartoon Animation

22 C: 'the only way to find his ideal job was to leave England …'
23 B: 'Grey has just given some funds to the university …'
24 D: 'the ability to develop the plot of a narrative …'
25 A: 'There is plenty of work around for people who can draw …'
26 D: 'he thinks the future of all that area of work lies with computers.'
27 A: 'animated characters for grown-ups …'
28 B: 'They fear large-scale projects will take away their freedom of action.'
29 C: 'something he feels is often neglected in schools.'
30 D: 'offer them a series of classes …'
31 B: 'the publicity industry has employed lots of people …'
32 A: 'Many of his ideas will be on show …'
33 C: 'I'd always dreamt of working in such a way …'
34 A: 'He would create images for his workmates …'
35 D: 'he has spent £10m on new machines …'

Questions **1–21** = 2 marks
Questions **22–35** = 1 mark
The total score is adjusted to give a mark out of 40.

Part 1

Question 1
Style: Formal letter. Avoid informal expressions.
Content: 1 Give information about the age, interests and level of fitness of the group.
2 Ask what experience is needed.
3 Ask whether canoeing is possible.
4 Ask if prices include food.
5 Ask for examples of appropriate clothes.

Part 2

Question 2
Style: Informal.
Content: Tell your friend how you organised the party and the difficulties you had. Include people, food, entertainment, your friend's reaction. Was it a success?

Question 3
Style: Semi-formal or neutral.
Content: 1 Include the reason why Peter was frightened. What had happened between them?

2 What Peter did after he saw Jack at the door.
3 How the story ends. Do they make friends?

Question 4
Style: Neutral or informal because the readers will be young people. Use a heading / title. Organise the article into clear paragraphs.
Content: 1 Describe your hobby (e.g. what you do, the things you need, etc.).
2 Say why you recommend it (i.e. is it entertaining / instructive / interesting?).

Question 5(a)
Style: Formal or neutral. Do not use informal expressions.
Content: Say whether you agree or disagree with the statement. Describe in your own words how the story ends. Give reasons for your agreement or disagreement.

Question 5(b)
Style: Formal or neutral. Do not use informal expressions.
Content: Say what character you think could be your friend. Describe the character (appearance / personality / opinions / feelings) and say why you think s/he would be a good friend.

The two parts of the Writing Paper have equal marks.
The total score is adjusted to give a mark out of 40.

PAPER 3   Use of English

Part 1: Trees for Life

1   D: 'as far as', 'as long as', and 'as soon as' do not make sense.
2   A: Only 'play' collocates with 'role'.
3   A: The expression is 'on a scale'. The other words do not collocate.
4   B: 'known' would need to be followed by 'as'; 'referred' would need 'to as'.
5   D: 'give out' means 'send out or emit'. 'Give in / away / up' have other meanings.
6   A: 'Bring' is the only one that collocates with 'benefits' here.
7   A: The phrase 'in turn' is the only one which means 'has the effect of'.
8   D: 'Opposite' and 'close' collocate grammatically but their meaning is wrong.
9   C: 'contact' collocates with 'with the world'. The others do not.
10   A: 'What's more' is a set phrase and no other word collocates here.
11   C: 'Without' is the only word that goes with 'we would lose the pleasure'.
12   C: 'Therefore' fits grammatically but not semantically. 'Whilst' and 'despite' are completely wrong.
13   B: 'come under threat' is an expression. The other words do not collocate.
14   C: We need an expression that means 'to bear': 'put up with'.
15   B: roots cannot be 'concerned'; 'interfered' would need 'with' after it; the meaning of 'involved' makes it wrong.

Part 2: Fit for Sports

16   *from (preposition)*: collocates with 'results'.
17   *which (relative pronoun)*: referring to 'the body shape and structure'.
18   *who (relative pronoun)*: referring to 'individuals'.
19   *on (preposition)*: collocates with 'dependent'.
20   *is (verb)*: singular, 'the aim … is'.
21   *and (conjunction)*: links two adjectives.
22   *this (pronoun)*: referring to 'to improve … both safe'.
23   *the (definite article)*: referring to specific physical demands: those of sport.

24   *what (pronoun, the subject of the sentence)*: means 'the point which'.
25   *in (preposition)*: only word that collocates in the expression 'in question'.
26   *taken (past participle)*: used in a passive construction, collocates with 'into account'.
27   *of (preposition)*: indicating belonging.
28   *these / such (determiners)*: referring back to all the points in the previous paragraph.
29   *at (preposition)*: collocates in the expression 'to work at it'.
30   *if / though (conjunctions)*: both collocate with 'even'.

Part 3

31   *wish I could (I was / I were able to)*: 'I wish' must be followed by a pronoun.
32   *advised Harry to cancel*: direct to indirect speech, 'advised' followed by 'to'.
33   *a small (tiny) number of*: 'small' collocates with 'number'.
34   *is going to be organised*: active to passive voice.
35   *was so confused (that) she*: testing collocation 'so + adjective + that'.
36   *(been) years since Peter saw*: from Present perfect to Past simple.
37   *accused John of stealing (of having stolen)*: 'accuse + of + verb -ing'.
38   *in case her son needs*: in case + pronoun + verb in Present simple.
39   *if she had not been*: third-type conditional 'would have told' + if + 'had not been'.
40   *put it off because*: to 'put off', to postpone, 'it' goes between 'put' and 'off'; 'because' when followed by a noun needs the particle 'of'.

Part 4

41   *themselves*: relax is not followed by a reflexive pronoun.
42   *such*: 'something more' does not need such.
43   ✔
44   *and*: wrong word separates adjective from noun.
45   *will*: 'unless' is never followed by a Future simple.
46   ✔
47   *very*: 'very much money' would be correct, but here 'very' is wrong.
48   *it*: you do not need the pronoun 'it' because you have 'the kite'.
49   ✔
50   *to*: you need the infinitive without 'to' here.
51   *that*: 'that' does not refer to anything here, the subject of 'making' is 'you'.
52   *more*: the expression is 'at the right moment'.
53   *by*: this particle is not used with 'higher'.
54   ✔
55   *be*: You can only have two forms of the verb 'to be' together in a passive voice (e.g. 'You are being watched').

Part 5: Florida

56   *laid* (infinitive to past participle)
57   *visitor* (verb to noun)
58   *belief* (verb to noun)
59   *unconnected* (verb to adjective plus negative prefix)
60   *impossible* (adjective to negative adjective by adding prefix)
61   *selection* (verb to noun)
62   *attraction* (verb to noun plus plural form)
63   *sandy* (noun to adjective)
64   *pointless* (noun to adjective)
65   *difficulty* (adjective to noun)

Questions **1–30** and **41–65** = 1 mark
Questions **31–40** = 2 marks
The total score is adjusted to give a mark out of 40.

PAPER 4   Listening

There is a mark for each correct answer in parts 1–4

Part 1

1 A   2 C   3 C   4 B   5 C   6 A   7 B   8 A

Part 2

9   play football
10   ballet teacher
11   competitions
12   make friends / fit in
13   kitchen(s)
14   two and a half hours
15   brilliant
16   arguments
17   The Circus
18   in silence / without music

Part 3

19 C   20 D   21 B   22 A   23 F

Part 4

24 B   25 A   26 B   27 C   28 C   29 B   30 A

The total score is adjusted to give a mark out of 40.

Test 2

PAPER 1   Reading

Part 1: The Good Buy Man

1   E: It was just meant to be a seasonal thing, but it turned out to be so successful …
2   B: A survey … found that … and this may go some way to explaining Bryan's success
3   A: Planning a shopping trip with military precision …
4   G: visit stores on their behalf … delivering goods … at a convenient time … return to the shops to exchange them.
5   D: Clients with a list of requests are given a quote …
6   C: Bryan's specialist knowledge means that clients usually get a good deal.

Part 2: The Ballet Sculptor

7   A: 'There is something amazing about all those graceful movements …'
8   D: Her dream is to join forces with them … and then hold an exhibition …
9   C: get the chance to sculpt from life … I can work more quickly
10   C: A worktop is a kind of table to work on.
11   B: This makes her pieces less expensive than solid bronze …
12   A: 'It' refers to making 'each one in the garden shed'.
13   D: I'd accept a lower offer … But I've learnt not to do that anymore.
14   D: All artists want some kind of recognition for their work.

Part 3: The Golfball Frogman

15   G: Link between 'began retrieving lost balls' and 'as a result' and between 'they just fall about laughing' and 'and you can't really blame them'.
16   A: Link between 'he's providing a valuable service to golfers' and 'Of course, Adam does also come across less distinguished balls'.
17   D: Link between 'he cleans them and sells them' and 'get the impression that it's easy money' and between 'It's dangerous … cold and smelly' and 'Most of the lakes … on the bottom it's impossible to see'.

18   B: Link between 'if he were to cut himself' and 'Another such danger is weed' and between 'Adam is well aware of the danger' and 'Fortunately, Adam's never been in any kind of difficulty'.
19   C: Link between 'keeping watch just in case' and 'Another thing to look out for is golfballs themselves' and between 'getting hit by one of those things' and 'Despite all these hazards'.
20   F: Link between 'I was under a lot of weed a couple of weeks ago' and 'On another occasion, when he was covered in weed' and between 'some poor unsuspecting golfer and yelled "Boo!"' and 'Luckily, nobody at the club has complained'.

Part 4: Women in Unusual Jobs

21   C: 'It was better paid than her present job but …'
22   A: 'I don't have any real contact with the large numbers of people I meet.'
23   D: 'the degree course … she started last year, but is confident she will finish …'
24   A: 'The one thing I resent is having to appear cheerful all the time …'
25   D: 'but they will get a written response from me.'
26   C: 'I've made many lasting friendships here …'
27   D: 'to organising events for retired employees …'
28   D: 'I've since climbed the ladder to become customer relations manager.'
29   B: 'It involved no talking, and that suited me down to the ground.'
30   C: 'time changes … it makes you feel physically unwell.'
31   A: 'For a while I trained promising young players …'
32   B: 'it was considered a job for men. "That is changing now …"'
33   C: 'she had always liked the idea of working on a ship.'
34   B: 'I liked my work too much to think of children … I have not regrets.'
35   D: 'performing taste tests on all chocolates to ensure …'

Questions **1–20** = 2 marks
Questions **21–35** = 1 mark
The total score is adjusted to give a mark out of 40.

PAPER 2   Writing

Part 1

Question 1
Style: Formal letter. Avoid informal expressions.
Content: 1   Ask if FCE-level English is acceptable or not.
2   Ask which jobs are on offer – waiting at tables?
3   Ask where you would be staying.
4   Ask if food is provided.
5   Add a question of your own, based on the information in the advertisement.

Part 2

Question 2
Style: Formal to neutral. Use a heading / title. Use neat paragraphs.
Content: 1   Explain what animals make good pets (e.g. dogs, cats, fish, rabbits). Give reasons.
2   Give advice on looking after pets (e.g. about health, diet, exercise).

Question 3
Style: Formal to neutral. Use clear paragraphs.
Content: Include the importance of the Festival, the time of year when it is held, how people react to the Festival, what your own contribution may be, etc.

Question 4

Style: Formal. Write clear paragraphs, maybe with sub-headings.
Content: 1 Talk about the museum and what you saw there.
2 Say whether it is of interest for all age groups. You need to refer specifically to the attractions for people of different ages in your school.

Question 5(a)

Style: Formal or neutral.
Content: 1 Compare the appearance, character, opinions, behaviour, etc. of your chosen characters.
2 Say which one you prefer and why.

Question 5(b)

Style: Formal or neutral.
Content: Say whether you would have preferred to see the film and not read the book. You must include examples from the book to back up your opinions.

The two parts of the Writing Paper carry equal marks.
The total score is adjusted to give a mark out of 40.

PAPER 3   Use of English

Part 1: Polar Adventurer

1 B: Only 'took' collocates with 'the sea route'.
2 B: Only 'widely' collocates with 'known'.
3 D: 'experiences' refers to everything that happened during the voyage.
4 A: The book cannot print, buy or produce copies.
5 C: 'own' is the only word that gives the idea that he built it himself.
6 A: 'set off' means 'left'.
7 C: 'spent' collocates with 'days', the others don't in this context.
8 A: 'out of necessity' is a set expression.
9 C: The other words cannot be used for this kind of journey.
10 B: 'avoid' is the only word that means 'preventing from happening'.
11 D: 'hitting' is the only one that collocates with 'an iceberg'.
12 C: 'consider', 'mind' and 'accept' do not fit grammatically or semantically.
13 B: 'strong' is the only one that collocates with 'wind'.
14 A: 'periods' is the only one that collocates with 'twenty-minute'.
15 D: 'in spite of' means 'although he had to face difficulties'.

Part 2: Good at Languages

16 *as (preposition)*: collocates with 'works'.
17 *Using / Speaking (verbal nouns)*: subject of the verb 'is'.
18 *like (preposition)*: links a noun and a pronoun.
19 *where (relative adverb)*: refers to 'Spain'.
20 *which / that (relative pronoun)*: refers to 'time spent abroad'.
21 *a (indefinite article)*: 'deal' is singular.
22 *being (verb form)*: it needs 'ing' after the proposition 'of'.
23 *with (preposition)*: collocates with 'dealing'.
24 *When (conjunction)*: It introduces a subordinate clause.
25 *they (pronoun)*: refers to 'customers from abroad'.
26 *no (adjective)*: you need to understand the whole of the sentence.
27 *most (superlative form)*: collocates with 'one of the'.
28 *in (preposition)*: collocates with 'changes'.
29 *her (possessive adjective)*: refers to Sarah's vocabulary.
30 *would (conditional form)*: 'would' + 'give', used with if + Past simple.

Part 3

31 *told Toby not to touch*: direct to indirect speech, 'don't' becomes 'not to'.
32 *apart from Tamsin had*: 'from' collocates with 'apart'.
33 *must have been pleased*: 'must have + been' means 'I'm sure she was'.
34 *not work extra hours unless*: 'unless' needs the negative form of the verb before it.
35 *turned down Max's*: 'offer' needs to be qualified by 'Max's' to make the meaning complete.
36 *has no objection to*: 'does not have any objection to' contains six words.
37 *has run out of*: you need the Present perfect to indicate what the situation is now.
38 *advised her to buy*: direct to indirect speech, 'advised' is followed by 'to'.
39 *are said to be*: active to passive form, 'said' is followed by 'to be'.
40 *as long as you are*: 'as long as' has the conditional meaning of 'if'.

Part 4: This Is My Hobby

41 *much*: 'enjoy making stories very much' but not 'enjoy much making'.
42 *a*: there is no noun to go with this article.
43 ✔
44 *these*: 'children's literature' does not need qualifying.
45 *am*: 'get' is in the Present simple and does not need 'am'.
46 *such*: there is no earlier reference to 'magazines' to which 'such' might refer.
47 ✔
48 *up*: 'up' cannot be used as an adjective here.
49 *from*: unnecessary preposition, 'waiting in a queue'.
50 *have*: 'having' would collocate, but not 'have'.
51 ✔
52 *them*: 'them' is not necessary because 'that' refers to 'languages'.
53 *given*: 'pleasure' is followed by 'of' and by a verb ending in -ing.
54 *how*: 'the way' in the previous line means the same as 'how'.
55 *will*: you cannot use 'will' in the 'if' clause of this conditional sentence.

Part 5: The Training Programme

56 *fitness (adjective to noun)*
57 *designed (infinitive to past participle)*
58 *development (verb to noun)*
59 *activities (verb to noun plus plural form)*
60 *knowledge (verb to noun)*
61 *gently (adjective to adverb)*
62 *intensity (adjective to noun)*
63 *impression (verb to noun)*
64 *painful (noun to adjective)*
65 *unwise (adjective to negative form by adding a prefix)*

Questions **1–30** and **41–65** = 1 mark
Questions **31–40** = 2 marks
The total score is adjusted to give a mark out of 40.

PAPER 4   Listening

There is a mark for each correct answer in parts 1–4.

Part 1

1 C   2 B   3 C   4 A   5 C   6 B   7 A   8 B

Part 2

9	*library*	14	*refreshments*
10	*grammar workshops*	15	*café*
11	*Programme Office*	16	*main lecture hall*
12	*tour of London*	17	*meet teachers*
13	*games*	18	*pronunciation practice*

Part 3

19 E   20 C   21 D   22 A   23 F

Part 4

24 F   25 T   26 F   27 T   28 T   29 T   30 F

The total score is adjusted to give a mark out of 40.

Test 3

PAPER 1   Reading

Part 1: Space Tourism

1 E: the first thing you should do … is save up …
2 A: So you can start university studies and try to get the sort of work experience …
3 F: Such tourism is … the quickest way to use the limitless resources of space to solve our problems on Earth.
4 B: It is possible to envisage a future … from thousands … to hundreds of thousands.
5 G: nearer to adventure travel than to luxury-style hotel.
6 C: It is possible to take an active role … asking airlines …

Part 2: Wakeboarding

7   A: I was more than a little taken aback so see how slight he was … Just 1.44m tall …
8   C: He didn't say that, of course. Maybe because he didn't want to seem bigheaded …
9   D: the organisers tried to persuade him … his first competition, thinking he'd be upset when he came last.
10 B: refers to 'practise for at least two hours every day'.
11 A: he can spot what I'm doing wrong in a second and put me right.
12 D: Contrast between 'relatively unknown' and 'it's on the up'.
13 D: wants one day to be a professional.
14 A: This is a global impression based on all the information.

Part 3: Marathon Running – A Recipe for Health?

15 F: Link between 'At first … she had problems' and 'within a couple of months'.
16 C: Link between 'tuned for jumping and running' and 'When it comes to …, however …'.
17 A: Link between 'you are starting to feel exhausted' and 'running gets really hard'.
18 G: Link between 'train sensibly … could even help you live longer' and 'This is …'.
19 B: Link between 'a small injury caused by falling' and 'most go home and …'.
20 E: Link between 'more likely to catch colds … in the week after …' and 'But this … is short-lived'.

Part 4: Wildlife Photographers

21 C: … By age 11 Roger was building his own telescopes …
22 B: You get used to it, he says.
23 A: I sold turtles … That money got me my first camera.
24 D: For each of his jobs, the steel structure has to go in river canoes …

25 B: And his efforts paid off when he finished his degree.
26 D: photograph animals which few people will ever see.
27 A: I'd now like a job where it's warm and sunny…
28 C: The camera made me comfortable around people.
29 C: He is aware of the risks involved in his assignments.
30 A: wrote an article for a wildlife magazine …
31 D: these creatures have to be protected … disappear altogether.
32 B: (he) said no to it in order to concentrate on photography
33 C: was building his own telescopes …
34 A: parents encouraged his enthusiasm …
35 B: They have been the basis for important pieces in scientific journals.

Questions **1–20** = 2 marks
Questions **21–35** = 1 mark
The total score is adjusted to give a mark out of 40.

PAPER 2   Writing

Part 1

Question 1
Style: Formal letter. Avoid informal expressions. Complain in a polite manner.
Content: 1 Say that the match was not disappointing.
2 Two players were sick.
3 Delays due to weather.
4 The team was prepared.

Part 2

Question 2
Style: Informal.
Content: 1 Give ideas for activities (e.g. sport, outings, visits, friends).
2 Give advice about clothes (e.g. according to weather, for parties, for sport).
3 Say if you want anything from England (e.g. a book, special food, stamps).

Question 3
Style: Neutral or informal.
Content: what happened in Clara's dream. It may be something frightening because she woke up with a shock (e.g. a light – a flying saucer – people in it invite Clara to visit it – Clara gets on – saucer takes off – Clara wakes up).

Question 4
Style: Formal or neutral.
Content: 1 Say what you saw (e.g. monuments, churches, parks, museums). Describe some of the things.
2 Say whether you think other students should go. Give reasons.

Question 5(a)
Style: Formal or neutral.
Content: 1 Good qualities of one of the characters.
2 Bad qualities of the same character. Do not choose a character that is only good or only bad.

Question 5(b)
Style: Formal or neutral.
Content: Say whether you think the plot was difficult to follow. Give reasons for your opinion and examples from the book.

The two parts of the Writing Paper have equal marks.
The total score is adjusted to give a mark out of 40.

PAPER 3   Use of English

Part 1: Singing for a musical life

1 D: 'age' collocates in the expression 'from an early age'.
2 B: You build (an understanding of music) on a good 'basis'.
3 A: The Foundation's ideas were influenced by the teaching of .... 'Behind' is the only word that communicates this meaning.
4 C: 'form' collocates with 'part' in the expression 'to form part of'.
5 B: The other three words do not collocate with 'is especially'.
6 A: 'expert' and 'skilled' do not fit grammatically. 'Fit' is the wrong meaning.
7 B: 'by heart' is a set expression.
8 A: 'to come to an understanding', 'reach' and 'arrive' do not fit grammatically.
9 C: 'although' introduces a subordinate clause and means 'some teaching of theory is part of this but ...'.
10 D: Music is written on a 'page'.
11 D: The Voices Foundation believes that .... Their 'belief' is that ...
12 D: The other three options do not fit grammatically.
13 B: Musicians have 'qualities' that we appreciate; 'appreciate' and 'qualities' collocate.
14 B: The expression is 'to set yourself a task'.
15 A: 'benefit' means 'do good to', 'favour' implies 'showing a preference for'. The other two options are completely wrong.

Part 2: The Birth of the T-shirt

16 *named / called (past participle)*: who was called / named.
17 *on (preposition)*: 'to go on stage'.
18 *pair (noun)*: a pair of trousers.
19 *had (auxiliary verb)*: the passive form 'had been seen'.
20 *but / except (prepositions)*: 'but' used with negative words: 'he is nothing but a fool' has the same meaning as 'except'.
21 *to / until (preposition)*: collocates with 'through'.
22 *from (preposition)*: 'come from' means 'originate'.
23 *so (adverb)*: used before adjectives and adverbs. It means 'to such an extent'.
24 *as (preposition)*: means 'so that it appears to be'.
25 *own (adjective)*: part of the expression 'in its own right'.
26 *for (preposition)*: collocates with 'wear' (wear something for warmth / comfort).
27 *or (conjunction)*: indicating an alternative.
28 *who (relative pronoun)*: refers to 'Brando'.
29 *the (definite article)*: 'release' is defined by 'of the film version of Streetcar'.
30 *by (preposition)*: used after the passive form 'that was to be adopted'.

Part 3

31 *to put up with*: to find (something) difficult + infinitive. 'Put up with' = 'tolerate'.
32 *I get bored*: to get bored + -ing form. You need a subject for 'get' = 'I'.
33 *tends to be very*: 'To tend' is always followed by an infinitive with 'to'.
34 *said to be a waste*: from active to passive voice.
35 *made a formal complaint*: 'to make a complaint', you need 'formal' to complete the meaning.
36 *get on my nerves*: 'to get on (somebody's) nerves' means 'to irritate'.
37 *wished he had not sold*: 'wished' (past tense) is followed by a verb in the Past perfect. It means the action in the past is regretted.
38 *advised Paul to buy*: from direct to indirect speech, 'advised' + noun / pronoun + to.

39 *as a surprise to Pauline*: the expression is 'to come as a surprise to (somebody)'.
40 *popularity of golf is increasing*: the verb 'to increase' is in the Present continuous to indicate it is happening now.

Part 4: TV Critic

41 *am*: I agree / I am in agreement.
42 *they*: the subject of the verb 'contain' is 'which'.
43 ✔
44 *on*: 'broadcast' is not followed by 'on' unless you mention a TV channel.
45 *it*: the subject of the verb 'is' is 'comedy'.
46 *the*: 'relaxation' is not qualified (e.g. 'the relaxation I need').
47 *that*: 'think' is an Imperative form here. 'So that' would need a pro(noun) after it.
48 ✔
49 *most*: 'most' does not fit grammatically between 'one' and 'thing'.
50 *there*: the subject of the verb 'is' is 'that'.
51 *up*: 'lecture up' is wrong, you 'lecture' somebody.
52 *to*: modal verbs are not followed by 'to'.
53 *so*: the expression is 'what's more', followed by a comma.
54 ✔
55 *with*: the expression is 'to take up verb + -ing'.

Part 5: Happy is Healthy

56 *laughter (verb to noun)*
57 *traditional (noun to adjective)*
58 *treatment (verb to noun)*
59 *entertainment (verb to noun)*
60 *successful (noun to adjective)*
61 *reduction (verb to noun)*
62 *tension (adjective to noun)*
63 *impossible (adjective to negative adjective by adding prefix)*
64 *unlikely (adjective to negative adjective by adding prefix)*
65 *illness (adjective to noun)*

Questions **1–30** and **41–65** = 1 mark
Questions **31–40** = 2 marks
The total score is adjusted to give a mark out of 40.

PAPER 4   Listening

There is a mark for each correct answer in parts 1–4.

Part 1

1 B 2 B 3 A 4 A 5 C 6 B 7 A 8 C

Part 2

9 *film (about it)*
10 *practical*
11 *very old church*
12 *reports*
13 *plans / photo(graph)s (i.a.o)*
14 *draw*
15 *how / why (i.a.o)*
16 *basements*
17 *diet*
18 *builders*

Part 3

19 E 20 D 21 B 22 F 23 A

Part 4

24 I 25 I 26 M 27 P 28 P 29 M 30 M

The total score is adjusted to give a mark out of 40.

Test 4

PAPER 1   Reading

Part 1: Across to Lundy Island

1   H: they'd have to spend the night on the island because the sea was too …

2   A: Its cliffs rise 400 feet … It is not surprising … resisted all attempts at invasion …

3   G: The clear blue water … made me think we must have taken a wrong turn …

4   B: I would certainly come to regret leaving behind … in favour of a smart …

5   F: You can choose between a 12-room castle … or … modest lighthouse …

6   C: the most frequent remarks were 'won't you get bored and lonely' … Lundy is deservedly famous …

7   E: You don't have to take part in … I went for rest and relaxation and …

Part 2

8   A: was weary after a long, hard day at the pottery factory …

9   C: 'pick up' means to collect somebody or something from a place.

10   D: she noticed a light flashing on and off in an upstairs bedroom.

11   B: Lisa's curiosity got the better of her and she decided to go back …

12   C: as the fury swelled inside her. She tore across the garden … shouting …

13   C: Ignoring her, the man fled across the garden.

14   A: 'I can't believe you were so foolish, Lisa,' scolded her father.

15   C: Lisa later remembered the name of the burglar … He was later caught …

Part 3: Herons

16   C: Link between 'they are quick to take to the air' and 'such nervousness is' and between 'persecution from fish farmers' and 'This cruel treatment is now'.

17   A: Link between 'consequently … there are … twice as many herons' and 'Another reason for this increase' and between 'reduction in water pollution' and 'This means herons can feed'.

18   E: Link between 'new areas of habitat have been opened up' and 'However, a hard winter will' and between 'a hard winter' and 'the one in 1963'.

19   G: Link between 'all is well for the heron at the moment' and 'similar increases have been recorded'.

20   D: Link between 'it is important not to be complacent' and 'there are still numerous threats'.

21   F: Link between 'The heron lives on fish' and 'The commonest hunting technique is' and between the latter and 'On other occasions a different tactic'.

Part 4: Tricks of the Trade

22   A: an attractive description but … a brochure won't give you a breakdown of the skills required.

23   C: work out a plan to carry your cash safely … not a good idea to stuff it in your pocket …

24   B: the people who handle luggage at airports are often very careless …

25   A: I find it's virtually impossible to take too little equipment …

26   D: keep a record of his passport number … makes copies of all holiday papers …

27   B: What I regret most … I ruined the walking experience for the others …

28   C: found that someone else had already taken my seat …

29   A: get information … from the abundant printed material available …

30   D: he admits to feeling uneasy when preparing for a trip …

31   B: gives them details about the type of walking he normally does …

32   C: with the local inhabitants and makes an effort to respect their customs …

33   B: Just a few words of the local language … if you try and speak their language.

34   D: people who have already climbed in the area … I talk to them and …

35   D: if you are as bad as I am at looking after your rucksack and things.

Questions **1–21** = 2 marks
Questions **22–35** = 1 mark

PAPER 2   Writing

Part 1

Question 1

Style: Formal letter. Avoid informal expressions.

Content: 1   Give information about your level of English (e.g. years of study, certificates, what you are good at, and not so good at). Ask if courses are available at this level.

      2   Ask for information about courses in the countries that interest you.

      3   Say you do not want to stay with a family.

      4   Ask about when there are courses.

      5   Ask for prices of student hostels and the cost of the course.

      6   Add one other question of your own.

Part 2

Question 2

Style: Informal letter.

Content: 1   Say how often you go (e.g. every day, three times a week, seldom).

      2   Mention the sports you do.

      3   Talk about the kind of competitions they organise (e.g. swimming, team sports, dancing).

      4   Talk about friends you have made (e.g. what they do, what they are like, when you see them).

Question 3

Style: Neutral to formal.

Content: Anna knocked on the door.

      1   What happened next? (e.g. The person who lived there was a thief.)

      2   What happened then? (e.g. Anna ran away, went to the police.)

      3   How did the story end? (e.g. Anna was given a prize for her courage.)

Question 4

Style: Formal to neutral.

Content: Describe your town (e.g. how old, inhabitants, houses, parks). Mention and describe the attractions for visitors (e.g. churches, museums, entertainment, walks).

Question 5(a)

Style: Formal or neutral. Do not use informal expressions.

Content: 1   Say which part of the story you liked the least (e.g. the beginning, the end, the description of a character).

      2   Explain clearly why you did not like it (e.g. it was frightening / boring / difficult to understand) and give examples from the text.

Question 5(b)

Style: Describe the character you have chosen (e.g. appearance, character, opinions).

Content: Say why you think the character is uninteresting and boring. Give examples from the story.

The two parts of the Writing Paper have equal marks.

PAPER 3   Use of English

Part 1: Whales

1 B: a 'beach' is a feature of a coast, 'seaside' is a place along the coast, often referred to as a 'resort'.
2 A: areas where whales can feed.
3 C: 'consider' is 'to take into account', 'think' does not fit grammatically, the other two options do not make sense.
4 D: 'lived' means 'existed' here, 'been' does not give that meaning.
5 B: 'come' collocates with 'as a surprise'.
6 D: 'to mistake something for', 'to confuse ... with', 'to mix up two things'.
7 A: 'to discover information about'. The other three options do not mean this.
8 C: 'hold' collocates with 'your breath'.
9 A: the 'dive' towards the bottom, '200 metres' refers to 'depth'.
10 B: 'known' collocates with 'as'.
11 B: 'touch' collocates with 'to keep in'.
12 D: 'to produce a noise' is 'to make a noise'.
13 A: the only option that collocates with 'of'.
14 B: 'last' means 'continue for'.
15 C: 'to get a chance to do something', to 'have the luck to ...', to 'have a choice (between ...)'.

Part 2: A Piano Around the House

16 *who (relative pronoun)*: refers to 'those (people)'.
17 *at (preposition)*: part of the expression 'at least'.
18 *do (infinitive verb)*: used after the verb *persuade + somebody + infinitive*.
19 *of (preposition)*: to be of interest to somebody.
20 *again / more (adverb)*: once again / more refers to something which is repeated.
21 *with (preposition)*: means 'who have'.
22 *all (indefinite determiner)*: used with plural nouns, 'every' used with singular nouns.
23 *get / become (infinitive verb)*: meaning 'grow to be'.
24 *ago (adverb)*: used with the simple past tense, means 'in the past'.
25 *like (preposition)*: similar to.
26 *in (preposition)*: collocates with 'huge numbers'.
27 *so (adverb)*: to such an extent.
28 *one (pronoun)*: refers to 'a piano'.
29 *worth (adjective)*: having a certain value.
30 *up (adverb)*: 'to chop up', to cut into pieces with an axe or big knife.

Part 3

31 *see the point of (to)*: 'see the point of something' = to understand its purpose.
32 *will have to be thoroughly*: active verb 'need' + direct object 'redecoration' replaced by passive form 'will have to be (redecorated)'.
33 *as long as you promise*: as long as = if.
34 *never able to get / not ever able to get*: to succeed + in + verb -ing, to be able + to-infinitive.
35 *a faster runner*: article 'a' before noun in singular, comparative form of 'fast'.

36 *had to be followed*: active to passive form, 'had to be + past participle'.
37 *in case it is / should be*: 'in case' followed by Present simple or modal 'should' to refer to future possibility.
38 *is unlikely to last*: to be unlikely + infinitive. It is improbable that it will do it.
39 *has difficulty (in) getting*: to have difficulty in + verb -ing.
40 *David forgot (to take) was*: forget + to-infinitive, 'was' is singular, in agreement with 'The only thing which'.

Part 4: How to be Animal Friendly

41 *how*: 'don't know much' about something, 'how much do you know ...'.
42 *them*: 'with facts' you do not need a pronoun between these words.
43 *written*: 'there are chapters ...', chapters are written ...
44 ✔
45 *for*: help + pronoun + to-infinitive.
46 *of*: 'some places', but 'some of the places we saw ...'.
47 *much*: 'so sad', 'so + adjective' but 'so much sadness', 'so much + noun'.
48 *mostly*: the animals themselves, no word between noun and pronoun.
49 *that*: not necessary because 'about' refers to 'what cruel people do ...'.
50 ✔
51 *been*: this is an active form of the verb 'save' in the Present perfect.
52 *such*: 'such' does not collocate grammatically with 'the'.
53 ✔
54 *as*: recommend something to somebody / for somebody.
55 *the*: 'people over seven years ....', no definite article before the number.

Part 5: On time

56 *importance (adjective to noun)*
57 *politeness (adjective to noun)*
58 *employers (verb to noun)*
59 *usually (adjective to adverb)*
60 *unsuccessful (noun to adjective plus negative prefix)*
61 *chosen (infinitive verb to past participle)*
62 *relaxed (verb to adjective)*
63 *stressful (noun to adjective)*
64 *impatient (noun to adjective plus negative prefix)*
65 *reasonable (noun to adjective)*

Questions **1–30** and **41–65** = 1 mark
Questions **31–40** = 2 marks

PAPER 4   Listening

There is a mark for each correct answer in parts 1–4.

Part 1

1 A **2** B **3** B **4** A **5** C **6** B **7** C **8** B

Part 2

9	concert hall	**14**	caves
10	(little) insects	**15**	30,000 / thirty thousand
11	paint	**16**	smile / laugh
12	expert	**17**	breathing
13	sound	**18**	art / culture (i.a.o.)

Part 3

19 F **20** E **21** A **22** D **23** B

Part 4

24 C **25** A **26** C **27** B **28** A **29** B **30** B

Test 5

Part 1: Ranger training

1 G: at a certain point … they will turn and fight.
2 A: buffaloes are the ones that scare the rangers most.
3 C: I wasn't tempted to swap the simplicity of the camp … I really felt a part of the bush.
4 D: The four of us … listened avidly to their tales from the wild side.
5 E: They provided an opportunity not only to take in the wild variety of wildlife … but also to gain an understanding …
6 F: To my great astonishment, I managed it.
7 B: There is no way that any of us would ever come close to being ready …

Part 2

8 D: Each … student took sole responsibility for a section of the car …
9 A: makes every other student … feel more than slightly envious.
10 A: He is convinced / certain that …
11 D: The most satisfying thing was actually getting to drive the car.
12 B: It's difficult relying on people finalising their part …
13 C: The idea … originally came from the students themselves.
14 C: The project has proved very successful.

Part 3: Bikes on Kilimanjaro

15 F: Link between 'which added to the weight (of the rucksack)' and 'When we'd got everything packed up' and between 'rucksacks to carry, stuffed to the brim' and 'And we had the bikes on top of that'.
16 C: Link between 'and there was total silence' and 'It was so quiet and calm' and between 'before we had really got started on the more exciting bits' and 'Nevertheless, our immediate objective had been fulfilled'.
17 A: Link between 'experimentation with the bicycles had to be abandoned' and 'Part of the reason for this had been …' and between 'Part of the reason …' and 'But principally … the constraints of time'.
18 G: Link between 'we sat down to consider what we had gained' and 'we knew that we had learnt' and between 'It is only by pushing ourselves' and 'And only by living under stress'.
19 B: Link between 'normally encourages a spring in the step' and 'However, … I was barely capable of lifting one foot'.
20 D: Link between 'I was sitting as far back as possible … could just reach the handlebars' and 'What I didn't realise …' and between 'I couldn't see where I was going' and 'After that incident'.

Part 4: Meet the Rising Talents

21 A: Such comments only give me more courage to do new and exciting things.
22 B: He found the work much less demanding than he thought.
23 D: to such an extent that his profits have doubled.
24 A: I owe my success to the arts instructor who …
25 A: brought him into direct contact with the landscape … his main subject matter.

26 C: My approach will be different from … the modern Head Gardener has to …
27 D: most of what he has learnt, he says, came from his day-to-day work …
28 B: Even at university, he knew where he was going.
29 C: being seen as a leader of a generation … I don't like that at all …
30 C: nervous about letting somebody else take over my job.
31 B: he turned down job offers from the national papers …
32 D: If your business is healthy … it has a beneficial effect on the community.
33 B: The only thing … dislikes … is finding … messages on his answering machine.
34 A: a number of negative comments from colleagues …
35 D: organising visits to the farm for children in the local schools.

Questions **1–20** = 2 marks
Questions **21–35** = 1 mark

Part 1

Question 1
Style: Formal letter. Avoid informal expressions.
Content: 1 Say how you plan to travel and request information on how to get to the camping site.
2 Say you would like to rent a tent and ask for details.
3 Ask if it's possible to walk to the village.
4 Ask about cooking facilities.
5 Say what you would like to do during your stay.

Part 2

Question 2
Style: Neutral or semi-informal.
Content: 1 Say what methods were useful for you (e.g. conversation, grammar lessons, listening to songs, reading a lot).
2 Say what books helped you (e.g. stories, novels, coursebooks, dictionaries).
3 Mention people who were helpful (e.g. teachers, English-speaking friends, family).

Question 3
Style: Neutral to formal.
Content: 1 You answered the phone (who was it? What did they say / want?).
2 The action taken (e.g. phoned the police, went to meet the person).
3 How the story ended (e.g. a discovery, a mystery solved, an unexpected turn of events).

Question 4
Style: Formal. Do not use informal expressions.
Content: Say how computers are changing our lives. Include:
1 The world of study (e.g. classroom computers, the Internet).
2 The world of work (e.g. people work from home, many jobs in computing).
3 Entertainment (e.g. games, contact by e-mail). Say how people feel about computers (e.g. they are useful / tiring / difficult).

Question 5(a)
Style: Neutral or formal.
Content: 1 Describe the character you least liked (feelings, appearance, opinions, actions).
2 Explain why you did not like the character's appearance, feelings, opinions, etc. Give concrete examples from the text.

Question 5(b)

Style: Formal or neutral.

Content: Give a brief introduction to the book. Say what type of young people would enjoy the book (e.g. studious, sporty, adventurous, shy, sociable, with a good sense of humour). Give reasons and examples from the text.

The two parts of the Writing Paper have equal marks.

PAPER 3   Use of English

Part 1: Music

1 A: recording music (on tape), there are no recordings so we cannot hear it.

2 C: to form an opinion without definite knowledge.

3 D: 'bang' collocates with 'on a drum'.

4 C: 'piece' collocates with 'of wood'.

5 C: Something takes (some) effort to do, somebody makes an effort to do …

6 A: 'look like' refers to the instruments as seen on wall paintings.

7 D: 'ways' of doing something.

8 A: belonging to times long past, 'ancient' civilisations.

9 B: 'based' collocates with 'on'.

10 C: 'mood' collocates with 'create'.

11 D: performers who played without accompaniment, 'unique' is 'special or 'outstanding'.

12 A: found over a large area. The other options do not convey that meaning.

13 B: 'spring' and 'turn' would need 'up'.

14 D: 'brought' is the only option that collocates with 'about', to cause to happen.

15 B: 'can be called', can be considered to be …

Part 2

16 *take (verb in Present simple)*: 'to take up a sport'.

17 *at (preposition)*: collocates in the expression 'at least'.

18 *If (conjunction)*: introduces conditional clause.

19 *with (preposition)*: in the company of.

20 *keep (infinitive verb)*: 'keep' followed by verb *-ing* = continue doing something.

21 *than (conjunction)*: used to introduce a comparison 'rather than (running) on hard surfaces'.

22 *used / accustomed (past participle)*: to be used / accustomed to something.

23 *need / have / ought to (verb in Present simple)*: here it indicates necessity.

24 *because (conjunction)*: introduces a subordinate clause, 'for the reason that …'

25 *sure (adjective)*: collocates with sure in the expression 'to make sure'.

26 *where (relative adverb)*: refers to 'from a shop'.

27 *like (preposition)*: means 'such as'.

28 *by (preposition)*: follows a passive construction, 'be influenced'.

29 *between (preposition)*: used when referring to the point in the middle of two things.

30 *pair (noun)*: a pair (of shoes)

Part 3

31 *in time for / in time to see / catch*: 'in time' + infinitive or 'in time' + 'for' + noun.

32 *they would rather have*: 'rather' is preceded by 'would' and followed by an infinitive without 'to'.

33 *she was / felt grateful for*: reported speech, 'to be grateful for' something.

34 *are said to be living / to live*: Active to passive form.

35 *are not widely read*: Active to passive form, 'widely' is between the negative particle and the verb.

36 *will not answer unless*: you need a negative construction before 'unless'.

37 *carry on walking because / as / since*: carry on walking = continue walking.

38 *to put off booking*: 'put off' is followed by a verb *-ing*.

39 *as soon as you*: without delay.

40 *long as it does not*: 'as long as' = if it doesn't rain.

Part 4: Students' Week

41 *which*: activities organised, does not need 'which'.

42 *them*: object of 'invited' is 'their parents'.

43 ✔

44 *of*: you 'enjoy something', the enjoyment of something.

45 ✔

46 *up*: to make preparations.

47 *be*: 'where they can put' is an active form, not a passive.

48 *that*: so = therefore, as a consequence.

49 *with*: people 'get together' with others.

50 ✔

51 *a*: 'fun' is uncountable.

52 *so*: = 'even when', 'It rained. Even so, we had a picnic'.

53 ✔

54 *the*: 'just in case', no article needed before 'case'.

55 *think*: the verb that goes with 'you' is visit, not 'think'.

Part 5: Rules for Wildlife Watchers

56 *following (verb to noun)*

57 *unforgettable (verb to adjective plus negative prefix)*

58 *advisable (verb to adjective)*

59 *disturbance (verb to noun)*

60 *frightened (noun to verb plus past participle form)*

61 *particularly (adjective to adverb)*

62 *patient (noun to adjective)*

63 *surroundings (verb to noun plus plural form)*

64 *unpleasant (adjective to negative form by adding prefix)*

65 *annoying (verb to adjective)*

Questions **1–30** and **41–65** = 1 mark
Questions **31–40** = 2 marks

PAPER 4   Listening

There is a mark for each correct answer in parts 1–4.

Part 1

1 A **2** B **3** A **4** A **5** B **6** C **7** B **8** C

Part 2

9	(the) balcony	**14**	Greek salad
10	Tower Bridge	**15**	(covered) terrace
11	Spanish cheeses	**16**	(elegant) lake
12	window (table)	**17**	(smoked) duck
13	Christmas lights	**18**	ice-cream(s)

Part 3

19 E **20** A **21** D **22** C **23** F

Part 4

24 T **25** F **26** F **27** T **28** F **29** T **30** T

Test 6

Part 1

1. E: the triumphant emerge from surprisingly varied quarters.
2. C: I realised that first I had to explore my own mind …
3. A: we come to the realisation that we either have to act now or dream on.
4. H: what I'm looking for now is an endeavour that scares me and may not …
5. D: The Norwegian sailors were the first to row the Atlantic …
6. B: New Zealanders … shot across to Barbados in an incredible 41 days.
7. F: As a schoolboy I had read about Blyth and Ridgway and about …

Part 2

8. A: if they ignored my often-repeated remarks …
9. D: they couldn't understand why he still had the same ambition to own a zoo.
10. C: after a number of unsuccessful attempts to convince local councils …
11. C: He would show me around the island and point out suitable sites.
12. D: he cocked an enquiring eyebrow at me and asked whether …
13. C: I could not imagine more attractive surroundings for my purpose …
14. B: at least it would rid her back garden of the assorted jungle creatures.

Part 3: Making Mirrors

15. D: Link between 'This was much admired by friends and …' and 'Before long, she was being asked to make'.
16. F: Link between 'into an office-cum-studio' and 'she works there'.
17. B: Link between 'Viv does everything herself' and 'This represents about a week's work'.
18. E: Link between '£3000 was spent on shells alone' and 'But Viv also had to think about'.
19. A: Link between 'Viv has now made contact with another company' and 'Together they can afford to'.
20. H: Link between 'a website on the Internet' and 'This is a very economical way of selling'.
21. G: Link between 'another year before her business starts to make money' and 'Once this happens'.

Part 4

22. B: has a large walk-in wardrobe where I put all my stuff.
23. D: I made the big mistake of going to … I'm stuck at my parents' house …
24. B: and the college has nothing of its own to offer you …
25. A: my room's just been re-carpeted, the furniture's new and …
26. C: I get a reasonably-sized room … and a sink.
27. D: I don't have the same amount of freedom or privacy …
28. A: The first thing I did … was buy myself a mini-fridge …
29. D: I even have to share a room with my younger brother.
30. A: we get room phones so I can ring friends …
31. C: an old wardrobe … a tiny desk … one shelf …
32. B: a rota for the washing-up, cleaning and putting out the rubbish …
33. D: they said they'd stop supporting me financially … had to give up the idea …
34. B: Cooking your own food is much cheaper than eating at college …

35. C: In the next block, there's a games room …

Questions **1–21** = 2 marks
Questions **22–35** = 1 mark

Part 1

Question 1
Style: Formal letter.
Content: 1 Say that you want a beginner's course.
       2 Ask for prices and discounts they offer students.
       3 Find out the number of hours per week and when the courses begin.
       4 Ask about the certificates you get at the end of the course.

Part 2

Question 2
Style: Formal or neutral.
Content: 1 Say what performance you attended (e.g. pop group, play, ballet).
       2 Describe the performance (e.g. the venue, the quality of the performers, the audience, the atmosphere).
       3 Say why you will always remember it.

Question 3
Style: Formal to neutral.
Content: 1 Describe the town (e.g. how old, location, inhabitants).
       2 Say what tourists can see (e.g. museums, famous spots, old churches, gardens).
       3 What tourists can do (e.g. eat in good restaurants, go for walks, have fun, swim).

Question 4
Style: Formal letter of application.
Content: 1 Say what area you are interested in.
       2 Explain in detail why you are a good candidate (e.g. you have previous experience, you are good at communicating, you have contacts with the right people, you are hard-working).

Question 5(a)
Style: Formal.
Content: 1 Say whether you think it is a good idea and why (e.g. teenagers interested in subject, a good lesson for teenagers, useful, lively plot, characters are young).
       2 Say what changes would be needed (shorter, fewer characters, a different ending, set in a different country / century).

Question 5(b)
Style: Formal.
Content: 1 Say what you (dis)liked about the book (e.g. the characters, the plot, the setting, the message), giving concrete examples from the text.
       2 Say what type of people would enjoy it (e.g. young, adventurous, romantic, interested in literature).

The two parts of the Writing Paper have equal marks.

Part 1: Teddy Bears

1 C   2 D   3 A   4 A   5 A   6 A   7 C   8 D
9 D   10 A   11 D   12 A   13 C   14 D   15 D

Part 2: Holiday Reading

16	thanks	**24**	their
17	between / among(st) / around	**25**	put
18	out	**26**	get
19	which	**27**	do
20	on	**28**	might / may
21	by	**29**	run
22	or	**30**	If
23	the		

Part 3

31 prevent the crowd from invading
32 were not / weren't allowed to leave
33 have been brought about / on by
34 oughtn't / ought not to request
35 if he had known
36 resulted from her
37 is said to be considering
38 is not as bad / poor as
39 in spite of eating
40 so that she could

Part 4

41	off	**46**	more	**51**	be
42	time	**47**	of	**52**	been
43	for	**48**	✔	**53**	the
44	then	**49**	much	**54**	going
45	✔	**50**	myself	**55**	✔

Part 5: Music in Schools

56 introduction (verb to noun)
57 musicians (noun to noun plus plural form)
58 survival (verb to noun)
59 solution (verb to noun)
60 argument (verb to noun)
61 childhood (noun to abstract noun)
62 uninterested (noun to adjective plus negative prefix)
63 performance (verb to noun)
64 explanation (verb to noun)
65 successful (noun to adjective)

Questions **1–30** and **41–65** = 1 mark
Questions **31–40** = 2 marks

PAPER 4   Listening

There is a mark for each correct answer in parts 1–4.

Part 1

1 C **2** A **3** C **4** A **5** B **6** A **7** B **8** B

Part 2

9	car park	**14**	(in) (the) winter
10	pink / grey (i.a.o.)	**15**	(a / the) berry / berries
11	face	**16**	gardens
12	north	**17**	(slightly) (rotten) apple(s)
13	lack of food / no food	**18**	(an) insect(s)

Part 3

19 C **20** B **21** E **22** F **23** A

Part 4

24 YES **25** NO **26** YES **27** YES **28** NO **29** YES
30 NO

Test 7

PAPER 1   Reading

Part 1: Waste Not, Want Not

1 G: soon scored top marks in a competition … to find the best farm shop …
2 A: is a trained chef and … she began offering a variety of prepared meals.
3 F: if the product is good, the public recognise this and buy it …
4 B: not wishing to see them get thrown away …
5 E: She spent much of the summer … doing presentations … As a result …
6 H: there was a huge untapped demand in London and …
7 C: Clara's next idea … These she thinks she might be able …

Part 2: Windsurfing around Britain

8 A: just for the fun of it I suppose … It was there to be done …
9 C: I didn't have that much time to prepare …
10 C: Kevin made do with an … and an old van manned by four friends.
11 B: made use of the camping equipment … and slept on the beach.
12 D: we had anything that was on special offer at the nearest supermarket.
13 C: 'gruelling' means 'very hard', therefore relaxation is important.
14 B: I'll be doing my best to be up there amongst the winners …

Part 3: All I had to protect me was a leaflet

15 F: Link between 'to avoid this one should whistle, talk' and 'To find out which of those was best'.
16 E: Link between 'may not be loud enough to do the trick' and 'So I decided to trust my own voice'.
17 A: Link between 'I didn't feel that brave' and 'I had experienced similar fears' and between 'is supposed to be safe' and 'Yet, here I was in a Niagara of sweat'.
18 D: Link between 'As many as five visitors have died' and 'The last one was in 1992'.
19 G: Link between 'He was British too' and 'This comment really made my day'.
20 C: Link between 'I can't say that I enjoyed it, I was too terrified for that' and 'But don't be discouraged from visiting'.

Part 4: You are what you wear

21 C: perhaps bordering on scruffy …
22 A: good quality suits that keep going for years.
23 D: I always get a reaction to the things I buy …
24 D: I'm also looking for bargains in the sales wherever I go.
25 A: What I have trouble with is casual wear …
26 B: the way I look can affect my opportunities and the parts I get.
27 C: My girlfriend usually comes with me because she has better taste …
28 B: rehearsals in jeans and T-shirts … at a film-sales company … smarter.
29 C: I'm hopeless at keeping things smart.
30 B: I like to browse at my own pace … try lots of things on.
31 D: I would describe my style … as individual … I know what I like.
32 B: I buy a lot of things in black and white …

33 C: I was in uniform for about twelve years …
34 B: I want a new look …
35 A: stylish even though I'm in my forties … I don't like to see older men wearing …

Questions **1–20** = 2 marks
Questions **21–35** = 1 mark

PAPER 2   Writing

Part 1

Question 1
Style: Formal letter.
Content: 1 Say you want to help and ask whether you can choose the kind of work. Say you are not keen on picking up rubbish and why.
2 Find out what they mean by 'mending walls' and the kind of training they would give you.
3 Ask if expenses include food.
4 Say when you can work and how many hours.
5 Say what work experience (if any) you have.

Part 2

Question 2
Style: Formal or neutral.
Content: Include reasons for your choice (e.g. in a gym: variety of activities, can do it on your own, can have professional advice, easy to get to; team sport: fun, competitions, weekend activity, make friends).

Question 3
Style: Formal or neutral.
Content: Narrate the unexpected events on that last day of the summer holidays (e.g. an adventure, an accident, a journey).

Question 4
Style: Formal.
Content: 1 Say what kind of films would be popular with students (e.g. adventure, thrillers, documentaries, comedy, musicals).
2 Give reasons for your choice (e.g. students like films that make them laugh, teach them, help them relax).

Question 5(a)
Style: Informal.
Content: Say why the book is or isn't a good choice for a summer holiday read (e.g. language level, plot, characters, length).

Question 5(b)
Style: Formal.
Content: 1 Say what passage from the book would be good for a class of young students and why (e.g. a passage that describes the main character).
2 Explain why young people would like that passage (e.g. the character is also young).

The two parts of the Writing Paper have equal marks.

PAPER 3   Use of English

Part 1: The Flying Aunties
1 C **2** C **3** C **4** A **5** B **6** C **7** A **8** B **9** D
10 B **11** A **12** C **13** D **14** B **15** A

Part 2: Liquorice Allsorts

16	*than*	**24**	*together / up*
17	*which*	**25**	*would*
18	*whose*	**26**	*but*
19	*in*	**27**	*was*
20	*over / around*	**28**	*ever*
21	*of*	**29**	*by*
22	*during / at*	**30**	*Despite*
23	*how*		

Part 3

31 *to borrow Ann's / if he could borrow Ann's*
32 *has not eaten anything since*
33 *impossible (for us) to find*
34 *had not turned down*
35 *do without Sheila's*
36 *if she had finished her*
37 *if we were expected to*
38 *which / that knocked the tower*
39 *so that the tourists could / might*
40 *if Martha had not held*

Part 4

41	*be*	**46**	*has*	**51**	*it*
42	*that*	**47**	*person*	**52**	✔
43	*did*	**48**	*from*	**53**	*much*
44	✔	**49**	*up*	**54**	✔
45	*of*	**50**	✔	**55**	*to*

Part 5: The Wild West

56 *various / varied (verb to adjective)*
57 *tourists (noun to noun plus plural form)*
58 *exhibitions (verb to noun plus plural form)*
59 *exciting (verb to adjective)*
60 *competitions (verb to noun plus plural form)*
61 *extremely (adjective to adverb)*
62 *indoor (noun to adjective)*
63 *performers (verb to noun plus plural form)*
64 *originally (noun to adverb)*
65 *cruelty (adjective to noun)*

Questions **1–30** and **41–65** = 1 mark
Questions **31–40** = 2 marks

PAPER 4   Listening

There is a mark for each correct answer in parts 1–4.

Part 1
1 B **2** B **3** A **4** C **5** C **6** B **7** A **8** A

Part 2

9	*rarest*	**14**	*(nature) reserve*
10	*fifty*	**15**	*local people / tourists* (i.a.o)
11	*(absolutely) fantastic*	**16**	*counting*
12	*eggs*	**17**	*(the) rat(s)*
13	*small / delicate (i.a.o)*	**18**	*bite / tooth / teeth*

Part 3
19 E **20** F **21** B **22** D **23** C

Part 4
24 C **25** B **26** A **27** B **28** A **29** C **30** B

Test 8

PAPER 1   Reading

Part 1: The Lady with Blue Nails

1 F: got fed up with not being able to find make-up … decided to set up …

2 H: I thought … the time was ripe for an alternative.

3 G: The more money you have … Sandy made her fortune in her former career.

4 E: As a founder … responsible for designing the eye-catching … that helped …

5 C: although they now do similar colours … people who want … still come to us.

6 A: aims its products at career women … a hit amongst Hollywood celebrities …

7 B: She is now turning her attention to her current projects.

Part 2

8   C: a mystery illness was beginning to …

9   A: Before he had hospital treatment …

10 C: it taught me the importance of getting the best out of what you've got.

11 D: everyone wants to listen to his voice …

12 A: they said only blind people listened to books on tape.

13 B: believe that I've really got a story to tell them …

14 C: Malcolm carefully does his homework …

Part 3: Face-to-Face with a Mountain Lion

15 C: Link between 'with my brother' and 'He encouraged me to tackle'.

16 F: Link between 'Farmers … were trying to rid the world' and 'And yet we knew almost nothing …'.

17 B: Link between 'This meant living in tents … intense cold' and 'But I was willing to give all that a try'.

18 H: Link between 'most of those had been shot by hunters' and 'So I moved next season as far from civilisation as …'.

19 A: Link between 'could not find enough lions for a valid study' and 'maybe my colleagues were right'.

20 D: Link between 'It was then that I felt those eyes' and 'I don't know how long we stared'.

21 E: Link between 'leapt into full view' and 'Then he was gone'.

Part 4: Just a Few Lines …

22   F: complaints or declarations of love … makes you feel better …

23   B: writes at least three letters each morning at a desk …

24   E: her secretary can type them up and fax them …

25   B: as important as talking to people.

26/7 E: Politicians … for them to use for letter writing …

26/7 F: is the agony aunt for a top weekly magazine …

28/9 C: I've got a cardboard box of them stored in the attic.

28/9 D: Fortunately, both parties have held on to the letters …

30   A: I include things in letters that I might not mention in conversation.

31/2 D: Even though a word-processor means … never quite so intimate …

31/2 F: I can't stand e-mail … they're so cold and concise.

33   D: the tone is lighthearted and amusing throughout.

34/5 A: What looks best is black ink on pure white paper.

34/5 C: He also chooses his note paper with care.

Questions **1–21** = 2 marks
Questions **22–35** = 1 mark

PAPER 2   Writing

Part 1

Question 1
Style: Formal.
Content: 1 Ask for an explanation of what the 'resource centre' offers.
  2 Ask if they have guided tours to see the wildlife and whether you can take your tent.
  3 Describe your interests (e.g. learn about birds, wild animals) and ask them to create a programme for you.
  4 Ask about sports you can practise and whether the price includes all food.

Part 2

Question 2
Style: Formal or neutral.
Content: 1 Say what you had done to prepare for the events that day (e.g. you had trained very hard).
  2 Say what happened on the day and explain why it was your greatest victory.

Question 3
Style: Formal.
Content: 1 Say whether fashion has become more formal / informal.
  2 Say what materials are used (e.g. leather, cotton), and whether it is comfortable (e.g. tight / loose fit).
  3 Say what colours are fashionable, what is the length of skirts, etc.

Question 4
Style: Formal or neutral.
Content: 1 Say what the advantages or disadvantages are (e.g. natural resources, future generations, mountains of litter, cost of recycling, time it takes).
  2 Give strong reasons to back up your opinions.

Question 5(a)
Style: Formal.
Content: 1 Say why you are recommending the book (e.g. well-written, interesting characters, thrilling plot).
  2 Give examples from the text to support your opinions.

Question 5(b)
Style: Formal.
Content: Say why you think the characters could / could not be real people. Consider their behaviour, feelings and emotions, their relationships and their appearance, in the context of their surroundings and the year / century when they lived.

The two parts of the Writing Paper have equal marks.

PAPER 3   Use of English

Part 1: The Earth Galleries

1 D **2** C **3** C **4** A **5** B **6** B **7** D **8** B **9** A **10** D
11 B **12** C **13** B **14** A **15** D

Part 2: Fading Memories

16	all	**24**	look
17	by	**25**	although / while(st)
18	for	**26**	at
19	signs	**27**	or
20	taken	**28**	make / help
21	up	**29**	them
22	to	**30**	stand
23	there		

Part 3

31 *too steep for me to*
32 *got away with stealing*
33 *not as / so popular as it*
34 *why she (had) called off*
35 *would be told / informed about*
36 *not to leave their*
37 *could not afford to buy*
38 *has lost interest in*
39 *not so / as easy as it*
40 *in case the car breaks*

Part 4

41	*prefer*	46	*one*	51	✔
42	*to*	47	*for*	52	*got*
43	✔	48	*it*	53	✔
44	*them*	49	✔	54	*ourselves*
45	*with*	50	*off*	55	✔

Part 5

56 *usually (adjective to adverb)*
57 *necessary (verb to adjective)*
58 *especially (adjective to adverb)*
59 *weight (verb to noun)*
60 *depth (adjective to noun)*
61 *alike (preposition to adjective)*
62 *variation(s) (verb to noun)*
63 *identified (noun to verb plus past participle form)*
64 *protection (verb to noun)*
65 *welcoming (noun to adjective)*

Questions **1–30** and **41–65** = 1 mark
Questions **31–40** = 2 marks

PAPER 4   Listening

There is a mark for each correct answer in parts 1–4.

Part 1

1 C **2** B **3** C **4** C **5** A **6** C **7** A **8** B

Part 2

9	*hairdresser's / hairdressers'*	14	*blue*
10	*beard*	15	*lawyer*
11	*budget*	16	*quiet / non-violent*
12	*film reviews*	17	*shy*
13	*doctor*	18	*make documentaries*

Part 3

19 C **20** E **21** A **22** F **23** B

Part 4

24 B **25** A **26** B **27** C **28** A **29** A **30** C

TAPESCRIPTS

Note: answers to questions are underlined in each script.

Test 1   PART 1

You will hear people talking in eight different situations. For Questions 1–8, choose the best answer A, B or C.

1

A: So, how was your briefcase stolen?
B: Well, I came into the restaurant and sat down over there, then I ordered lunch …
A: And you put the briefcase under the table?
B: Yeah, and I looked out of the window for a while, at all the people walking down the street. Next thing I look down and the briefcase is gone.
A: You'd better come to the police station with me. We'll need a full report.

2

Wondering whether a career in IT is really for you? Come along on Thursday 24th June, find out what is involved and get a free Technical Basics course. This will cover a full explanation of what is inside your PC. Networking will be discussed, and the way computers interconnect and communicate across local or international networks. All the basics of the world of computing will be introduced so this one day may be your chance to get a good start …

3

This is an amazing collection of stone figures, not just because the materials come from all over the world, but it's the way they've been arranged, in wonderful combinations of shapes and colours. Deep blues next to pure white, for example. It's similar to the effect of paint on a canvas, you really have to see it to believe it. My only criticism is that we are not told exactly what areas the materials come from. It would be good to have photos of each stone in its original environment.

4

We are looking for young people who are interested in work experience. Now, this is not as difficult as some youngsters think. They often have the idea that we won't accept them unless they're proficient at computers. In fact, we believe those skills can be learnt as you go along. What we absolutely insist on is that they should come to us knowing how to produce a letter without mistakes. Of course there'll be lots of problems to begin with, because working for the first time is difficult. But we'll teach them how to overcome these.

5

A: So, may I ask you how you found out about our hotel?
B: Oh, it was recommended by a friend of mine. I think she'd found the information on the Internet, but I'm not sure.
A: Oh, yes, we've had our own Web page for about a year. We're also listed in the *Best Guest Houses of the Year* book …
B: Are you? I've got a copy but I must say I seldom look at it!

6

I lived in a flat with other students and we were attending classes for three hours in the morning. Unfortunately the course level wasn't high enough for me, mostly I was revising what I already knew. But I'm pleased I went because before this trip I always thought I wouldn't be capable of managing on my own, and it helped me realise that I can … I would have liked to see the country … there was little time for that during the week and at the weekends we usually went to museums and galleries …

7

Let me start by saying this is not a book about fashionable eating habits. It's about how food production developed through the centuries. It is aimed at youngsters and so it contains lots of cartoons that give it a lightness of touch. Adolescents have long been exceptionally interested in food, largely because eating is so tied up with appearance and health. But they'll be disappointed if they buy it thinking it'll tell them what is good or what is bad for them.

8

When you go dancing, you don't want to have to take a taxi back home, that would make it a very expensive evening, so it's a good idea to arrange a lift back home with friends or take a bus if it isn't too late. But the main thing you have to remember is you'll be there for hours and dance to all sorts of music … you may not like some of it but you'll still want to dance all the time! So you'll need to put on something you'll be comfortable in all night. If your feet hurt, for example, you won't be able to enjoy yourself …

Test 1   PART 2

You will hear an interview with the dancer, Darren Fairweather. For Questions 9–18, complete the sentences.

Interviewer: With me today to talk about his life and work is the well-known dancer, Darren Fairweather. Darren, how did you come to take up dance as a child?

Darren Fairweather: Well, I had a childhood illness which left me rather weak on my legs and my father was keen that I should be able to play football, and be as good as other boys, and so he sent me to dance classes to strengthen my legs.

Interviewer: But why dancing classes?

Darren Fairweather: It was pure accident. At that time, the family was living in a town on the coast, and we were living next door to a ballet teacher, and it was she who suggested it.

Interviewer: And clearly, you got on well there.

Darren Fairweather: Yes, I went on to win a number of competitions, at first locally and then later at national level, which was how I came to be offered a place at the main College of Dance in London.

Interviewer: So, at the age of 16, you went to London to study dance, did you fit in easily?

Darren Fairweather: I did not. I was a poor boy from the provinces; I didn't have the same social background as most of the other students. So, I didn't make friends easily and I found myself being rather aggressive to cover my shyness.

Interviewer: So, it was difficult.

Darren Fairweather: Yes. But, the daily instruction in dance was so satisfying that it was all worthwhile. I had very little financial support, but the people working at the school were kind, they let me have classes for free as long as I worked in the kitchens at lunchtime, and I stayed with an aunt and uncle outside London because we couldn't afford accommodation in the city itself.

Interviewer: You must have spent half your time travelling.

Darren Fairweather: Yes I was up at around half past five in the morning and I travelled two and a half hours per day, six days a week. I did that for three and a half years. I probably wasn't getting enough sleep, but somehow you survive.

Interviewer: But you came to the notice of one particular teacher, the famous Lily Partridge, didn't you?

Darren Fairweather: Yes, I was very fortunate to have such a teacher, she was brilliant, although many people found her very strict, but that's not how I saw it.

Interviewer: She pushed you, didn't she?

Darren Fairweather: Yes. I was, I suppose, her favourite, and of course other people were jealous of that too.

Interviewer: How hard did she push?

Darren Fairweather: She didn't know the word tiredness, neither in relation to herself or others. She dedicated her whole life to dance and expected the same from her students.

Interviewer: People have said it was a fiery relationship, is that the case?

Darren Fairweather: Very. And I think she enjoyed people fighting back, she tended to destroy people who didn't. I don't understand why she didn't fire me, actually, because we had so many arguments. But at the same time, in rehearsal, I would work for her until I couldn't stand up.

Interviewer: So, would you go as far as to say that if it hadn't been for her, you wouldn't be where you are today?

Darren Fairweather: Oh I think that's certainly true.

Interviewer: So, you became a star when you were 22, dancing the lead role in a modern ballet. Tell me about that role.

Darren Fairweather: It was called 'The Circus' and it's a wonderful piece to dance. There are very few major roles in modern dance that can really fulfil you as that role does. But I remember just being very surprised by the excitement of the audience and the success of the piece, and all the fuss that was made afterwards.

Interviewer: And, since then you've made your name dancing without music, haven't you?

Darren Fairweather: Yes, I'd always thought that the dance was as important as the music as an art form, and you can almost create your own music if you perform in silence. And if there is music, I like the type of music that allows the dancer to be in control, I don't like to feel that I'm being led by any particular rhythm or direction in the music.

Interviewer: Darren Fairweather, thank you for being with us today.

Test 1   PART 3

You will hear five different women talking on the subject of happiness. For Questions 19–23, choose from the list A–F what each speaker says. Use the letters only once. There is one extra letter which you do not need to use.

1

My friends are forever worried about not having enough time to take it easy, and they praise me for my happy frame of mind. I tell them that a good laugh can in fact produce the same effect as a 15-minute rest, and with family and friends there are always plenty of chances! And it doesn't mean making fun of others, just seeing the funny side of things, even when something happens that's not exactly wonderful news.

2

I think what makes me a happy person is the fact that I always find something encouraging to say to people I like, about their successes, about how well they're doing, and it never fails to bring a smile to their faces … We all like to receive such comments from others. And, don't laugh, I've now decided to make a list of the people I care about, and of what they have achieved recently!

3

I greet each morning with a positive thought, it's my way of looking forward to the day. I know that from 9 to 5 there'll be very little time for relaxation, but that won't be a problem if I'm prepared for it. For lots of people, it's a fast coffee, a search for socks, catching the news headlines, trying to find the keys … I think of the sort of day I want to have, and I plan it that way. My day will be what I want it to be … I think that's the key to my happiness.

4

Why am I happy? Well, I should say that I have as many problems in my life as other people, but I suppose I always look on the bright side of things. Lots of people, if you ask them how they are, will say 'not so bad', or something like that. I always celebrate my successes, and I choose to talk about the positive things that have happened to me, work, holidays, whatever. It doesn't matter if they're only small things. And I'm never afraid I'll be laughed at …

5

I used to spend my days running around doing hundreds of things, and expecting everyone to agree that I was very good at everything … Then I decided certain things were important for me, and other things weren't. I now focus on these things only and give them all my energy. My days are still full, but the good news is I'm a happy person. I must say I sometimes laugh when I remember my former way of life!

Test 1   PART 4

You will hear an interview with the television actor, Simon McGregor. For each of the Questions 24–30, choose the best answer A, B or C.

Interviewer: My guest today is Simon McGregor, star of three of the most popular television series of recent years. But you haven't always been an actor, have you Simon?

Simon McGregor: Well, when I left school I wasn't sure where I was going.

Interviewer: But you did well at school, didn't you?

Simon McGregor: I passed all my exams, yes, but I knew I didn't want to go university. I thought I'd like to be an actor, actually, but I lacked the courage at that age to do anything about it. So eventually I went to a careers advisor, somebody whose job it is to advise young people about training opportunities, etc.

Interviewer: And was he able to help?

Simon McGregor: Well, he said, 'What do you want to do?' and I said, 'I'd like to be an actor' and he said, 'Well, there's no future in that, you know, what else do you want to do?' and I foolishly said, 'I'd like to be a big business tycoon' not really knowing what I meant by that. And he said, 'Oh right, accountancy's the thing for you then' and within three days I was a trainee working for one of the largest accountancy firms in Newcastle.

Interviewer: But the wrong thing for you?

Simon McGregor: Not really. It was a big firm which handled the accounts of lots of companies. It was fascinating, actually. I saw a huge slice of working life, you know, shipbuilding, food factories, big offices. I wouldn't have missed it for the world.

Interviewer: And you did that for a couple of years?

Simon McGregor: Three and a half. I was just six months away from qualifying.

Interviewer: Really? So it was a huge decision to quit. Has there been a time since, though, when you've thought, 'Should I have given it up like that'?

Simon McGregor: Not for a second.

Interviewer: But something must have led to a decision like that?

Simon McGregor: Well, in the meantime, I'd joined an amateur theatre club. We did about six plays a year, and I found that I was living for the evenings and weekends. The work I did during the day, although it was interesting, didn't mean anything to me at all. I got a place in drama school and, although it was tough, I've never looked back.

Interviewer: And whilst at drama school you worked as a busker, as a street musician, why?

Simon McGregor: <u>Financially it was a necessity, it supported me through drama school</u>. I used to play my guitar and sing in the underground stations in London during the Friday morning rush hour and I'd earn enough to buy food and stuff for the week.

Interviewer: And this interest in performing goes back to your grandmother, doesn't it?

Simon McGregor: Yes, <u>apparently she had once worked in the theatre</u>, although I never knew her. But what we did have at home when I was a child was a tin of theatrical make-up which had been hers. It fascinated us as little kids. My elder sister used to write plays for all family occasions and we would cover ourselves in this make-up and act them out, dressed in bits of old clothes.

Interviewer: And you describe yourself as a very shy person. Why so shy if you spent your young life performing?

Simon McGregor: I don't know. I also spent a lot of time walking alone on the hills with my dog.

Interviewer: But why do you want to perform if you're shy?

Simon McGregor: I suppose nobody likes being shy, not being able to cope in social situations, so <u>shy people are always looking for a way of joining in somehow</u>.

Interviewer: So does that mean that, as a shy person, you enjoy playing more exciting roles, because you can have a go at being the type of person you're not in real life?

Simon McGregor: Well, I'm not lacking in energy. I do put a lot of energy into my work and I like playing all sorts of characters.

Interviewer: But, on the other hand, presumably you play a role better if there are some similarities between you and the kind of guy you play.

Simon McGregor: Yeah. <u>I don't think that, on screen, you can play a character unless you find those similarities actually</u>. The audience knows if the actor is having to try too hard, it doesn't work.

Interviewer: I see. Simon McGregor thank you for joining us today …

Test 2   PART 1

You will hear people talking in eight different situations. For Questions 1–8, choose the best answer A, B, or C.

1

I'm drinking far too much coffee, and I know why. It's all this pressure at the office. I'd really appreciate any advice you can give me on how to cut down. Although probably what I should do is try to reduce my workload – I could discuss it with my manager. <u>At my last appointment</u> you advised me to replace it with a fruit tea. Problem is that's the same advice I've had from my mum ever since I was a teenager. It didn't work then, it doesn't work now.

2

We were four men in two small boats, I can tell you it was scary. Because in an instant you can find yourself thrown out of your seat and into the river, wondering when you'll have your next breath of air. Not easy to get back on the boat because for miles and miles <u>the river runs much faster than normal</u>. Luckily this part is also relatively shallow, and the river bed is sandy. At least we knew we weren't going to hit any big stones.

3

Patrick Stokes, star chef and restaurant owner, sets out to educate even the most timid of cooks. He offers sound advice on how to select the best fresh fish and shellfish from what is available in local stores and guides us through basic preparation techniques <u>with the</u>

<u>aid of clear step-by-step illustrations. This recipe collection</u> builds on the ideas he shared with us in last year's fish series on Channel 4. I'm sure he will have us all dashing out to buy lots of fresh fish!

4

Look, do you mind if we change the subject? We've been talking about your problems for a couple of hours, and we could go on and on for the whole day. There's nothing I'd like better than to be able to do something for you, but I find what you're telling me a bit sad … <u>To tell you the truth it makes me realise that I should have tried to help you a long time ago</u>. Anyway, I'm glad we've been able to talk without getting into a fight.

5

Have you ever asked yourself why it is that whenever we look in glossy magazines, we see nothing but pictures of rooms large enough to play football in, when most of us are struggling to find the elbow-room to play cards? If you're looking for ideas that are more than just dreams, <u>then look no further than Jenny Palmer's Compact Living. This is a gem of a little book</u>: practical, inspiring and, most importantly, realistic. There are some nicely thought-out ideas for storage as well as decorating schemes if you want to create the impression of greater space, and all on an affordable budget.

6

The bedroom is the first room I worked on when I did up my house and I still think it's the most successful because it's great for relaxing in. It's gorgeous in summer when it's hot – with the windows open you can look out on sky and rooftops all around you. I did it all myself, actually, I even fitted the radiators. I did something really silly when I put the shelves up there, though. I thought I'd measured the height of all my box files, but if I did, I got it wrong. <u>I had to cut every single one down so they'd fit</u>!

7

Everything to do with bats is the subject of a workshop in Cambridge later this week. The workshop is being led by Derek Dainton of the *National Bat Conservation Society* and it will include a slide show and the use of the latest technology <u>to allow people to first hear and then learn to interpret the calls made by these little flying mammals</u>. There will also be a chance to learn how to use an electronic bat detector. The day-long workshop will end with an evening walk, once darkness falls, along the river, when it should be possible to observe these fascinating little creatures in their natural environment.

8

A: Sorry Tom, we weren't expecting you so early, your room's not ready yet.

B: That's OK, all I need is a table where I can just sit down and do a jigsaw puzzle. <u>I need to unwind after the drive</u>.

A: Really? But can you concentrate when you're so tired?

B: Oh very much so. If I've had a stressful day, to sit down with a small 200-piece puzzle, perhaps with some music playing, is wonderful.

A: This is just one of those ordinary little cardboard jigsaw puzzles?

B: Yes. <u>It soothes one completely</u> and then, feeling that you've achieved something, you go off to bed feeling happy.

Test 2   PART 2

You will hear someone welcoming students to an English School. For Questions 9–18, complete the notes.

Once again it is time to welcome all the newcomers to International English School. I hope that at Reception you were all given your own complete guide to the activities we have prepared for you for the month you'll spend with us. If you haven't got one yet, don't despair, although <u>the Reception's run out of copies, there are plenty of them in the library</u>.

Now, you're all here to improve your business English skills and you'll be expected to attend two one-hour conversation classes each day, followed by grammar workshops. Don't worry, we've also allowed time for relaxation, and I'll tell you about that in a minute, but first let's get the serious matters out of the way.

Some of you may be unsure about the level of the course you've been put into. We've placed each of you at the level we think is ideal, based on the information you sent us about your previous studies. However, any concerns about your course will be dealt with by our Programme Office, and you are welcome to pay them a visit at any time.

This weekend, which is your first in London, we'll offer you what we call 'an orientation weekend' to help you get used to your new surroundings in an unusual and exciting way. So starting with Friday, in the morning we thought you'd want to get better acquainted with this city – we know that some of you've already visited a few museums in the neighbourhood – so a tour of London seemed like the ideal activity, and we've organised one for those of you who are interested.

In the afternoon we've planned games that'll help you get to know your fellow newcomers, as well as the School's current residents. You'll all be rather tired by dinner time so we thought you might like to see a film, which is free to all International School members.

On Saturday we are taking you further afield. Our Travel Club have organised a day out in Bath, a historical city. We'll be setting off at 10 a.m., on board a bus which we've hired for the day. Everything will be provided for you except refreshments which you'll need to get yourselves before leaving.

Talking of leaving, last year we had a problem when a few students did not turn up for the trip because there'd been a misunderstanding about the meeting place. To avoid a repetition of that, this time we'll all gather in the cafe instead of in the street outside the school. And please can I ask you all to be punctual, so that we can start off on time.

Right. Now on Sunday, we've left it entirely up to you how you spend the day, the morning and afternoon. Most of you will want to prepare yourselves for the beginning of your classes on Monday. On Sunday evening, however, at about 6 p.m., I'll ask you to come to the main lecture hall. No, it won't be another long talk by me, no. And it isn't a party either … it's for you to collect your study materials and meet your teachers. Don't you think that's a good idea? There'll be plenty of time for parties later in the month …

OK, that's all for now. Can I just remind you that for those of you who feel you want to make the most of your summer course in England, there are a number of extra classes you're welcome to attend. I'd advise you to try the Pronunciation Practice class which will help you feel more confident in oral interaction. If I were you, I'd avoid the advanced level special classes until your teacher tells you they're all right for you. Thank you for coming and welcome to our School …

Test 2   PART 3

You will hear five young swimmers talking about what's happened to them in the past year. For Questions 19–23, choose from the list A–F what each speaker says. Use the letters only once. There is one extra letter which you do not need to use.

1

I'm fifteen and I'm competing in the senior championships. Last year I had a shoulder injury, and it took a while to mend … I still swam every day, but I wasn't allowed to spend much time in competition. It was a bit disappointing not to be able to take part in tournaments and things. As usual, a lot of my time was spent preparing for my college exams because I've promised my parents I won't neglect my studies. They know I'd rather be in the swimming pool than the classroom!

2

Last year was an important time for me. I went to the European Championships in April and I came third in the 100 metres competition … Which was very good because I wasn't expecting to win any medals, I was very happy that I qualified to take part … And after the Championships I was invited to swim in a series of competitions in South America, and had a good month swimming in five different countries! My real medal ambitions are focused on 2004 …

3

Well, at first I thought it would be a difficult year because my trainer was out of action for a couple of months with a back problem. But I carried on training on my own and he was surprised at my progress when he came back. There was a national college competition in June – that was perhaps the biggest event for me – representing your university is a big responsibility. I hope to be able to do that again in New Zealand and Australia next year.

4

Oh, the past twelve months have been good and bad really … I broke my 100 metres personal best record in January and I knew I had the best chance of a medal for years … but then I started worrying about my future. I wanted to finish my exams and apply for a place at university. So in fact what I did was interrupt my training completely for several months. Didn't come near the pool … Now I need to work hard to get back to the level I had a year ago.

5

The past twelve months? Oh, they've been almost too busy, I had to be careful because the last thing I wanted was an injury … I got the Continental Cup in France and came first in the national summer tournament. I was really pleased about it all, because I started my swimming training when I was at school and then at college, and you know how some people believe that school sport can't produce champions … I'm always grateful to them for the encouragement they gave me years ago.

Test 2   PART 4

You will hear a radio interview with Ricky Foyles, a singer and songwriter. For Questions 24–30, decide which of the statements are TRUE and which are FALSE and write T for True or F for False in the boxes provided.

Interviewer: With us today is Ricky Foyles, a songwriter you might be familiar with if you are under 20 … Ricky, your songs are really extraordinary. Are they about real people?

Ricky Foyles: Well, yes, there's nothing in them that I've invented. For example my latest song, 'Sara Jane', is about a young woman I know well, and it's basically about her strength in a difficult situation. My subjects are people and events I'm familiar with, but not the well-known personalities everyone would recognise …

Interviewer: And people like that kind of subject matter …

Ricky Foyles: Yes, though you often have to listen three or four times to one of my songs before you realise that it's about something completely different from what you thought it was about. That's because I use everyday words, so you understand their meaning straight away. It's the message behind them that's more complex, what the song as a whole is really saying. I suppose the advantage of that is you don't get bored and tired of a song so quickly …

Interviewer: Would you say you're more popular now than you were when your album *Rocket Love* appeared last year?

Ricky Foyles: Mmm … I've always dreamt of selling millions of records, but that hasn't happened of course. I've got faithful followers, though, and I know that I'd be able to fill a 500-seat concert hall now, just as easily as I did two or three years ago. When my next album appears, that will certainly change things, that'll be in about six months' time

Interviewer: So you might make a fortune then …

Ricky Foyles: Well, funnily enough I've always written my songs for the pleasure of it. The financial side of it has never been the driving force.

Interviewer: So is your new album very different from what you've done so far?

Ricky Foyles: Well, for a start, I took into account what some of my fans had said about my songs. They'd said I only write about what's unhappy, you know, they asked me to be a bit more optimistic. Well, I find that strange, because on the whole I think my songs are about real life, and in real life it's not always summer time … But I've tried to give it a more positive flavour, see what happens.

Interviewer: Do you like meeting your fans at concerts?

Ricky Foyles: You know I've mixed feelings about that. I think most of my fans buy all my albums but few have actually seen me perform. You know, there are 40,000 people out there who just love me. They've got all sorts of expectations. Now coming face to face with me is often a bit of a let-down, they don't expect that I'll be grey-haired and clearly well into middle age … But we manage to have a very good time together in spite of that …

Interviewer: So are you writing more songs at the moment?

Ricky Foyles: Oh, sure, I need to have a new challenge all the time. I'm convinced my next album is going to be better than anything I've produced so far.

Interviewer: Well, we all wish you the very best of luck. Ricky Foyles, thank you for talking to us today …

Test 3   PART 1

You will hear people talking in eight different situations. For Questions 1–8, choose the best answer A, B or C.

1

Following the success of last night's performance by the New York Dance company, we'll have the pleasure of talking to one of its brightest stars after the 6 o'clock news. Clive Franceschi and his group delighted the audience with the grace and speed of their movement and we are sorry this was their last night on a London stage. So if you want to find out more about them, tune in after the news!

2

We need to have a serious discussion about this. Your design for the school is excellent, but we've found a few problems. We liked the office areas in particular because it'll give tutors the space they need. However, some of the students are not happy with the study rooms you are proposing, they think they're too small. Do you think you can still do something about that? I can have all these points typed up for tomorrow.

3

We know pollution is destroying the planet. We have more than doubled the amount of harmful substances in the environment, destroying plant life in the process. We may wipe out two-thirds of animal life on earth within the next 100 years, that is most birds and butterflies, for example … A major problem is that we don't know enough about many of them, some have not even been recognised scientifically. We need more research about them to be able to protect them.

4

We all know the school is facing financial problems, so as from next week we've been told everyone using the school's computer services will have to pay a small sum. This applies to those of us on the staff

as well. I've been asked to give you the information and to report your reactions to the Head … I can understand your frustration because I was also a student here in the days when nobody had to pay for anything.

5

For me this is the ideal tent. I spend a weekend in it at least once a month. I paid £400 for it, and as you see, it isn't the kind of tent which gives you lots of space. But then that's not what I was looking for when I bought it. The main thing is that it is stable, so it won't let me down in bad weather. The last thing you'd want is a leak, isn't it? It takes me about an hour to put it up, probably longer than other simpler ones, but I don't mind that at all.

6

Kangaroos are Australia's favourite animal. They're most famous for the way they get around – by hopping. They cover vast distances and travel quickly without getting tired. Special tests to study kangaroos as they hop have been given the go-ahead by animal experts. The tests are vital in the study of these amazing animals in their own habitat. The animals won't suffer at all and it's a good way to see how much energy they use when they're on the move when compared to humans who soon run out of breath.

7

Weather for tomorrow? Well, it should begin fine and dry, though with cloud increasing during the afternoon which could bring a small risk of a light shower after the sun goes down. Temperatures? Well, a touch up on today's, rising to 19 or 20 degrees Celsius by midday and then falling off slightly. There will be moderate, occasionally fresh, south to south-easterly winds all day. So that's the weather and I'm Colette Crowther at the Eastern Weather Centre.

8

Newsreader: Two fire crews from Denbridge were called to a blaze in a chicken shed containing 3,000 birds just before midnight last night. None of the chickens in the shed in Upwell Road was injured and the fire was quickly brought under control. It's thought that an electrical short circuit in a refrigeration system was the cause. The owner, Doreen South, who lives nearby, first reported the incident. She had praise for the fire service.

Doreen South: I was standing in the kitchen, washing up, when I noticed the smoke. I called the emergency number and I must say the engines were here in about 10 minutes. They were brilliant … just wonderful.

Test 3   PART 2

You will hear an archaeologist talking about her job. For Questions 9–18, complete the sentences.

My name's Anna Sage and I'm an archaeologist. What does an archaeologist do? Well, an archaeologist studies the remains of ancient civilisations, and these remains are usually found buried in the ground. When I was about 13, what first made me want to become an archaeologist was seeing a film about it.

History was a favourite subject of mine at school, but sitting in the library reading facts was not enough for me. With archaeology, you're involved in finding things and it attracted me because I'd always wanted to do a practical activity. I now work for the Museum of London's Archaeology Service. My office is right in the centre of London, and that's wonderful because this area is rich in ancient remains. The Service employs about 200 archaeologists and last month, during an excavation, we discovered a very old church. You could even see the street pattern, because we had dug up a very large area.

But my work is not always so exciting. I work in an office as well as in the excavations, so I spend much of my time working with the reports that the senior archaeologists write. I have to read them and put them in files.

In the last year, we have worked at about 200 different 'sites' – that is what we call the places we dig in search of remains. Now, for each of those sites, you have to find the person who did the work and make sure the plans and photos of the excavation are all where they should be. Sometimes they aren't, and that means you have to chase the person to get the material you need. It can be very frustrating …

When I'm working at a site, typically I start at around 8 a.m., I start digging and when I find an interesting piece, say a piece of pottery, the first thing I need to do is clean it and after that I draw the piece. This may sound strange but it's got to be done because we need to understand the piece found in relation to the site.

What we tend to find most frequently is not so much pottery, although there is a lot of that as well, but tools. There are lots of those, sometimes five metres below the modern surface of London, or very near the surface when you are near the river Thames. Sometimes I could spend a day just cleaning a wall that was built 900 years ago, and that may sound boring, but it isn't when you think you're finding out how and why it was built.

It's hard physical work if you're digging all day. At a busy site, you often have to work in a basement. This can be most unpleasant as it's very hot and dusty there. But on the whole I enjoy my job. It is surprising the amount that's still there left to dig up. When we find the remains of people who lived hundreds of years ago, thanks to scientific techniques, we can now even find out what their diet was.

Much of the work that the Archaeology Service does involves giving help to builders. They have to understand and respect the law that protects archaeological sites, so if they're planning, say a new road, we have to be involved as well.

I suppose a very good aspect of this job is that you work with very enthusiastic and motivated people. Generally, there isn't a lot of money in it. It isn't well paid compared to what a lot of graduates get. I earn about £14,000 a year. But then I'm doing a job that I'd do for pleasure, so I'm not complaining.

Test 3   PART 3

You will hear five people saying why they became professional artists. For Questions 19–23, choose from the list A–F what each speaker says. Use the letters only once. There is one extra letter which you do not need to use.

1

I began painting portraits when I was eighteen, but to begin with I was an amateur, I wasn't thinking of taking it up as a profession. At school I'd been good at a number of things, and my teachers all thought I'd be a lawyer one day. I'm sure that would have been a more profitable career, because artists don't make much money. As it happened, by the time I left school, I'd had enough of books and research and was keen to devote my time to something more practical. My parents weren't too happy with my decision, but are now pleased that I'm doing something I like.

2

Oh, my decision to become a professional sculptor was a bit of an accident … I studied art at college and then took on a teaching job, teaching young people how to make things out of stone. At the time I thought my teaching skills were better than my skills in sculpture. Then a very successful sculptor who lives in the north of Scotland contacted me to say she could do with somebody to help out in her studio, would I consider becoming her partner. Well, she didn't need to ask twice, I knew immediately that I wanted to do it. I never even asked what sort of income I could expect!

3

I wouldn't have become a professional painter had it not been for my family. I was in my early twenties when I discovered that I had a gift for painting, but at first I never even thought it might be the career for me. I had a job as an assistant in a local shop and the money I earned there was badly needed at home. The job in the shop was time-consuming and finally I decided to ask two of my aunts, who were well-off, for a loan so I could give it up and open a studio. Now I get lots of orders from galleries and private collectors.

4

Oh, becoming a professional fashion designer was not easy. I did computer studies at college, and had always been brilliant at mathematics, so you can imagine that design was not what I had in mind as a profession. However, one day I was invited to design clothes for a college performance and what I produced was considered to be pretty impressive. The first suggestion that I could become a successful designer came from a friend who had a job in the fashion industry. It took her a few days to make me see the idea in a positive light, but she succeeded.

5

Why did I decide to become a professional painter? Well, I didn't have much of a choice. My grandparents and my parents were all artists, but found it extremely hard to make a living out of it and would have given anything to make sure that I chose a different profession. However, I was good at painting, and when I lost the job I had as a secretary in a lawyer's office I found that although I spoke foreign languages and could type well, there were no jobs for me in the area where I lived. I knew then that I had to turn my attention back to painting.

Test 3   PART 4

You will hear a conversation about three films, 'Imitation', 'Midday Train', and 'Postman Gregg'. For Questions 24–30, decide which of the following is said about each film. Write I for 'Imitation', M for 'Midday Train' or P for 'Postman Gregg'.

Man: That was really a record for us, seeing three films in one weekend. *Imitation* on Friday, *Midday Train* on Saturday, and *Postman Gregg* on Sunday …

Woman: Yes, but they were three films we very much wanted to see, weren't they? And they'd all been strongly recommended … To tell the truth, I found *Imitation* a bit disappointing in some ways. The characters are such … unpleasant people … their personalities … the way they behaved, I wish there'd been at least one I could say I liked. Very different from *Postman Gregg* – in that I felt you could really identify with the characters.

Man: Well, I agree with you about *Imitation*, but you must admit it's superbly acted, particularly the leading roles. I'd be surprised if one of them didn't get an Oscar. Same can't be said about *Midday Train*, though. What did you think? The leading actor wasn't convincing at all … he seemed to be making too much of an effort.

Woman: Yes, you may be right. But isn't it an amazing story … this man whose life depends on the arrival of the train. It's very well done. And a lot of it's true as well, that's what makes it interesting. The real man only died last year. Did you know that?

Man: No, I didn't. That's weird, isn't it? I must say I hadn't read much about *Midday Train* … I'd expected it to be about a train journey. But I was wrong there, wasn't I?

Woman: I had read a lot about it, actually, which was a pity because I already knew how it ended …

Man: Well, it's a predictable end, really, not surprising – the train does arrive and our hero is saved …

Woman: Yes, I suppose you're right. It's the kind of film where you expect a happy ending, and sure enough, you get it. <u>Not like</u> <u>Postman Gregg. Who'd have thought he'd finish up in prison</u>?

Man: Exactly. But you come to expect that kind of a twist with certain directors … so that didn't bother me at all. I liked it actually. What did bother me, I don't know about you, was <u>that you had to</u> <u>concentrate all the time, and even then I often lost the thread of</u> <u>the story</u>. I suppose it's because it kept moving between the past and the present all the time.

Woman: Yes, I had the same difficulty. In that respect I prefer *Imitation* <u>where the story follows the adventures of the three young</u> <u>men and their journey through Europe</u>. I liked all the thrills and action in it. I only wish they'd shown more of the countries they go to, you know, the landscape and the people. I thought I might be able to recognise a few places …

Man: Yes, there wasn't much of that, was there? That's what I liked about *Midday Train*. The main character never leaves the small town, <u>but what wonderful views you get of the area, those</u> <u>amazing hills and lakes</u>, they add so much beauty to the film.

Woman: Precisely. With *Postman Gregg* you don't expect to see anything much, because most of the film takes place inside courtrooms and police stations. There are hardly any open-air scenes. It's a good film, though, in spite one or two odd bits …

Man: Oh, yes, I wouldn't argue with that. I prefer *Imitation*, though.

Woman: Mmm, my favourite is *Midday Train*, no doubt about that!

Test 4   PART 1

You will hear people talking in eight different situations. For Questions 1–8, choose the best answer A, B or C.

1

Let me just repeat our competition of earlier this morning. This is to win yourself one of those lovely burgundy-coloured T-shirts with the name of the programme on it, plus a key-ring with a rather fine bird of prey on it. And the question is, <u>what was the name of the</u> <u>screen heroine</u> who gets swept up in a whirlwind and finds herself in a magical land. First name will do, full name even better. Write it on the back of a postcard or envelope to the usual address which I'll give you in just one moment …

2

The time is just coming up to twelve minutes to eight. No travel bulletin, I'm afraid, this morning for us, for reasons beyond our control – <u>no one is available in the travel section</u>. But I can tell you some travel news, so far, things are quiet on the roads and we hope it stays that way. And we will have up-to-date travel bulletins throughout the rest of the day here on Radio 236 at the regular times of quarter to and quarter past the hour.

3

It's the latest must-have item for the style conscious amongst you. Hackers are made from heavy-duty nylon so they're <u>tough enough</u> <u>for even your heaviest, dullest schoolbooks</u>, but they are also packed with the sort of design detail that cybersurfers demand. So if <u>you'd like to throw the ultimate statement of post-millennium</u> <u>techno-cool over your shoulder</u>, then the number to call for Hacker stockists is 7011 871 3505.

4

Well, the island itself is sub-tropical with mountains, lakes, streams, etc. In terms of wildlife, there's a bit of everything there and <u>it</u> <u>would really be a great place for people to go and study all kinds of</u> <u>natural things</u> because there is very little human activity there at all. The only real risk to the place comes from a plan to build a holiday resort there which would have the effect of turning the island into a kind of holiday paradise for those that could afford it. For me that would really endanger what is, after all, a world heritage site.

5

Actually, two of my favourite bits of the festival are probably <u>bits</u> <u>where the music hasn't actually got under way yet</u>; which would be early on the Friday night when, you know, the bands are unpacking and tuning up and <u>there's that air of expectation all around</u>, and then one of the loveliest moments is the Sunday morning, I think, if you've been camping there, you get up and <u>everything's just so</u> <u>relaxed after all the excitement</u> of the big-name performances of the night before.

6

Outdoor shopping will get a boost in the city of Dorrington today with the opening of what's called a farmer's market. This is a new movement, already popular in the USA, which is now being widely introduced in a variety of areas in Britain. The idea is that local farmers can sell their produce direct to the customer. Farmer's Market stalls must be attended by the person who actually grew or produced everything on sale, <u>meaning that shoppers can talk to them directly</u> <u>and be sure that what they buy is healthy</u>. All goods must have been grown or produced within a 50 kilometre radius of the city.

7

I was canoeing down the river with a friend. I saw there were hippos on the bank – they were coming into the water. There were hippos underwater, coming up to look at us. It was getting a little scary. Hippos make these noises and you feel the vibrations up through the canoe. I saw this big, beautiful hippo come off the bank, mouth open, water spraying, charging right toward us. I quickly started pushing my oar onto the water with no results. My companion also slammed his oar on the water and broke it. <u>Our screaming and</u> <u>yelling did the job</u>, and the hippo went underwater and away.

8

There are many reasons why we should reject this proposal for a new restaurant so near our primary school. This development would only encourage car use and my primary concern is over <u>the impact</u> <u>of traffic on the children</u>. The supporters of the proposal are arguing that there aren't enough restaurants in this area which provide food of the quality and standard we all expect. I believe this is untrue, we have enough quality restaurants and food shops and I would like to ask everyone who agrees with me to reject the proposal.

Test 4   PART 2

You will hear an interview with a man who plays the traditional Australian musical instrument called the didgeridoo. For Questions 9–18, complete the sentences.

Interviewer: The didgeridoo is the traditional musical instrument played by the aboriginal peoples of Australia. Today didgeridoo enthusiasts from all over the world will be gathering in England for a celebration of their favourite instrument. So, just before things got started, <u>I went along to the concert hall where the meeting is being</u> <u>held</u> to find out all about it from the organiser, Bob Corbett. Bob, it's such an incredible instrument, first of all, can you describe it for the listeners?

Bob: Yes, sure. They are made from eucalyptus wood and this comes from particular <u>trees that have actually been hollowed out by</u> <u>little insects</u>. What in fact happens is that these attack the live wood, eating through the middle of the tree, so that you're left with a tunnel inside. And then an aboriginal chap will come along, cut the tree down and get all the insects out, so that they don't continue to eat the wood. And <u>he'd finish it off by applying paint to</u> <u>the outside of it in a traditional pattern</u> because these instruments aren't carved or stained in any way, it's just a piece of tree that's been painted.

Interviewer: So it's a long, hollow tube of wood basically?

Bob: That's right.

Interviewer: Now, you're something of an expert on the instrument, I know Bob, but you're not actually Australian, are you?

Bob: No, that's true, I'm English, but I wouldn't say that I'm an expert, I've just organised the event here in England.

Interviewer: So how did you become interested in didgeridoos? Was it the history of the instrument, or what was it?

Bob: Well, I've always liked the sound. It's very different to western instruments because it doesn't really play a tune, it's just very wonderful. Although the instrument is very ancient as well.

Interviewer: Do we know how far back it goes in history?

Bob: Well, there are various estimates and they are based on images found drawn on the walls of caves in Australia where people appear to be playing didgeridoos. The skills are passed down from generation to generation amongst aboriginal people.

Interviewer: And how old are those images?

Bob: They are thought to be around 30,000 years old. But given the nature of the instrument, and what they're made of, none of them actually survive that long.

Interviewer: And it's a living tradition?

Bob: Oh yes, they're being made and played today.

Interviewer: Tell me. How easy is it to learn to play?

Bob: I think it's relatively straightforward to get a sound out of one, as long as you've got someone to show you. The only thing is, you've got to stop yourself from laughing because if you smile, you won't be able to do it at all.

Interviewer: So it's a serious business?

Bob: You've got to look serious and, once you've got a noise out of it, you've got to keep the note going and to achieve that you need to learn to control your breathing. That can take a bit longer to learn.

Interviewer: I think I'll leave that to the experts then. But tell us about some of the things that are happening at today's event.

Bob: We've got workshops for people who want to learn to play, from absolute beginners upwards. Then we've got a 'make and play' workshop where people will be able to make their own instrument and take it home with them at the end of the day. And we've also got displays of aboriginal art and culture.

Interviewer: Everything to do with didgeridoos in fact?

Bob: That's right and a bit more besides.

Interviewer: I was talking to Bob Corbett, and if you're interested …

Test 4   PART 3

You will hear five writers giving advice to young people who want to start writing stories. For Questions 19–23, choose from the list A–F what each speaker says. Use the letters only once. There is one extra letter which you do not need to use.

1

It's difficult when you're asked to give advice to youngsters … because they may want to be different, and maybe they think, well, I don't need advice. What I can say to them is that knowing exactly what you're going to write about, that's important … and making sure that the subject you've chosen is something you're really familiar with. When I wrote my latest book, there was going to be an elephant in the story, so I read a lot about them and even visited the zoo to take a closer look at them. If you've done the hard work, then the writing itself is easy, the language will just flow …

2

Oh, well, I know exactly what I'd say to new writers … We all started our writing careers by imitating the authors we admired, and there's nothing wrong with that … sometimes we copied their style, or even their stories … Developing your own will come later, so to begin with it is essential to write down all the little things that happen to

you day after day, keep a record of all that, because it will enrich your writing. Never mind if they seem unimportant and boring, good stories are often made up of apparently insignificant details …

3

When I started writing I found that managing my own time was difficult. I had lots of ideas, and thought, well, this is such a good story line and nobody's ever written anything like it … But my mind was all over the place, and writing was just one of my interests, so I'd say when you write, do as I did in the end … I chose to have a rather unusual view out of the window – a brick wall! Anything to make sure you don't get distracted. I kept a record of how many words I wrote a day, and that helped too.

4

I didn't read a book until I was about eleven … it was then that I discovered the pleasure of reading … and then I'd read any stories I came across, sometimes I barely understood the language, so many long, difficult words I didn't know … I'd spend hours looking them up. I didn't mind that as long as the stories were different and special. New young writers should try to produce stories which are their own, seeing the world through their own eyes, not those of the writers they admire. We can give advice, but only up to a point.

5

When somebody decides to write stories, it's usually the case that they've been reading stories for a long time, and maybe thinking, well, I could do this just as well, or even better. Trouble is young writers often think that in order to be better, they've got to use lots of long words and complex sentences. That's their idea of originality. Nothing is further from the truth. Keep your attention on getting the message across, whether it's an everyday personal experience or a science-fiction story that's involved days of library work in preparation for writing.

Test 4   PART 4

You will hear an interview with a young TV soap opera star, Jack Benton. For each of the Questions 24–30, choose the best answer A, B or C.

Interviewer: Hello and welcome to *One to One*. In the studio with us today is Jack Benton, who plays the leading role in the TV soap opera *Teenagers*. Jack, have you always wanted to be an actor?

Jack: Well, I've always wanted to act – it's the only thing I knew I wanted to do. I started acting when I was still at school. One day I went along to a TV studio to meet a TV star with a friend. As we got there, we heard one of the actors had suddenly decided to accept a job offer in another studio. Believe it or not, I was offered the job then and there. I'd planned to go to drama college and get a degree in cinema studies, but things just happened differently.

Interviewer: Do you find acting difficult or is it fun?

Jack: I really enjoy acting, not just because *Teenagers* is the first acting job I've done, but because I really get into it and it's a real challenge acting side by side with all the big stars. I find it hard learning what I have to say, though, I need to read through the scripts several times! I play the part of a really nasty guy, and I'm often asked if that's hard. It's not, really, and I won't suddenly turn into somebody like that!

Interviewer: Do you ever worry that fame may go to your head?

Jack: No – my mum's definitely going to keep my feet on the ground. She still makes me do the washing-up, you know. And she insists I keep doing the usual things, like going round my mates' houses and sitting in the front room watching films and things. She's read lots of books about what fame can do to people, how an actor can have a real change of personality.

Interviewer: What type of clothes do you like to wear when you're not playing your TV role?

Jack: I love really casual clothes. And I love the 'old school' type of trainer – I don't really like all the new multi-coloured ones. I'm not after the latest fashion at all. My friends say some of the things I buy went out of fashion years ago! The truth is I can now afford all the gear that I wouldn't have dreamed of a few years ago. The price is no longer an issue.

Interviewer: You have a group of very good friends. What is it you like best about them?

Jack: Oh, I don't know what I'd do without them. I like to be able to have a laugh with them and forget all the stress of work, they're great at that. You see, fans are OK, but they're not real friends. When they come up to me, I often run in the opposite direction. Friends are different, well, mine are, anyway. They often tell me what's bothering them, for example, and I know they're not thinking I'm a big star, I'm just a friend.

Interviewer: Jack, you seem to be very fit. Is the gym one of your favourite places?

Jack: No, the gym's a place I never ever go to, as it happens! I'm afraid my excuse is simply lack of time. I'm sure it would do me a lot of good, although as you say I basically look really fit, in fact I'm not as strong as I look. At school I used to play a number of sports and was never much good at any, I'm afraid. I couldn't understand how my friends found them so exciting!

Interviewer: One last question, Jack. What are your dreams for the future?

Jack: Well, like most young actors, I have quite a few! Getting an award for my role in *Teenagers* is top of my list at the moment. And I've been offered the opportunity to play a minor role in a film, which is tempting because it might lead to other cinema roles. Also films are shown all over the world. You might think this sounds strange, but I'm not keen on that kind of success, it is too frightening.

Interviewer: Thank you, Jack, it's been wonderful to have you in our studio.

Test 5   PART 1

You will hear people talking in eight different situations. For Questions 1–8, choose the best answer A, B, or C.

1

Scientific discovery can inspire and fire the imagination whether you're a leading scientist of the day or a small child discovering how something works for the first time. When you walk into *Wonderworld*, you're in an interactive experience which offers you the chance to touch exhibits and so extend, in an entertaining way, the knowledge of the world you've gained through reading. The team at *Wonderworld* has worked hard to create an environment where all visitors are able to embark on a journey of discovery and participation by making active use of the facilities available.

2

The old man lived in a small house in the village. He was said to be unpopular with the younger inhabitants because he was always telling them how to do this and how to do that. 'You should use a different type of wood to build a fence like that' he'd say to the local carpenter. Can you imagine? The man had almost finished making the fence. His answer is said to have been: 'Give me exact instructions and I'll follow them next time.'

3

Mark was in the area for just one day. He wanted to go up what's called Black Mountain which can be rough going, rockfalls sometimes blocking the paths. He asked for my advice and I said, 'Don't do it.' I'm usually reluctant to give advice, especially if I don't know how fit the person is, but that wasn't the problem in this case because Mark does a lot of walking. There was a long walk just getting to the base of the mountain, let alone the time it takes to go up and then down again, so it couldn't be done in a day, even if the paths *were* clear.

4

I go to *The Barn* restaurant fairly often. It's the sort of old-fashioned place where you know you'll get good generous helpings. It's also good ordinary food, nothing exceptional, if you know what I mean, but tasty and healthy. But then I took a friend there the other day, and we ordered the usual steak and roast potatoes, and I couldn't believe my eyes when I saw the half-empty plates they put in front of us. The prices seemed to have gone up too, although I couldn't say for sure because my friend picked up the bill at the end and paid for us both.

5

Well, everyone wonders what it is that I do in the dance company. There are twenty-five dancers at the moment, all employed full time. I work as an assistant to Mike Braggs who is the one who actually teaches the movements for the various pieces we do. My role is to go through the hundreds of applications from dancers wishing to join the company so that I can interview and pick out the ones we want. It takes up a lot of time, so we've now taken on somebody extra to make the travel and accommodation arrangements when the company's on tour, because I used to do all that myself too.

6

The greatest asset in any organisation is those people who continuously increase their knowledge and abilities, at least that's what the authors of the book, 'Training and Promotion' say and I entirely agree. I give my employees time off for keeping up-to-date because I believe you can't expect them to both do that and work an eight-hour day. And I make a point of going through their work once or twice a week to show them there's somebody in the organisation who actually takes an interest in their performance.

7

If you sail to see the dolphins in one of Terry's Boats, satisfaction is guaranteed. After twenty years of running these trips, Terry's confident of finding dolphins somewhere in the bay. But, if you should happen to be disappointed, a full refund will be offered. During the trip you can also enjoy a three-course meal in the restaurant on board as the boat takes you through some of the finest coastal scenery in the world. What's more, there's no charge for children under five and Terry will give you a free repeat trip if you come back with a group of friends.

8

I always say to young people, it's not easy when you're starting out. Trying to make a living out of writing is just as difficult as trying to make a living on the stage, and I should know as I've tried to do both. Indeed, that's what young writers and young actors have in common. Strangely, most of them will need to supplement their income by training others. I certainly had to do that, although in my case it eventually turned into a full-time occupation. Others have managed to combine it with other theatre work or writing, but I'm afraid that's not something I was able to do.

Test 5   PART 2

You will hear part of a radio programme about restaurants in London. For each of the Questions 9–18, complete the notes.

Tonight we're taking a look at three of the city's leading restaurants. Our idea was to find places where not only is the food good and the service all you'd expect it to be, but where you also get a good view at the same time.

Well, the first restaurant on our list was *The Blue Restaurant*. Now this is not a new place, but if you've been before, then you might like to give it another try because there have been a number of improvements here in the last few months. The glassing in of the balcony is certainly a plus as far as the view is concerned. We'd advise you to sit on the balcony and enjoy the excellent views of the River Thames, whatever the weather. If it gets too hot, the glass slides back and you're in the open air, but if it gets chilly or starts to rain, then you can quickly be covered up again. Another advantage is that, from here, you get excellent views of Tower Bridge, which is not really visible from the indoor tables.

The resident chef, Jamie Heybridge, has a passion for fresh ingredients and this is reflected in the excellent menu. Look out for dishes with a strong Mediterranean flavour and we'd like to particularly recommend the Spanish cheeses, which are really exceptional. If you prefer to go for something sweet rather than cheese to finish your meal, however, then you can't get more traditional than apple pie, and nobody can match Jamie when it comes to this truly English delight.

Our next stop is at *Tamsin's* restaurant. Those lucky enough to book a window table can enjoy a wonderful view; the length of one of London's most fashionable shopping streets laid out before them, because *Tamsin's* is situated right in the heart of the city's West End on the eighth floor of an elegant eighteenth-century mansion. What's more, if you visit in the wintertime, this is also absolutely the best place in London to sit and enjoy the Christmas lights. It's warm and comfortable and you couldn't be closer.

As far as the menu is concerned, it's the starters that really grabbed our attention. The chef is Greek and there's a strong Greek flavour to many of the dishes. The Greek salad was actually one of the best we've ever tasted outside Greece. We had just the right quantity and the mix of flavours was just right. *Tamsin's* also offers an excellent mushroom soup served with delicious slices of home-made bread. The main courses are all worth trying and vegetarians are well catered for here.

Finally, in contrast to the fashionably casual atmosphere in *The Blue Restaurant* and *Tamsin's*, *The River Restaurant* has been trading on its particular mix of formal dining and comfortable service for decades. Don't be taken in by the name, however, the view is fantastic, but it's actually not of the river this time. The best place to sit is on the covered terrace which has wonderful views over London's most beautiful park. And dominating that view, just below the restaurant is the elegant lake. You could be miles away from the city in this wonderfully peaceful setting.

When it comes to the food, you can choose between Italian and Far-Eastern cuisine. We would most definitely recommend the smoked duck to anyone who hasn't tried it. Nowhere in London does this sort of food better and everything is so beautifully served. The most important thing, however, is not to go mad on too many courses because it would be a shame not to leave room for *The River Restaurant's* real speciality, its incredible ice-creams. These are a real work-of-art, and have to be seen to be believed. If you can bear to spoil the intricate designs, you'll find the mixture of flavours out of this world.

So, three restaurants with a view as well as good food and service. Next week, we'll be …

Test 5   PART 3

You will hear five tour guides saying why tourists value their work. For Questions 19–23, choose from the list A–F what each speaker says. Use the letters only once. There is one extra letter which you do not need to use.

1

Well, I think what tourists most want is to have a good time. They're usually well-read about the historic sites and the attractions of this area because there are so many publications now, and they buy them and read them before they leave home. But when it comes to finding reasonably-priced amusement in the evening, I know all the best shows in town. Tourists don't need guides to take them to museums because most museums have their own guides, and for tourists who don't speak English they've got recorded commentaries in different languages.

2

I don't expect tourists to speak English, and they appreciate that. Sometimes I get groups of four or five different nationalities, and here my knowledge of their languages is put to good use. They are so pleased they don't even mind when I'm unable to answer some of their questions about historical events! Good tour guides have to be very sociable people and I've always been shy, so it hasn't been easy. There are tourists who'll expect you to join them for an evening's entertainment as well. Frankly, after a whole day spent on my feet, all I look forward to is a good night's rest.

3

Most people believe a good tour guide must have the answer to every question. Well, I'm not ashamed of telling tourists I need to find out the information they want. I've never had any complaints, though. On the contrary, I've had letters from tourists who've gone back home, saying how much they appreciated my services. And I think it's because I always take into account the interests of the tourists I'm helping. You don't take a group of adolescents to museums all day, but that may just be what an older group wants. You need to be flexible.

4

Why do tourists consider me a good tour guide? I always make an effort to ensure that they get their money's worth, and that means paying attention to detail, because tourists want everything to go smoothly. I take groups of tourists on excursions to different cities and I plan everything personally, from departure to arrival back at their hotel. I even hire translators for people who don't speak English, because my own knowledge of languages is very limited. And for tourists who may be interested in a particular subject, I get experts who take them to museums or historical sites.

5

I'm not that good at working with the younger tourists. I believe that they're more interested in having fun in the evening than in learning about the history or the architecture of this wonderful city. The tourists who really like my style are the older ones, who appreciate my commentaries, which are well-organised and documented, even if sometimes a bit long. I moved to this city four years ago, so I'm not a local, so to speak. Even so, I think I've become an expert in the development of the city from the Middle Ages to the present.

Test 5   PART 4

You will hear a radio interview with Ella Webster, a fashion photographer. For Questions 24–30, decide which of the statements are TRUE and which are FALSE and write T for True or F for False in the boxes provided.

Interviewer: Ella, every time a member of your fashion team sets off on a trip to some exotic location, we all feel very envious …

Ella: Yes, most people would consider it one of the best jobs in the world. At the beginning of a season I can stick a pin in a map and go off to some glamorous destination. So how can I tell you that without fail, each time I have to go away, the days before I go are filled with a sense of dread. Seems a waste, but I'd live without all the jetting around if I could.

Interviewer: So once you're at your destination, can anything go wrong?

Ella: Well, there's a lot of pressure to come back with photographs that will transport the reader to paradise. This is not an easy task when the models are in a bad mood, the hairdresser's depressed, that sort of thing. All of this has happened to me and yet the editors, understandably, want happy, smiling, pictures, with blue sea and blue skies. You can't blame them for that, they're only doing their job.

Interviewer: You've just returned from Mauritius. That place really is paradise, isn't it?

Ella: Oh, yes, but we were there to work, remember? We needed to shoot three different fashion stories, one was the Paris collection, then swimwear, and last the casual travel collection … so we had several assistants, the make-up and hair team, and four models. What we were not expecting is that because it's so gloriously hot and sunny, we couldn't shoot between midday and four in the afternoon. Sounds good until you have to get up at four-thirty in the morning to be ready as the sun rises.

Interviewer: And then I understand you had an unpleasant experience on the way back?

Ella: Yes, the flight lasts 13 hours, four to Nairobi, then there's an hour's stopover there, and then another eight hours to London. Well, three hours into the flight the captain told us there was a problem and we wouldn't be able to land at Nairobi. A plane skidded on the runway and wouldn't move. I suppose we would have felt worse if he'd told us there was something wrong with our plane …

Interviewer: So you flew direct to London?

Ella: No, because we did not have enough fuel, so we landed again four hours later, in Uganda. We were then told we had to stay in Uganda at least eight hours for the crew to rest. I wouldn't have minded that so much, except that we had to take all our luggage with us. Locating all our suitcases and bags and loading them on to minibuses was a nightmare, 25 suitcases containing thousands of pounds worth of clothes, plus three trolleys with expensive photographic equipment …

Interviewer: So it was one of those trips when absolutely nothing goes well …

Ella: The photos were OK, so it was worth it in the end. I think, though, that the true value of the experience is what it taught me about the members of my team, it was wonderful to see how supportive of each other they were. I'd had this idea that in this profession it was everyone for himself so to speak. So, in that respect it's been very positive.

Interviewer: So you think you'll continue in this job for the foreseeable future?

Ella: In spite of everything, I know I'd find it difficult to do a nine-to-five office job, even if that job was a well paid one, so I don't have any ambition to become a magazine editor or anything like that. On the other hand, I realise that it is time to look around for a job that's physically less demanding. I'm in the process of making my mind up.

Test 6 PART 1

You will hear people talking in eight different situations. For Questions 1–8, choose the best answer A, B, or C.

1

Woman: Peter! At last! So how did you get here?

Man: By train. Then I walked from the station, it's only about ten minutes. By the way, this place looks a bit dark, doesn't it? And it's almost empty. Do we really want to eat here?

Woman: Well, there's a better restaurant down the street, if you'd rather go to that. It's right by Benton's grocery store.

Man: Yes, let's try that. And I can buy a couple of things I need on my way back. I tried the station shop but they didn't have them.

2

Hi, there. It's Jack Brown speaking. I'm phoning about the report you asked me to write. I know I'm late, I should have finished it by now, but I haven't been feeling well for the past two days. I promise it'll be on your desk on Monday without fail … yes, I know an important contract depends on it, I'm aware of that. Anyway, the medicines I'm taking seem to be working, so I hope I'll be back in a few days.

3

I've been hiring cars from this company for years and up to now I'd never had any complaints. I haven't always had the latest models, but that's fine. I've told them that I hate driving very large cars along these narrow roads, it's true. But that doesn't mean I wanted one with hardly any room for a piece of luggage, which is basically what they've given me! Well, I'm a good customer, a careful driver who never goes above the speed limit. You'd think they'd try to keep a customer like myself happy!

4

Goodness, that was an expensive vase that got smashed. Now, we need to explain what happened to the hotel manager. We were both going upstairs, right? And somebody was coming down, and the vase was on a shelf where the stairs turn. The woman who was coming down was carrying a rucksack on her back, and I moved aside to let her pass. Yes, there's no doubt about it, is there, it was my elbow that knocked it down, the woman never even touched it. And you did your best to save it when it toppled down the stairs. OK, let's go and see the manager.

5

You know David, don't you? Well, he's got a car now. He's just passed his driving test. Yesterday, I was driving along with my daughter when I noticed he was right in front of me, driving his car. Now, can you believe this, his two dogs were in the back of his car, jumping around, you know. My daughter thought it was really funny but I'm afraid I failed to see the joke. I was concerned he might pull up in front of me, because I wasn't sure he was paying attention to his driving. Well, I thought, he'll be wiser when he's a bit older …

6

Well, I'd go for the Dorian Hotel if I were you. It's a difficult choice between the Dorian and the Windsor, I agree. Both have pleasant and helpful staff, and large seating areas, which is important if you're forced to stay indoors in bad weather. Now, you're going on holiday with children, so what you need is a hotel that's within walking distance of the main places of interest for visitors, and there's no better than the Dorian in that respect. As long as you don't expect the breath-taking views you get from the Windsor, the Dorian should be ideal for you.

7

Now, you might be lucky and have a huge and fertile vegetable patch, or you might have very little space in your garden, but have you thought of putting in spinach with your sunflowers or cucumbers next to the chrysanthemums? Well, Tanya Pollard is a well-brought-up cook, she learnt at her mother's knee that you must eat your greens, and she's just written a book on the subject. Jenny Harris is the author of *Creative Vegetable Gardening* and she's bursting with tips on how to cultivate your summer salads. Jenny, how nice can you make a garden look that has lettuce or rocket in amongst the flowerbeds?

8

The college building is brand new. You see, it's got everything you could possibly need from a first-class library to a state-of-the-art sports centre. And now they're building a new media centre too which is good because it's going to attract large numbers of students. I only wish they'd also enlarged the academic staff. We are really overworked trying to cope with the growing numbers in classes. I mean, after all, when they get snowed under in the admin section, they bring in a temp, don't they?

Test 6 PART 2

You will hear part of a wildlife programme which is about birds called waxwings. For Questions 9–18, complete the sentences.

Interviewer: In today's programme we are featuring a bird that is only rarely seen in Britain. They are called waxwings and have appeared suddenly and in unusually large numbers over the last few weeks in eastern England. I went to the small town of Ferringham earlier this week and met up with local expert Paul Baker. Before long we came across a group of around <u>twenty waxwings resting in a tree in the town's car park</u>. I talked to Paul there.

Paul Baker: What we are seeing is really a mass invasion of waxwings into this country. This has happened during the last two weeks, but it seems the birds are still arriving.

Interviewer: They are such colourful birds, as they fly by, you can see <u>they are largely pink and grey</u>, but they have red and yellow tips to their wings and tail.

Paul Baker: Yes and these tips look as if they've been dipped in wax, hence the name waxwing.

Interviewer: I can't believe how close they are coming. I can see <u>they also have really beautiful black marks on the face</u>, it looks almost like a mask.

Paul Baker: Yes. They are similar in size to the common blackbird, but rounder in shape.

Interviewer: Where do they come from, Paul?

Paul Baker: Well, people look at them with their parrot-like colours and assume that they must come from the tropics or somewhere to the south, but these are birds that have actually come here <u>from the north of Europe</u>.

Interviewer: So they come here just at certain times. Is it something to do with the weather, do you think?

Paul Baker: I think it's less to do with the weather than it is with the fact that there must be <u>a lack of food in the places where they normally live</u> this time of year, and that could be due to a number of factors.

Interviewer: So there might be some years when they don't come to Britain at all?

Paul Baker: There are plenty of years when we don't see them at all and, although <u>I think a small number do come here every winter</u>, you'd never see them in the summer months. But I think this year we're talking about thousands of birds, and to see so many at once is exceptional.

Interviewer: So why do they stay together in such large numbers like this?

Paul Baker: Because they're looking for something to eat and at this time of year, <u>for waxwings that means berries</u>, they do eat other things, but they are not so keen on seeds as some birds. And that's why they travel in groups because they're all looking for the same thing.

Interviewer: And the really good thing about these birds is that you can get a really good look at them without having to go out into the wilds to find them.

Paul Baker: <u>Yes they appear regularly in people's gardens</u>, we've had lots of reports of that locally in the last few days. So they are not the sort of birds which are shy of people or who avoid built up areas at all.

Interviewer: And if people want to attract waxwings into an area, what would you suggest they do?

Paul Baker: Well, a good tip is to <u>get a slightly rotten apple and hang it from a tree</u>, it's not their favourite, but it's the sort of thing they'll happily come and feed on as they pass through.

Interviewer: And as we're talking, I can hear this beautiful birdsong all around us, is that the waxwing's call?

Paul Baker: Yes, it is. It's a very distinctive call and probably the first sign you get of waxwings in your area is when you hear that call. People say that <u>it sounds more like an insect than a bird</u>.

Interviewer: Yes it's lovely. Well, something to listen out for then, because I'm sure all of our listeners will be hoping to see waxwings in the next few days.

Paul Baker: Oh yes, everybody loves to see them.

Interviewer: I was talking there to Paul Baker in Ferringham.

Test 6 PART 3

You will hear five people saying why they like reading novels. For Questions 19–23, choose from the list A–F what each speaker says. Use the letters only once. There is one extra letter which you do not need to use.

1

Oh, I love novels, especially if they have a good plot. I started reading them when I was 12, encouraged by my parents who were hoping I'd be a writer myself one day … As it happened, reading so much at an early age had an effect on my studies, my compositions were always very good! And I still read at least one novel a week. <u>My own life isn't terribly exciting</u>, apart from my work, which is very interesting, nothing much happens. In the novels I read there's always a lot going on, lots of thrilling events, <u>and I can share in the experiences and problems of the characters</u>.

2

Well, I used to read only short stories. That changed when I moved to a new city and found myself in a job I didn't really enjoy. I would get back home at about 5 p.m., make some supper and sit down to read a novel for the rest of the evening. Many of them are pretty unbelievable stories, and not particularly well-written. It's not as if you can imagine yourself in any of those situations, but <u>the thing is they take my mind off whatever's worrying me</u>. I've had long conversations about this with friends who think I should read better quality stuff, but I know what I'm doing.

3

Why I like reading novels? I remember as an adolescent, I used to read novels <u>just so as to see how my favourite characters solved their problems</u>. I thought I could then apply that to my own problems! And I'm not ashamed to say <u>that's still the case</u>, that's what I'm looking for in the novels I read, and that's my reason for reading them. I always choose novels that are in a clear style, because I find complicated language difficult. And also I like the stories to be about countries and cultures I know well, because then I can understand the characters better.

4

I think reading novels is helping me a great deal in my studies, and although I haven't got much spare time, I always make a point of reading a couple of hours in the evening. I'm in my last year at secondary school, and frankly, <u>reading novels is an excellent way of learning how people live in other countries</u>, how they communicate with each other, what problems they have. That's why I prefer novels with characters who are true to life, not the ones who have impossible adventures. I'm very lucky because my best friend also likes reading and we can often discuss what we've both read.

5

I like reading novels because they <u>help me develop the ability to write myself</u>. I used to have real problems in producing a good piece of writing. It wasn't that I lacked ideas, no, my teachers always said my compositions were interesting. <u>But I couldn't get my tenses right. That's where reading novels helped</u>. I don't think you can learn much about other things from novels, because the situations are usually so unrealistic. Some people say that's OK, if your life's boring, you need the excitement of fiction. Well, my life's exciting enough, so that's not my problem.

Test 6 PART 4

You will hear two people talking about holidays. For Questions 24–30, decide which of the views are expressed by either of the speakers and which are not. In the boxes provided, write YES next to those views which are expressed and NO next to those views which are not expressed.

Sally: Hello, Tom. You look very relaxed.

Tom: Do I?

Sally: Did you have a good holiday?

Tom: Well, I have been in the sun, abroad actually.

Sally: Really?

Tom: Yes, although as you probably know, I spend most of my holidays in this country with my family. But I had a reason for changing that this year. Until last Christmas, I was the manager of a football team. And then I resigned, you know, I got fed up with it. Anyway, I thought the team might ask me to go back to the job, so I decided it was best to be out of the country at the beginning of the football season.

Sally: So you wouldn't be tempted?

Tom: That's right.

Sally: Oh I see. So, where did you go?

Tom: I've been to Ibiza, the island in the Mediterranean.

Sally: Oh really. I went there myself once.

Tom: Did you?

Sally: Yes. I didn't pay, mind you. I got it free.

Tom: How come?

Sally: It was about ten years ago. I remember it was a travel company which has since gone bankrupt, which is hardly surprising actually, and they were being criticised in the press for the way they organised their package tours to such places and so what they did, they paid for a whole party of journalists like myself to go to Ibiza.

Tom: Great!

Sally: Well, we had a really dull time there actually.

Tom: You didn't like it?

Sally: Oh it's a lovely place, no it wasn't that, it was because they insisted on entertaining us, you know, they wouldn't leave us alone to enjoy it. For instance, one day, I think it was the Sunday, they suddenly announced that we were going on a trip to a salt works. You know, those salt evaporation places. As it happens, I'd already been to one and once you've seen one, well, I mean, they're all alike. It was so boring.

Tom: But I can't imagine you liking a beach holiday, I have to say.

Sally: You're quite right. I set out with good intentions, you know, with magazines to read, towels to lie on and all that, and I sit there. But you can't get comfortable, whichever way you turn you start to get burnt, so you put on that sticky stuff and then you get sand in everything, and so I generally give up after half an hour or so.

Tom: Well, there's a slightly more civilised way, you know. I tend to sit at a poolside with a sun lounger and a chair, so there's no sand and you can read if you want to, and if you start to get too hot, you can jump in the pool to cool off.

Sally: I know a lot of people who like that and I wish I did, but it's funny, I find it difficult to sit by a swimming pool and do nothing. I think of all the streets I haven't walked and the hills I haven't climbed and the shops I haven't looked round, you know, I can't get comfortable just sitting in the sun. I've got to have someone to talk to or something to do.

Tom: But I'd have thought you were quite a reader.

Sally: I read slowly.

Tom: But you could read for three or four hours couldn't you? If you had a good novel?

Sally: Anywhere but on a beach.

Tom: Really? So what's your idea of a good holiday then?

Sally: The best holidays I ever had were the ones I spent in Ireland. I've got such happy memories. It was spellbindingly beautiful, I just loved the countryside and then there was the …

Test 7 PART 1

You will hear people talking in eight different situations. For Questions 1–8, choose the best answer A, B, or C.

1

Complaints about the country's railways are at their highest level ever. The National Rail-user's Committee says it received 19,000 complaints last year, 27% more than in the previous 12 months. Delays, cancellations and overcrowding were the most common concerns. However, David Driver, the committee's chairman, says that in fairness to the railway companies, it must be said that the last quarter of this year has seen an improvement, which is a step in the right direction, but that a great deal more remains to be done to provide a better service.

2

It all started when I bought a washing-machine from a superstore and arranged for it to be delivered the following Saturday morning. When Saturday lunchtime came and nothing had turned up, I phoned the shop. The manager made enquiries and promised to get the machine delivered the next day, Sunday. Fifteen minutes later, however, the new washing machine arrived, so I phoned the manager, who expressed surprise, and said that he would cancel the Sunday delivery. Then, on Sunday, yes you've guessed it, a second machine turned up. Well it was hardly my fault, and I'd been very polite up till then, I mean, what would you have said in my place?

3

We've been very impressed by the community spirit of people in the Orville region. We've collected more than a thousand signatures from people concerned about the building of houses on the woodland and many people have come forward to actually help with the delivery of leaflets and that sort of thing in the hope of stopping it going ahead. I think it reflects the strength of opinion locally about what is a valuable site for wildlife populations, and people want an answer. I'm sure that when the council finally meets to decide this issue once and for all, the voice of local people will have to be taken into consideration.

4

Woman: I've officially closed the business now.

Man: But why, when it was going from strength to strength, why close it when you could have sold it to someone?

Woman: Well, I'd done it for nine years and it became, in that time, the largest of its kind in Europe. Although to be honest, it was all in my head, so there was only the goodwill to pass on really, and the phone numbers, so it wasn't that big. No, I just got fed up with it and thought it was jolly well time to try my hand at something else.

5

The City Library is set to introduce round-the-clock opening for a trial period of six months. The rapid growth of information technology in recent years has made it possible for customers to access the services they need without the help of staff. Customers will be able to issue and renew their own loans outside core hours using the new technology in the same way as the banks offer services to their customers through cash machines. The library will continue to operate a fully-staffed service during normal opening hours.

6

Woman: As a writer, you rely absolutely on your imagination. How do you separate the good ideas from the bad?

Man: You put them down, you work on them, and you see if you can make them into something that will appeal to someone else's imagination. If it doesn't work, you put them into a little notebook called 'ideas'.

Woman: Really? And do they stand the test of time?

Man: If you leave them long enough, until you've done other things, had other thoughts, and you come to them afresh, then they may mean something else to you. It's like having a new idea.

7

Until 1997, Jason Foreman was safely settled in a teaching career. He spent his days helping youngsters achieve their goals while his own creative ambitions went unrealised. Then, one day, in a move that few of us would be brave enough to make, he gave it all up and took up his wood-working hobby professionally. For most of us, facing the life of the artistic designer with all its insecurities, would not be at all easy. But luckily for us, Jason hasn't looked back and the exceptional wooden bowls and vases he makes have been an overnight success.

8

Woman: And our next caller to the advice line is Tom Smith. Hello, Tom?

Man: Yes, hello. I've just redone my sitting room and I'm short of an old leather sofa to complete the look, if you know what I mean. I'm after something that's both comfortable and well-seasoned, you know, something that's seen a bit of life! Where should I start?

Woman: Well, I know exactly the sort of thing you mean. They are very sought-after these days, I'm afraid, so you'll find it will set you back a bit financially.

Test 7　PART 2

You will hear part of a wildlife programme about a snake which comes from a group of islands in the Caribbean. For Questions 9–18, complete the sentences.

Interviewer: Almost exactly a year ago, five racer snakes from a small Caribbean island began their journey from their native land to the Wildlife Preservation Trust in Britain. All part of an emergency rescue operation by the trust to save one of the world's rarest snakes from extinction. With only about fifty of them left living in the wild, it was hoped that the snakes would breed safely in Britain and the babies could be returned to the island. With me is the leader of the project, Martin Dale, who has some good news I think?

Martin Dale: Absolutely fantastic news. As you say, it's twelve months since I very nervously carried five adult racer snakes across the Atlantic to Britain.

Interviewer: How did they settle in there?

Martin Dale: Very nicely and we had eggs by last autumn, after which we had to keep our fingers crossed for a while as we waited to see if they would hatch. Now we can actually announce the great news that we have five baby racer snakes, which represents a 10% increase in the world population. This is better than we could ever have hoped for.

Interviewer: And are they male or female, or a mixture of both?

Martin Dale: At this stage we can't tell. We can't handle them because they're too small and delicate at the moment.

Interviewer: Well, obviously, you're very pleased, but this is just the start of the project, isn't it?

Martin Dale: Oh yes. The whole point is to take the snakes back to the Caribbean, and there we're looking to move the project forward in a number of ways. Firstly, in the Caribbean people are working on the establishment of a nature reserve on the island itself.

Interviewer: That's the island these snakes come from?

Martin Dale: That's right. And then they're also working on

education. A public awareness group is working on the island, and not only with the local people, because the island attracts around 20,000 tourists each year, although it's only very small.

Interviewer: Really?

Martin Dale: Yes. It's quite a busy place actually. Then, thirdly, in terms of research into the snakes themselves, we have a leading researcher, Dr Heather Dayton, who is currently counting the snakes on the island. And the first signs are, again, very positive. The population is beginning to increase there too.

Interviewer: And why is that?

Martin Dale: It's because we've been successful in removing the rats and the mongoose that were attacking the snakes. Both of these animals were introduced to the island at the time of the sugar plantations and they have attacked the native wildlife. But we seem to have got rid of them now.

Interviewer: How do you know?

Martin Dale: Well, the young racer snakes that we are finding now don't have all the teeth marks that are left after such attacks, if the snake survives.

Interviewer: I see. Well, I hope that you'll keep us informed, Martin, because we'd love to know when the little snakes finally do return to the island and how they get on there.

Martin Dale: It'll be a pleasure.

Test 7　PART 3

You will hear five students who want a summer job in an office saying why they are suitable for the job. For Questions 19–23, choose from the list A–F what each speaker says. Use the letters only once. There is one extra letter which you do not need to use.

1

I think this is just the job for me, working in an office is boring for some people 'cos you need to do the same thing again and again, like writing letters and stuff like that. I've always liked to make sure that what I write is perfect, and I'm not saying my grammar or my spelling are very good, but I check everything several times, for even the smallest mistakes, if necessary I'll look up a word or ask somebody if I'm not sure, even if it's only a comma. And I always do that at college, too, when we work in groups.

2

Well, maybe the first thing to admit is that I'm not the sort of person who'd enjoy working with a lot of other people in a large office, but I'm sure I'd adapt quickly. I've devoted hours to finding out about this job that's on offer, and about the structure and development of the company – I found lots on their website – and I feel I understand it though I've no real experience of work. I think it's important because I've discovered, for example, that they have started a number of new projects that I'd love to be involved in.

3

Oh, I'm very keen on getting this job for the summer, it would be really exciting and a great way to gain some experience of work. I don't know a great deal about this company but I've been told they are involved in research, and I think I have a lot to offer in that field, I've developed lots of projects at university. I'm quite good at planning them and seeing them through to completion. And my final reports have always been praised for being concise and clear, though I admit my grammar and spelling often needed some improving.

4

I think for this job, well, probably I'm a good candidate. I have no difficulty whatsoever in producing a piece of writing, say a report, that's accurate, you know, something you can read easily and understand without problems. It just comes naturally to me, and I never need to check it for errors. I'm not terribly good at working under pressure, though, particularly if I'm part of a team and I'm expected to work quickly. But from the little I know about this company, they seem to have a very relaxed attitude.

5

What makes me good for this summer job? Well, I've got lots of enthusiasm, which is important, I may not be brilliant at communicating with people, and my eye for detail could be better … I know that employers value all this but I believe that what they value even more is an ability to be part of a working group where everyone's contribution is important. I have a lot of confidence in myself when it comes to sharing responsibility with others. That's definitely my strong point and if I get this job, I'm sure my other skills, including language, will improve greatly.

Test 7   PART 4

You will hear a radio interview with Dominic Austin, a science-fiction writer. For each of the Questions 24–30, choose the best answer A, B or C.

Interviewer: With us in the studio today is Dominic Austin, a science-fiction writer who has delighted readers of all ages … Dominic, I read somewhere that you found it very easy to get published …

Dominic: It's true. I was very lucky. But with *Return to Nothing*, my first book, I had a problem. I sent it to a firm of publishers and they kept it for about six months. They finally sent it back to me, saying the way it was written was very original and the story was amazing, but they were unwilling to publish it because it was rather a large book and they were a tiny company. They advised me to contact another publisher who they knew were looking for science-fiction writers. I had no trouble after that.

Interviewer: In *Return to Nothing* the three central characters are completely imaginary, aren't they?

Dominic: That's right. My characters are different from real people. The main thing is that in a good adventure story the characters must have some sort of evolution, for example they come to have knowledge that they lacked to begin with. And it doesn't mean they always go from being bad to being good at the end of the story. I don't believe in that. My heroes are not particularly loveable.

Interviewer: After *Return to Nothing* you went on to write a series of three other books with the same central characters. Why?

Dominic: I started *Return to Nothing* with one book in mind. It sort of progressed from there, and it went to another book, then it went to a third book. The publishers knew they'd be an instant success. But writing a good series of books has one unwelcome consequence: I get a lot of requests from readers for more books in that series. I love the fact that they bother to write to me about it. But I also need to do something different and recharge my batteries.

Interviewer: Your success has not yet led to any literary prizes. Do you regret that?

Dominic: Not in the least. I'm a story-teller, and story-tellers want an audience. The more people who read me, the happier I am. So all the other stuff to me has no meaning. I've always believed that when writers win prizes, their careers are over. But everyone seems to think I'm dying to win awards. I read a lot of fiction, too, and sometimes I wish I'd written some of that. But I know I'm just as good, only different.

Interviewer: I understand you regret having allowed your book series to be made into a film …

Dominic: Most definitely. It was a moment of foolishness when I thought: 'There's no one in the science-fiction field who's ever been offered this chance.' I somehow knew I was making a mistake, but my pride got in the way, and then it was too late. It was a difficult experience because the director was asking me to change parts of the book all the time. I knew from the beginning there'd be little

money in it anyway. Maybe the only advantage is that it was an experience I could use in my writing.

Interviewer: That's very interesting. Can I ask you, as child, were you an avid reader?

Dominic: Yes, I think I was. My childhood background in reading is rather strange. My mother was a history teacher and very much wanted to introduce me to all the interesting historical characters she was so familiar with. Those were her bedside stories! She got me into that habit, and as soon as I could read myself I was rereading all that. I also went through a phase when I liked reading poems, but by that time I was an adolescent.

Interviewer: Finally, Dominic, there are so many novels on the market, readers are often at a loss what to buy. Any advice?

Dominic: Oh, yes. First, ignore what the critics say. They are frequently wrong, or rather, they don't know what you like. Some readers like to have information about the writer, a kind of biography of the author. I'm against that approach because it won't tell you much about the book you're interested in. A more reliable method is to skim through the first few pages of the book to see if it holds your attention.

Interviewer: Dominic Austin, thank you …

Test 8   PART 1

You will hear people talking in eight different situations. For Questions 1–8, choose the best answer A, B, or C.

1

Man: They're never included in the price, you have to buy them separately.

Woman: Of course. How silly of us not to have thought of it in the shop.

Man: Silly of us? You're joking. I don't see why they can't sell you the batteries at the same time, or at least tell you when you buy the thing that you'll need them.

Woman: Toby's going to be so disappointed if he can't play with it in the morning.

Man: I know. I've a good mind to write to the shop, I mean it's just not good enough, is it?

2

I know some people complain about having to do it, but actually I don't agree with them. What with our lives getting more and more isolated by computers and telephones, not to mention cars, opportunities to meet people are getting fewer and fewer. So I think, as long as you're not in a hurry or anything, it can be quite fun. Of course, you have to make the effort to talk to the people in front or behind you, but if you do, they usually respond. I've made some really good friends at places like ticket offices and bus stops, you'd be surprised.

3

The thing about hats is that no one of my age wears one, except maybe baseball caps, and I've never even had one of them. But then I had to wear the full gear for a wedding recently, and I hired a suit and all that and, of course, the top hat came with it. They measured me up for it, you know, so it was the right size and everything. But when it came to it, I carried the hat round most of the day, because it made me feel like a fool. Everyone said how nice it looked, but I just couldn't get used to the idea.

4

I was brought up in the city, but was dragged off to a country cottage at the weekends. I hated those weekends. I mean what's the point of sitting in the country when everything you might conceivably want to do takes place in the city. The obvious feature of the countryside is that there are very few people there compared to the city. But since other people are what makes life worth living, I can't see the attraction of it. Peace and quiet is OK occasionally, even I can enjoy the odd day of relaxation, but it gets anyone down after a while surely?

5

I've got an eight-year-old son and when I pick him up from school, and I'm waiting for lessons to finish, I'm able to look through a window into the classroom. And whenever I see him in that way, I feel as if I'm spying on him because I'm thinking, 'Is he listening?', 'What's his body language telling me?' and I must say I feel incredibly doubtful about doing this. I instinctively feel that it's not right, if I want to know how he's getting on at school, I should go and ask his teacher or whatever. I feel I'm spying on him, looking into his world without his consent.

6

This afternoon I'm going to be joined by Arthur Shilton, whose series of science-fiction novels have won him respect all over the world. But he's not going to be talking about them, he's going to be giving listeners some handy hints on writing books. So any budding authors, or people who just want to record their memories, or whatever, should give us a call if they'd like their chance to put questions to Arthur Shilton, the famous science-fiction author. And here's the number …

7

Eating out on holiday is often a time for special treats and rich food. But a survey by the Health Authorities suggests that 97% of people want the choice to eat healthily when they are out. We asked a team of nutritionists to evaluate the menus available at a range of tourist attractions around the country with a view to assessing how much choice and healthiness was on offer. Their initial findings reveal a number of shortcomings, especially in children's menus. The most common problem was the lack of fruit and vegetables and the predominance of high-fat items. In today's programme, a representative of …

8

So, it sounds like something of a recipe for disaster this evening. The appalling conditions are set to continue, I'm afraid with quite widespread falls of sleet on top of the impacted ice and we've already got some trouble in the Pelham area where a lorry has shed its load of onions after skidding in the blizzard. You're advised to take great care if you're out and about, although all routes are clear at the moment. The only other thing to report so far is that efforts are still being made to right that overturned milk tanker I told you about earlier, although most of the milk has now been cleared from the carriageway.

Test 8   PART 2

You will hear an interview with the actor Alex Beringer. For each of the Questions 9–18, complete the sentences.

Interviewer: Hello and welcome to *Film File*. With us in the studio is Alex Beringer, who has gone from daytime soaps to roles in Hollywood films. Alex, you started in a rather unexpected manner, didn't you?

Alex: Yes, it was my birthday and I was going to have a party in a music club. I'd decided to have my hair cut and I was sitting in the hairdresser's, when this man came in and said he thought I had the face he needed for one of his films. Next day I was in a studio …

Interviewer: Wonderful! But I understand you were asked to make a small change …

Alex: Oh, yes. It was funny because I'd dressed in the best clothes I had, in fact a pair of faded jeans and jacket. He gave them a disapproving look but made no comment about them. My beard was a different story. I had to shave it off at his request.

Interviewer: Is it true that you were not paid for this part?

Alex: Only a small amount as the budget was small. The big money would come later, I knew that. It had nothing to do with my being inexperienced, as has been suggested.

Interviewer: Had you ever imagined you might take up acting?

Alex: My mum was a cinema-goer, and there was always conversation at home about film stars. She would read film reviews to me, while my Dad was busy reading science fiction! So when I became an actor she was really pleased …

Interviewer: Was your father pleased?

Alex: My father's a doctor. At that time I suppose I saw his work as very trying, and he knew how I felt. He'd say to my mother how pleased he'd be if I followed in his footsteps … She usually said she'd rather I was an architect! Anyway, he was pleased when I got my first part in a film.

Interviewer: And after your first film you wanted to play other similar roles?

Alex: Not really. I wanted to change myself in some way. I had two days off between finishing one film and starting another and the roles were totally different. I wanted to do something drastic so I dyed my hair blue. The producers almost had a fit. In the end it wasn't too bad because the actress who played my girlfriend had pink hair.

Interviewer: You have played a number of nasty characters, haven't you?

Alex: In my first film I was a factory worker who didn't get on very well with his boss, and then, I was a youth who gets into trouble with the police in another one. But if you look at later roles, they're very different. In my latest film, I'm playing the part of a lawyer who has to defend a rich businessman.

Interviewer: And what sort of characters do you enjoy the most?

Alex: I have to admit I'd rather play quiet characters. Of course, I've played violent types as well, and quite successfully. But not out of choice, if you know what I mean.

Interviewer: Do you get on well with your colleagues, other stars you meet on the set?

Alex: Oh, I'm a very polite sort of person, so I tend to get on with people. Famous stars are often shy, that's a fact. They can appear to be cold and indifferent, but when you get to know them, you discover that's not the case at all. Being famous isn't easy.

Interviewer: Do you find fame difficult to deal with?

Alex: My girlfriend is a star herself. It used to be that we could go out to dinner and no one would care much. Now we can't go to the movies on a Saturday night anymore. The late show on Wednesday, maybe, but you can tell when people sitting round you are trying to catch what you're saying.

Interviewer: Have you any unfulfilled ambitions?

Alex: I'm not going to say I want to write a book! Because it's not a question of sitting at your PC for a day and producing a best-seller … in fact I've never given up the hope that I might make documentaries. At the moment I'm doing some research into the subject, and I'll see how it goes.

Interviewer: Alex, thank you for coming …

Test 8   PART 3

You will hear five students saying what makes them successful in their studies. For Questions 19–23, choose from the list A–F what each speaker says. Use the letters only once. There is one extra letter which you do not need to use.

1

What makes me successful in my studies? I'm certainly not somebody you could describe as studious, you know, the kind of student who will devote serious time to reading and rereading stuff … Probably I don't need to do that, <u>I'm always wide awake when the teachers are explaining things</u>, I can take in a lot like that. I think that's it really. All I need to do later is have a glance at the notes I've made, to make sure I'll remember things, otherwise I'd soon forget them.

2

Well, I think my approach to studying is a bit different … At college you're expected to read and study a lot of stuff, and honestly, <u>quite a lot is not really essential. I don't bother with all that</u>. That means I've got time to concentrate on the rest … I could spend hours reading all sorts of additional information, which is no doubt very interesting, but I choose to ignore it. I often try to help friends by telling them to do it my way, but what works for me may not work for others, of course.

3

The secret of my success? I'm not terribly good at learning new things … as a child I'd learn things by heart, like poems for example, but then my parents would give a hand … Now I'm on my own of course, and I know perfectly well that <u>I need to devote more time than others to my studies</u>. And that's what I do, <u>I give it as long as it takes</u>. Some of my fellow students concentrate better than me during lectures, maybe that's why they don't need the extra study time.

4

Well, <u>whatever I read stays in my head</u>, so it does. I must admit my mind's often somewhere else when I'm in class, but then I know it won't take me very long to look at things at home, maybe a couple of hours a day, which is less than most students need, that'll be enough. <u>Next day I can even recall the unimportant details</u> … My teachers want me to make the most of this ability and they give me extra stuff to read. But I can't be bothered to tell you the truth. I'm doing well enough as it is.

5

I think I'm a successful student because I don't rely 100% on my own abilities. I know what my weaknesses and strengths are, so <u>I don't study on my own</u>. I'm good at maths and physics, for example, but a disaster at writing. <u>I wouldn't be any good without a hand from classmates who are good at that</u>, who can read a literary essay, say, and understand its main points in no time at all. And I'm useful in other subjects. People sometimes waste a lot of valuable time trying to be good at everything.

Test 8   PART 4

You will hear a radio interview with Dave Salter, a deep-sea diving instructor. For Questions 24–30, choose the best answer A, B or C.

Interviewer: Dave, you've been a diving instructor for many years. Now, teaching new divers the basics cannot be an easy job. What made you choose this unusual career?

Dave: Well, deep-sea diving was simply a leisure activity for me. Then the local Diving Centre needed instructors and I got a job during the peak tourist season. I gave it a try though the pay wasn't much. I must say that my first experiences with students left me wondering if this was the career for me at all … Probably <u>what decided me was that the next season there were a number of happily returning divers who wanted me as an instructor again</u> …

Interviewer: So what standards are expected of instructors like yourself?

Dave: Well, instructors will set off in boats, with their students, to find a good spot to dive. Now, you can't expect us to have detailed local knowledge of all the dive sites in an area. However, you <u>are expected to fully understand the effects of strong wind and storms</u>, because you need flat water, that is, not many waves. When conditions are not suitable, some inexperienced instructors panic, because their students want action, no matter what.

Interviewer: Is it difficult to keep students under control?

Dave: I'll tell you what makes me very nervous. Once, I had six students with me. We all went under water, got everybody settled, and wallop, all six of <u>the students suddenly went in different directions! Now, that's worrying</u>. I quickly rounded up four of them, but couldn't find the other two. Then I saw bubbles in the distance so I swam after them, grabbed, got them in line. They were kicking and struggling and I suddenly realised they weren't my students. I let them go and found my own halfway up the boat.

Interviewer: Well, it must be difficult with everyone wearing the same kind of outfit …

Dave: It certainly is, and sometimes that can lead to strange situations … One day a girl, Elaine she was called, went missing while we were inspecting a wreck. My group were coming up after a good dive when other divers went past, down on their way to the wreck. In the confusion, <u>Elaine thought one of them was me</u>, and followed whoever it was back down. Not that she wanted another look at the wreck! I went back down and I came across a diver in black I had never seen before, and behind him, my lost student, who looked very upset.

Interviewer: Have you ever made a serious mistake with your students?

Dave: Mmm … Training new divers is tricky, particularly if your students know more about a subject than you do. I had a couple once, Mr and Mrs Jones, they were doing OK, but when it came to life-saving they were not doing it to the right standard. I just kept saying to them, 'What you're doing is OK, but it isn't up to our standard.' When we met in the bar later, I found out they were a doctor and nurse. I just <u>wished the ground would open up and swallow me, I felt so stupid</u> …

Interviewer: Do you find any part of your job boring?

Dave: Most definitely. <u>Possibly number one is swimming around in a few metres of water for my students to be able to take photos of each other to show to their friends</u>. But apart from that, I know that students can't be expected to get things right from the beginning, and I'm a patient teacher. Unlike many of my colleagues, I don't find that part of my job tiring at all. In fact, I'm glad to be doing the routine things which don't involve much action.

Interviewer: Are you planning any career changes?

Dave: I'd love to move on to a quieter sort of job. Some people have suggested I should try to get a job with a film company, taking photos and doing documentaries of shipwrecks and fish. I feel I'm not young enough for that sort of job. I'd like something where I can use the administrative skills I have, ideally <u>running a busy dive centre</u>, where I'd organise the work of other instructors …